VEGETABLES FROM AN ITALIAN GARDEN

SEASON-BY-SEASON RECIPES

VEGETABLES FROM AN ITALIAN GARDEN

SEASON-BY-SEASON RECIPES

Φ

FROM THE GARDEN

Vegetables are at the heart of Italian cooking, and Italians have a natural instinct for selecting fresh produce at its very best and making the most of whatever is in season, whether it comes from the garden or the market. Everyday, homecooked dishes are typically straightforward, combining a few ingredients in which the natural flavors are celebrated instead of being smothered by rich sauces or elaborate garnishes. What could be simpler or more delicious than Tomato and Basil Risotto (see page 214), Linguine with Zucchini, Almond, and Mint Pesto (see page 195), or Spiced Pumpkin with Parsley (see page 312).

Italian cuisine is by no means vegetarian, but vegetables play an important and integral role in every meal. This is partly because historically meat was very expensive, but it is mainly due to the immense richness of the Italian harvest. Markets all over the country are stocked with spectacular and colorful displays of tomatoes, bell peppers, globe artichokes, broccoli, fennel bulbs, asparagus, chicory, carrots, eggplants—whatever is in season. With this array of readily available vegetables, it is hardly surprising that many favorite dishes use little meat, and Italians show remarkable ingenuity and skill in their treatments of vegetables. In fact, the first step of many recipes is to soften a mixture of vegetables—usually finely chopped onion and celery, but sometimes including garlic, carrot, and herbs—before adding the meat or fish. This mixture, called a *soffritto*, from *sotto friggere* (to under-fry), must be cooked gently in olive oil to release the flavors without any bitterness. Vegetable accompaniments are rarely boiled in water and served plainly.

Peas, for example, are often poached gently in stock and often flavored with onion and ham while asparagus is broiled and served with Parmesan cheese.

Cooking with vegetables helps to maintain a nutritious diet. With an array of dishes that incorporates everything from stems and shoots to leafy greens and roots, making sure you eat enough vegetables is easy when you cook the Italian way. Vegetables are also economical and easy to grow, ensuring a supply of mouthwatering ingredients all year round—just follow the growing tips at the beginning of each chapter.

THE ITALIAN MEAL

The *primo* and *secondo* (first and second courses) are the foundation of both lunch and dinner. Vegetables are regularly used in first course dishes such as soups, risottos, pasta dishes, pies, layered bakes, and savory custards and flans—see, for example, the Cream of Carrot and Fennel Soup (see page 320), Asparagus and Pancetta Risotto (see page 87), and Pumpkin Gnocchi with Orange Butter (see page 308). Vegetables also play an essential part of the *secondo*. Meat or fish dishes are often flavored with vegetables and herbs—even fried or broiled meat or fish is usually served with a lovingly prepared vegetable accompaniment, or *contorno*. This might be something as simple as Fava Beans and Mint (see page 95), Pea Puree au Gratin (see page 103), or Roasted Zucchini, Potatoes, and Tomatoes (see page 196). Alternatively, a salad may accompany a *secondo*, and these are as imaginative and delicious as cooked vegetable accompaniments: the Frisée Salad with Green Beans and Red

Currants (see page 174), Belgian Endive Salad with Caper Dressing (see page 125) or Marinated Cherry Tomato Salad (see page 212).

An *antipasto* (hors d'oeuvre or appetizer) may be served before the *primo* at a more formal or special occasional meal and at restaurants. *Antipasto* means "before the meal" and not, as is often mistakenly believed, "before the pasta." This usually consists of a platter of cured meats or shellfish and may also include broiled bell peppers or eggplants, vegetables cooked in tomato sauce, stuffed hard-cooked eggs, and a dish of olives.

Family meals usually end with fresh fruit, but wonderful desserts and ices are served at celebrations and special occasions, and vegetables and herbs may even play a part in these. Pumpkin Flan (see page 307), Avocado, Yogurt, and Honey Cream (see page 112), and Mint Ice Cream (see page 167) are just some of the ingenious recipes for sweet treats.

GROWING YOUR OWN

Vegetables from an Italian Garden shows how simple it can be to grow and cook your own vegetables. The book is divided into the four seasons, with each section featuring seasonal vegetables that are typically used in Italian cooking, with tips on how to grow and prepare them, followed by a collection of Italian recipes. All recipes are vegetarian unless indicated otherwise with an animal or fish symbol next to the title. Although the vegetables are commonly used in Italy, not all of them are indigenous: the tomato originally came from South America, but it would be impossible to imagine Italian cooking without this ubiquitous ingredient. There are also some inclusions that are not strictly speaking vegetables: for example, chestnuts are included because they are important in Italian cooking, and mushrooms because Italians are passionate about all kinds of wild and cultivated fungi.

Even if you have a small vegetable patch or only some pots on the windowsill, you can discover the joy of harvesting and eating the freshest possible vegetables prepared and cooked in the Italian way. Herbs are easy to grow and maintain in small spaces. Many cool-weather loving crops, such as lettuce, broccoli, and spinach, can be sown in spring for a late spring/ early summer harvest and again in late summer/fall for a fall/ winter harvest in many areas. By sowing these crops more than once, you can ensure having a more continual supply of these vegetables.

If you're buying your vegetables at the market, it's worth looking for locally grown seasonal vegetables, because these are much less expensive and environmentally friendly than imported ones. There is a genuine and long-forgotten pleasure to be found in greeting each new season's crop. Asparagus in winter will always be a disappointment, but your patience will be rewarded and your pleasure doubled if you wait for it until the late spring. You may even encounter some vegetables that are completely unknown in your kitchen, such as cardoons and scorzonera, but which are a popular and well-known part of Italian cooking. *Vegetables from an Italian Garden* shows all home cooks how to take inspiration from Italian cuisine, and to get the very best out of vegetables.

Vegetable	SPRING			SUMMER		
	Early	Mid	Late	Early	Mid	Late
Spinach						
Swiss chard						
Wild greens						
Artichokes						
Asparagus						
Fava beans						
Peas						
Radishes						
Avocados						
Onions						
Belgian endives						
Herbs						
Arugula						
Green beans						
Eggplants						
Zucchini						
Cucumbers						
Tomatoes						
Bell peppers						
Fennel						
Corn						
Lettuce						
Celery						
Chestnuts						
Mushrooms						
Truffles						
Pumpkin						
Beets						
Carrots						
Potatoes						
Scorzonera						
Turnips						
Radicchio						
Cardoons						
Cabbage						
Brussels sprouts						
Broccoli						
Cauliflower						
Leeks						
Celery root						

Sow time ◇◇◇◇◇◇◇◇◇◇   Harvest time ▬▬▬▬▬▬

	FALL			WINTER			
Early	Mid	Late	Early	Mid	Late		Vegetable
							Spinach
							Swiss chard
							Wild greens
							Artichokes
							Asparagus
							Fava beans
							Peas
							Radishes
							Avocados
							Onions
							Belgian endives
							Herbs
							Arugula
							Green beans
							Eggplants
							Zucchini
							Cucumbers
							Tomatoes
							Bell peppers
							Fennel
							Corn
							Lettuce
							Celery
							Chestnuts
							Mushrooms
							Truffles
							Pumpkin
							Beets
							Carrots
							Potatoes
							Scorzonera
							Turnips
							Radicchio
							Cardoons
							Cabbage
							Brussels sprouts
							Broccoli
							Cauliflower
							Leeks
							Celery root

SPINACH

SWISS CHARD

WILD GREENS

ARTICHOKES

ASPARAGUS

FAVA BEANS

PEAS

RADISHES

AVOCADOS

ONIONS

BELGIAN ENDIVES

SPRING

SPRING

After the cold of the winter, the Italian garden flourishes
dramatically in spring, and many of the fruit and vegetables
grown throughout the year are now at their very best because the
young shoots are at their tastiest. As ever with Italian cooking,
the key to maximizing flavor is to use the freshest produce.

During spring, cultivated and wild greens begin to grow
in abundance, taking over from the hardy vegetables of winter.
Spinach is an Italian favorite found in simple dishes, such
as Spinach Salad with Bacon and Beans (see page 52) and
Spinach and Mushroom Salad (see page 54), which allow the
earthy flavor of freshly picked young spinach to shine through.
Puntarelle (a variety of chicory with serrated leaves), escarole (a
broad-leaf chicory) and watercress add texture, color, and crisp
flavors to light meals, and more unusual wild greens, such as
nettles, can be added to soup or ravioli.

In spring, Italians love to eat the earliest fava beans straight
from the pod with fresh pecorino cheese. A classic springtime
risotto is always prepared with arborio or carnaroli rice, but this
speciality is distinguished by ingredients such as Belgian endive,
asparagus, or Swiss chard, which provide a unique character.
Asparagus and globe artichokes send up spears and shoots early
in the season. Prized for their versatility, both can be prepared
in a variety of ways—from Asparagus in Lemon Butter (see
page 91) and Asparagus and Pancetta Risotto (see page 87) to
Sorrentino Artichokes (see page 72) and Artichoke Lasagnette
(see page 79). And while most root crops are thought of as
winter vegetables, radishes are an exception and the crunchy
roots are delicious eaten straight from the garden or as a peppery
addition to salads.

To grow spring vegetables successfully, add generous
amounts of compost to the garden early in the season. While

spring vegetables like cool, moist conditions, soil that is too wet and cold can cause the seeds to rot. This can be avoided by making raised beds 10-inches high. Sow greens, radishes, and even peas in these beds. The soil will dry out and warm up more quickly in raised beds, making the seeds less likely to rot before germinating. Keep newly planted beds well weeded and watered. As the seedlings grow, thin them out to give them space to expand. You can use the thinnings in salads, getting your first taste of what is in store in a few weeks' time in the spring garden.

Greens are sweetest and tenderest if they are allowed to mature while temperatures are still low. If exposed to heat or drought, they can become tough and bitter. Harvest greens in small quantities as and when you need them, and they will grow back for multiple harvests during the spring months.

In addition, prepare your garden for the upcoming season. "Hardening off" is the process of adapting a plant that has been grown in a greenhouse, indoors, or under protective shelter to full outdoor exposure. This is the time to move cool-season crops from the windowsill, greenhouse, or cold frame to the garden. This is also the time to sow annual herb seeds, start off tomatoes, peppers, eggplants, and cucumbers, and begin planting early potatoes.

SPINACH
SPINACI

First cultivated in Persia several thousand years ago, spinach is popular the world over both as a salad green and cooked vegetable. Sharp and distinctive, its flavor complements dairy products, warm spices, eggs, ham, and bacon, and it also makes a great accompaniment to fish and shellfish. Whether in a frittata or risotto, a pie or soufflé, spinach offers incredible diversity to spring dishes. Spinach is often paired with ricotta as a filling for ravioli or savory tortes.

Although spinach is at its best in spring, it is available around the year. Look for firm, deep green leaves with no blemishes, insect damage, or signs of slime. Store in the refrigerator and use within 1–2 days of purchase.

Because spinach reduces dramatically with cooking, allow 9–11 ounces per serving (half the quantity if serving uncooked baby spinach). Wash well and cut off coarse stalks. Cook in just the water clinging to the leaves after washing with a sprinkle of salt in a covered pan until wilted. Drain thoroughly, pressing out the excess liquid, then chop.

IN THE GARDEN Plant seeds in late winter for a spring harvest or in fall for a late winter/early spring harvest. Soak the seeds overnight in warm water to encourage quick germination. Prepare the soil by adding compost and sow the seeds 1 inch apart in rows spaced 1 foot apart. When the seedlings are 2½ inches high, thin them to 6 inches apart, and serve the thinnings in salads. Start harvesting individual leaves or whole plants 30–50 days after planting. Keep harvesting individual leaves until the plant starts to bolt, when it should be removed.

SPINACH RECIPES ON PAGES 46–57

SWISS CHARD
BIETOLE

Swiss chard is a leafy green vegetable often referred to as "greens," with fleshy white or ruby red ribs and fan-shaped leaves, and a taste similar to spinach or beet greens but with a stronger, more pronounced flavor. Highly nutritious, it is ideal in salads and savory dishes, such as Swiss Chard with Anchovies (see page 61) or Swiss Chard au Gratin (see page 58).

Choose Swiss chard with firm ribs and fresh, vivid green leaves. The stalks are tougher than the leaves and require longer cooking time. To prepare the vegetables, cut out the ribs with scissors and slice and shred the leaves. For a simple yet nourishing dish, cook the ribs in salted boiling water for 10–15 minutes, adding the leaves for the last 5 minutes. After draining, the ribs can be sautéed gently in butter and/or oil and served sprinkled with grated Parmesan. Serve the leaves dressed with olive oil and lemon juice. Avoid cooking Swiss chard in an aluminum pot because it will react with the metal and discolor the pot.

IN THE GARDEN Swiss chard is one of the easiest vegetables to grow because it can tolerate poor soil and withstand frost and mild freezing. When all danger of frost has passed, sow seeds in beds with added compost 2 inches apart in rows 2 feet apart. When the plants are 6 inches tall, thin them to 12 inches apart. Use the thinnings in salads. Keep plants well weeded and watered, and mulch with straw once they are established. Start harvesting the outer leaves when they are about 4 inches long. The more you pick, the more the plant will produce up until frosty weather. Swiss chard does not bolt.

SWISS CHARD RECIPES ON PAGES 57–61

WILD GREENS
ERBE

Italians are voracious foragers of edible wild plants. Dandelion, a type of wild chicory, is one of the most popular. Use only tender young leaves for salads, because older ones will be very bitter. Shredded leaves may be boiled for 15 minutes, then drained and served with melted butter and grated Parmesan or drizzled with olive oil and lemon juice. Dandelion leaves are also used in gratins and risotto. The puntarelle, a variety of chicory with serrated leaves, is traditionally soaked in water until the leaves curl attractively, then served with an anchovy dressing.

The sweet-flavored tops of young nettles are used for making soup, risotto, gnocchi, and even filling for ravioli. Nettle has a flavor like mild spinach and may be used in the same way. Wear gloves to handle. To prepare, wash the leaves thoroughly. Cook in a covered pan with just the water clinging to the leaves for 4–6 minutes; this destroys the sting.

IN THE GARDEN Forage for wild dandelion and, in the West for nettle tips, in fields and lawns that have not been treated with herbicides and are far enough away from roads to avoid traffic pollution. Harvest individual leaves or the whole plant of young dandelions when the leaves are less than 10 inches long. Harvest the top 4 inches of 4 foot tall nettle plants while the leaves are still young. Wear gloves to avoid stings. Lambsquarter is a tasty annual weed found in cultivated gardens in the summer. Pick the leaves when the plants are 6 inches tall.

WILD GREENS RECIPES ON PAGES 61–67

ARTICHOKES
CARCIOFI

With an exquisite nutty flavor, artichokes are much used in Italian cooking. Look for firm specimens with a good bloom on tightly wrapped, unblemished leaves. Some varieties are almost round and pale green, while others are elongated with purple-tinged leaves. Violetta, the mild-flavored Italian heirloom variety, is worth seeking out, and tender young artichokes of any variety are a joy because they can be eaten whole.

To prepare, fill a bowl with water mixed with a little lemon juice. Break off the stems, remove any coarse outer leaves, and scoop out the hairy chokes (the mass of immature florets in the center of an artichoke bud), if any, with a teaspoon. Trim ½ inch from the remaining leaves, adding them to the acidulated water to prevent discoloration. Cook them in salted boiling water for 30–45 minutes, until a leaf comes easily away from the base. Serve with melted butter, garlic butter, mayonnaise, or vinaigrette. To eat, pull off a leaf, dip it into the sauce, and pull off the fleshy base between your teeth. Finally, eat the heart (the edible base). Tender young artichokes may be sliced or cut into wedges and fried, or thinly sliced and served raw in salads. Artichokes may also be stuffed and baked in a preheated oven, 375°F, for 20–25 minutes.

IN THE GARDEN Globe artichokes are perennial. Plant seedlings in spring when all danger of frost has passed. Space them 5 feet apart in a sunny well-drained site with added compost. Feed throughout the summer and keep well watered and weeded. Cut the plants to ground level in fall and mulch in winter. To harvest, cut just below the heart before the leaves open.

ARTICHOKE RECIPES ON PAGES 68–85

ASPARAGUS
ASPARAGI

Asparagus has a delicious and delicate flavor. Its short season from late spring to early summer makes it a luxury vegetable that deserves a starring role. Thin, young asparagus, called sprue, can be stir-fried and added to salads, or served, Italian style, sprinkled with grated Parmesan. Asparagus pairs nicely with eggs and is also tasty in risotto. Alternatively, cook on a broiler pan brushed with oil or under the broiler for 5 minutes, or drizzle with oil and roast in a preheated oven, 350°F, for 8–12 minutes. Cooked asparagus can also be served as a cold appetizer, drizzled with olive oil and lemon juice.

When buying, look for tightly furled tips and straight, fresh-looking stems. To cook, cut off the lower woody part of the stems—use for soup—and scrape off any tough skin. Trim the spears to the same length. Tie in a bundle and stand upright in a tall pan of salted boiling water with the tips protruding. Cover and cook for 6–10 minutes, until tender.

IN THE GARDEN There are many varieties of asparagus. Green asparagus is most popular in the United States. White asparagus, a European favorite, is a green variety that has been blanched (deprived of light during growth). To grow asparagus, dig an 8-inch-deep trench in a sunny site with well-drained sandy loam soil. Plant asparagus crowns (the base and the roots of a year-old plant) 12 inches apart, add a phosphorous-rich fertilizer, and cover with 3 inches of soil. After the first shoots emerge, continue to cover the plants with soil until the trench is full. Spread mulch around plantings to keep them weed free. For the first two years, let the shoots grow to 6 feet to strengthen the plant. Begin to harvest in the third year.

ASPARAGUS RECIPES ON PAGES 86–94

FAVA BEANS

FAVE

Very few vegetables are as versatile as the fava bean. Early in the season, the beans are tiny and tender enough to be plucked from their skins and, in Italy, eaten raw with pecorino. Freshly picked fava beans have a sweet flavor and work best with simple, clean flavors, including fresh herbs (mint, summer savory), lemon juice, and leafy greens, and even mild cheese, such as mozzarella. They are equally delicious in purees, soups, casseroles, risotto, and as a filling for omelets. When dried, they make a good winter staple.

When buying, look for pale green pods with a satin bloom and a tender texture. Eat as soon after purchase as possible. Shell all but the very youngest beans and boil or steam them for 5 minutes, then toss with olives and melted butter. Older beans are best skinned to remove the slightly bitter flavor. Simply pop them out of their skins by gently squeezing between finger and thumb.

IN THE GARDEN This tall, attractive, cool-season legume crops throughout the winter in mild climates, producing green pods with large white, green, or brown beans inside. Sow the seeds in spring for an early summer harvest in cold areas or in fall for a winter and spring harvest in mild regions. Plant them 2 inches deep in rows 8 inches apart. Beacuse they can grow tall, support newly emerged seedlings with a fence. For the sweetest flavor, harvest when pods are 2–3 inches long.

FAVA BEANS RECIPES ON PAGES 95–98

PEAS
PISELLI

The sweet flavor of fresh peas makes their short season in the spring and early summer worth waiting for. The term "peas" covers several types: those that are shelled before cooking, those with plump pods that are eaten whole (sugar snaps), and those with flat pods that are eaten whole (snow peas).

Peas are a favorite accompaniment to meat, especially duck, although in Italy they are usually poached in stock instead of boiled in water. They feature in a wide range of rice, pasta, and baked dishes.

Look for bright green, satiny pods. Any that look withered will be old with starchy peas. Use them as soon after purchase as possible. Shell by popping open the bottom of the pod and pushing out the peas with your thumb. Cook in boiling water (or stock) or in a covered steamer until tender for 8–10 minutes (5–8 minutes for snow peas and sugar snaps). You can also stir-fry or cook them in butter in a covered pan.

IN THE GARDEN Peas grow 2–8 feet tall, depending on the variety, so most will need support. Plant in spring or in late summer for a fall harvest. Add compost to the soil and form raised beds. To hasten germination, soak pea seeds in warm water the night before planting. Sow seeds 2 inches apart in rows 10 inches apart. Harvest snow peas about 7 days after flowering while the pods are still flat. Harvest other peas when the pods are filled, but before the seeds mature. Plants will continue to grow and produce as long as the weather stays cool.

PEA RECIPES ON PAGES 100–108

RADISHES
RAVANELLI

Round, red radishes and elongated red and white radishes have delightfully crisp, white flesh and a peppery flavor with an underlying nutty sweetness. They are almost always served raw in salads, as a garnish, or simply with bread and butter. Long, white mooli, or daikon, radishes, mainly used in Chinese and Japanese cuisine, are less peppery with a slightly bitter taste. They are eaten raw but are also good when cooked.

Preparation is simple—just trim off the leaves, wash, and serve whole or sliced. Radishes go well with yogurt and cheese dressings and are especially tasty with salty ingredients, such as olives and capers.

Radishes are available all year round. Look for small, brightly colored specimens with no bruises or blemishes, preferably with crisp green leaves still attached because this is a sign of freshness. Store in a tightly sealed bag and keep refrigerated for a few days.

IN THE GARDEN Plant seeds in the spring or fall to mature during cool weather. Plant in a loose, raised bed on well-drained soil 1 inch apart in rows spaced 1 foot apart. Thin small varieties to 2 inches apart and winter radishes to 4 inches apart when seedlings are 1 inch tall. Thinning too late or insufficiently causes stress, resulting in smaller roots with a more pungent flavor. So too does lack of water or too much heat. Check the roots periodically by removing some soil from under the plant, and harvest when the roots are big enough to eat. Then remove the tops and taproot, and scrub clean.

RADISH RECIPES ON PAGE 109

AVOCADOS
AVOCADI

This pear-shaped fruit with its melt-in-your-mouth buttery texture is best served in salads, sauces, dips, canapés, and *antipasti* and can also features in dessert recipes. Heat makes the flesh taste bitter so it is never cooked. There are over 400 varieties, with the best-known including the small 'Hass', with purple knobby skin and pale yellow flesh, and the larger 'Ettinger', with thin, smooth, mid-green skin. Avoid buying avocados with damaged skin, bruises, or a squashy texture.

To prepare avocados, slice in half lengthwise with a stainless steel knife, cutting around the central pit. Rotate the halves in opposite directions to separate them, then remove the pit. Scoop out the flesh with a spoon or peel and slice, depending on the recipe. Prepare avocados at the last minute and sprinkle the flesh with lemon or lime juice to prevent discoloration. Avocado halves can be served simply with a spoonful of vinaigrette or mayonnaise in the pit cavity.

Because ripe avocados perish rapidly, mature fruit is picked before ripening and usually sold when still quite hard. They will ripen at room temperature within 3–5 days. Test an avocado by cradling it in the palm of your hand; if it yields to gentle pressure, it is ready.

IN THE GARDEN Not a common garden plant, avocados can only be grown outdoors in frost-free areas. However, some avid gardeners have had success growing them in containers indoors. The prime season is late winter and early spring, but they are produced in both hemispheres, so they are available all year round.

AVOCADO RECIPES ON PAGES 110–112

ONIONS
CIPOLLE

Few vegetables are so essential to such a wide range of dishes as the onion, whether the pungent brown, mild white, or sweet red variety. Cooking onions until golden brown before adding other ingredients provides a more distinctive sweet-savory undertone. In the Italian kitchen, the *soffrito* is the basis of myriad dishes: Finely chopped onion, celery, garlic, and carrot are softened in olive oil and/or butter before the main ingredients are added. Onions also feature in dishes such as soup and tarts, roasted or fried in rings as an accompaniment, and added raw to salads. Roasted onions, peeled and sliced, then served with olive oil and salt, are a favorite winter snack in Italy, while red onions feature in salads, and little white ones are blissful in *agrodolce* (sweet-and-sour sauce).

Choose firm, dry onions with a thin, papery skin. Avoid any with damage, damp patches or green shoots. Store in a cool, dry place. To prepare, remove the papery skin and the first layer underneath it. Cut into wedges or slice through the rings widthwise. To dice, slice the rings again lengthwise.

IN THE GARDEN Onions can be planted as seeds, plants, or sets on raised beds in well-drained soil. Sow seeds 3 inches apart in rows 1 foot apart, and thin to 4 inches apart when the seedlings are three to four weeks old. Plant sets or transplants 4–6 inches apart. Keep beds well weeded and watered. Harvest bulbs when half of the tops have naturally fallen over. Cut off the leaves just above the bulb and store in mesh bags in a dark room at 40°F. Sweet onions keep for 1 month and pungent onions for up to 4 months.

ONION RECIPES ON PAGES 115–120

BELGIAN ENDIVE
INDIVIA BELGA

The large chicory family includes many edible plants and there is sometimes confusion over names. The Belgian endive described here is the light colored, compact, spear-shaped plant also known as witloof (white leaf) or chicory. With a slightly bitter taste and a crisp texture, it is perfect raw in salads with bacon, capers, or citrus fruits. It can be simply dressed with olive oil and balsamic vinegar or cooked with strong flavors, such as chile, nutmeg, ham, and cheese.

Look for crisp, fresh white heads with yellow tips in tightly packed cones. Avoid any that are beginning to open or have green tips. To prepare, simply separate and rinse the leaves for salads. For cooking, remove the core and any damaged leaves, rinse well, and halve or quarter according to the recipe. Belgian endive is usually blanched before braising or baking, but can simply be boiled in salted water for 20–30 minutes. Young Belgian endive can be broiled.

IN THE GARDEN Sow seeds 2 weeks before the last frost date in the spring on raised beds filled with well-drained, compost-enhanced soil. Thin seedlings to 6 inches apart when they are 1 inch tall. In fall, after a frost, dig up the roots, remove the leaves, and let the roots dry overnight. Fill a pail with slightly moist sand and place the roots, top end up and barely touching, in the pail. Cover with a cloth and store in a cool, dark place. In the winter, transfer the pail to an indoor location with a temperature of 60°F, water, and keep covered with plastic. In 3–4 weeks, the roots (chicons) will sprout leaves that can be picked as needed.

BELGIAN ENDIVE RECIPES ON PAGES 123–126

SPINACH QUICHE WITH SALTED CHEESE AND FETA

PHOTO PAGE 47

QUICHE AI GERMOGLI DI SPINACI, PRIMO SALE E FETA

Preparation time: *15 min*
Cooking time: *30–40 min*
Serves 6

— 9 ounces puff pastry dough,
   thawed if frozen
— all-purpose flour, for dusting
— 4 eggs
— 7 ounces ricotta salata
   or salted soft cheese,
   crumbled
— 3½ ounces feta cheese,
   drained and diced
— ¼ cup pine nuts
— 2⅓ cups chopped spinach
— olive oil, for drizzling
— salt and pepper

Preheat the oven to 400°F. Line an 8-inch tart pan with parchment paper. Roll out the dough on a lightly floured counter and use to line the prepared pan. Prick all over with a fork. Beat together the eggs and ricotta, then stir in the feta. Season with pepper and lightly with salt, and pour the mixture into the pie shell. Sprinkle with the pine nuts, add the spinach, and drizzle with oil. Put the pan on a baking sheet and bake for 10 minutes, then reduce the oven temperature to 350°F and bake for another 20–30 minutes, until set. Remove the pan from the oven and serve the quiche lukewarm as an accompaniment to mixed cold cuts, such as ham, speck, and very thinly sliced mortadella.

CREAM OF SPINACH SOUP

CREMA DI SPINACI

Preparation time: *10 min*
Cooking time: *30 min*
Serves 4

— 4¼ cups vegetable stock
— 3 tablespoons butter
— 2 onions, finely chopped
— ⅓ cup all-purpose flour
— 1 pound 2 ounces fresh
   spinach, chopped
— 3 tablespoons lemon
   juice, strained
— 2 tablespoons heavy cream,
   plus extra to garnish
— salt and pepper
— hot paprika, to garnish

Bring the stock to a boil. Melt the butter in another pan, add the onions, and cook over low heat, stirring occasionally, for 5 minutes, until softened. Stir in the flour and cook, stirring continuously, for 2 minutes, then gradually stir in the hot stock. Add the spinach and simmer for about 20 minutes. Stir in the lemon juice, then transfer to a food processor or blender and process to a puree. Pour into a pan, season with salt and pepper, stir in the cream, and simmer briefly. Remove from the heat, cover, and let stand for 5 minutes. Serve the soup sprinkled with paprika on top as a garnish.

SPINACH QUICHE WITH SALTED CHEESE AND FETA

RICE WITH SPINACH

RISO ALL'ONDA CON SPINACI

Preparation time: *30 min*
Cooking time: *28 min*
Serves 4

— 3 tablespoons olive oil
— 7 ounces small onions,
  very thinly sliced
— generous ½ cup risotto rice
— 2¼ pounds spinach, coarse
  stalks removed, chopped
— 2 tablespoons butter
— salt and pepper

Pour 3 cups of water into a pan, add a large pinch of salt, and bring to a boil. Meanwhile, heat the oil in a large pan. Add the onion and cook over low heat, stirring occasionally, for 5 minutes, until softened and translucent. Stir in the rice and cook, stirring continuously, for 1–2 minutes, until all the grains are coated in oil. Add the spinach and cook, stirring, for 5 minutes. Pour the salted boiling water into the pan and bring back to a boil, then reduce the heat. Cover and cook for 18 minutes, until the rice is tender. Remove from the heat, add the butter, and let it melt, then season with pepper and serve immediately.

SPINACH AND TOMATO RISOTTO

RISOTTO CON SPINACI E POMODORI

Preparation time: *30 min*
Cooking time: *25 min*
Serves 4

— 3 plum tomatoes, halved
  lengthwise
— 2 tablespoons olive oil,
  plus extra for drizzling
— 4¼ cups vegetable stock
— scant 1 cup dry white wine
— ½ tablespoon butter
— 1 small onion, finely
  chopped
— 1 small carrot, finely
  chopped
— 1 stalk celery, finely
  chopped
— ½ clove garlic, finely
  chopped
— 1⅔ cups risotto rice
— 2⅓ cups chopped spinach
— ½ cup grated Parmesan
  cheese
— salt and pepper

Preheat the oven to 400°F. Put the tomatoes, cut side down, on a baking sheet, season with salt and pepper, and drizzle with oil. Roast for 10 minutes, then remove from the oven and set aside. Pour the stock, wine, and scant 1 cup of water into a pan and bring to a boil. Melt the butter with the oil in another pan. Add the onion, carrot, celery, and garlic and cook over low heat, stirring occasionally, for 5 minutes. Stir in the rice, season with salt and pepper, and cook, stirring continuously, for 2 minutes, until all the grains are coated. Add a ladleful of the hot stock mixture and cook, stirring continuously, until it has been absorbed. Continue to add the hot stock mixture, a ladleful at a time, stirring continuously until each addition has been absorbed. When about half the stock mixture has been absorbed, stir in the tomatoes and, after a few minutes, stir in the spinach. Season with pepper. Continue adding the stock mixture and stirring as before until it has all been absorbed, for about 18–20 minutes. Remove the pan from the heat, sprinkle with the grated cheese, transfer to a warm serving dish, and serve immediately.

PANSOTTI FROM MAGRO

Preparation time: *1 ¼ hours, plus 1 hour resting*
Cooking time: *30 min*
Serves 6

— 3 ½ cups all-purpose flour, plus extra for dusting
— 1 tablespoon dry white wine
— salt

For the filling:
— 4 ½ cups borage leaves
— 9 ounces spinach, beet, or Swiss chard leaves
— ½ clove garlic
— scant 1 cup ricotta cheese
— 2 eggs
— ⅔ cup grated Parmesan cheese

For the walnut sauce:
— ¾ cup fresh bread crumbs
— 2 tablespoons milk
— 1 ¼ cups shelled walnuts
— ½ clove garlic
— ⅔ cup olive oil
— 1 ½ tablespoons butter
— 1 cup grated Parmesan cheese
— salt

To make the pasta dough, sift the flour and a pinch of salt into a mound on a counter and make a well in the center. Pour ½ cup of water and the wine into the well and gradually incorporate the dry ingredients with your fingers. Knead well, then shape the dough into a ball, cover, and let rest for 30 minutes.

Meanwhile, make the filling. Bring 2 pans of lightly salted water to a boil. Add the borage leaves to 1 pan and the spinach, beet, or Swiss chard leaves to the other. Cook the borage leaves for 2–3 minutes, then drain. Cook the spinach, beet, or Swiss chard leaves for about 5 minutes, until tender, then drain. Reserve the cooking liquid. Finely chop all the leaves together with the garlic. Transfer to a bowl and stir in the ricotta, eggs, and Parmesan. Roll out the pasta dough into a thin sheet on a lightly floured counter and cut into 4-inch squares. Put 1 teaspoon of the filling into the center of each square and fold in half diagonally, pinching the edges together firmly with your fingertips to seal.

To make the sauce, put the bread crumbs into a bowl, add the milk, and let soak for 10 minutes. Meanwhile, bring a pan of water to a boil. Add the walnuts and blanch for 5 minutes. Drain, turn onto a dish towel, and rub off the skins. Drain the bread crumbs and squeeze out any excess moisture. Put them into a mortar, add the walnuts and garlic, and pound to a paste with a pestle. Gradually add the olive oil in a thin steady stream, stirring continuously, until the sauce has a pouring consistency. If necessary, add a little of the reserved cooking water. Bring a large pan of salted water to a boil. Reduce the heat to a simmer, add the ravioli, and cook for about 10 minutes. Drain and transfer to a warm serving dish. Pour the walnut sauce over, dot with the butter, sprinkle with the Parmesan, toss lightly, and serve immediately.

SPINACH AND FONTINA SOUFFLÉ

SPINACH AND FONTINA SOUFFLÉ

SOUFFLÉ DI SPINACI E FONTINA

Preparation time: *1 hour*
Cooking time: *50 min*
Serves *4–6*

— 1¾ pounds potatoes
— 2 egg yolks
— 1½ tablespoons butter,
  plus extra for greasing
— ⅓ cup grated Parmesan
  cheese
— 11 ounces mild fontina
  cheese, diced
— 6 tablespoons fresh
  bread crumbs
— 11 ounces spinach,
  coarse stalks removed
— 1 tablespoon olive oil
— 1 clove garlic, peeled
— salt and pepper

For the béchamel sauce:
— 3 tablespoons butter
— ⅓ cup all-purpose flour
— 2¼ cups milk

Put the unpeeled potatoes into a large pan, pour in water to cover, add a pinch of salt, and bring to a boil. Boil for 30–40 minutes, until tender. Drain, peel, and then mash in a bowl. Stir in the egg yolks, butter, and Parmesan, and season with salt and pepper.

To make the béchamel sauce, melt the butter in a pan. Stir in the flour and cook over low heat, stirring continuously, for 2 minutes, until the mixture turns nut brown. Gradually stir in the milk and bring to a boil, stirring continuously. Cook, stirring continuously, until thickened and smooth. Season to taste with salt.

Remove from the heat and stir in the fontina. Preheat the oven to 400°F. Grease a soufflé dish with butter and coat with the bread crumbs, tipping out any excess. Cook the spinach in just the water clinging to the leaves after washing, for 2 minutes, then drain, and squeeze out the excess liquid. Heat the oil in a small skillet. Add the garlic clove and cook over low heat, stirring frequently, for a few minutes, until golden. Remove and discard. Add the spinach and cook, stirring occasionally, for 2 minutes, then remove from the heat and stir into the béchamel sauce. Spoon a generous layer of the potato mixture into the dish to cover the bottom and sides. Fill the center with the béchamel sauce mixture and top with the remaining potato mixture. Bake for 50 minutes. Remove from the oven and serve the soufflé immediately straight from the dish.

HERB GNOCCHI

GNOCCHI ALLE ERBE

Preparation time: *45 min*
Cooking time: *20 min*
Serves 4

— 1 pound 5 ounces spinach
  or borage, coarse stalks
  removed
— 2 tablespoons butter
— 1 cup ricotta cheese
— 1 cup all-purpose flour
— 4–5 mint leaves, chopped
— 2 eggs, lightly beaten
— 2 tablespoons grated
  Parmesan cheese
— 2–4 tablespoons fresh
  bread crumbs
— salt and pepper

For the dressing:
— 6 tablespoons butter
— 2 cloves garlic, peeled
— 4–5 sage leaves
— ⅔ cup grated Parmesan
  cheese

Cook the spinach in boiling water for 2 minutes, or until wilted. Drain well, squeeze out the excess moisture, and chop. Melt the butter in a skillet. Add the spinach and cook, stirring occasionally, for 5 minutes. Transfer to a bowl and let cool slightly. Add the ricotta, flour, mint, eggs, and Parmesan. Season with salt and pepper and stir in just enough bread crumbs to produce a firm mixture. Scoop up nut-size portions of the mixture and shape these into dumplings. Bring a large pan of salted water to a boil, then reduce to a simmer. Add the gnocchi, in batches, and cook for 7–8 minutes, until they rise to the surface. Remove, drain on a clean dish towel, and transfer to a warm serving dish.

To make the dressing, melt the butter with the garlic cloves and sage leaves in a small pan and cook over low heat, stirring frequently, for a few minutes, until the garlic is golden. Remove and discard the garlic and sage. Pour the aromatic butter over the gnocchi, sprinkle with the grated cheese, and serve immediately.

SPINACH SALAD WITH BACON AND BEANS

INSALATA DI SPINACI CON FAGIOLI E BACON

Preparation time: *10 min*
Cooking time: *5 min*
Serves 4

— 3 ounces smoked bacon,
  chopped
— 5 ounces baby spinach
— ¾ cup white beans,
  soaked, boiled, and drained
— 1 small onion, thinly sliced
— olive oil, for drizzling
— red wine vinegar, for
  drizzling
— salt and pepper

Preheat the broiler. Line a baking sheet with parchment paper and spread out the bacon on it. Cook under the broiler for 5 minutes, until crisp, then remove and set aside. Put the spinach, beans, and onion slices into a salad bowl, drizzle with oil and vinegar, and season with salt and pepper. Toss gently, then sprinkle the bacon on top and serve.

RICOTTA AND SPINACH CREPES

Preparation time: *20 min*
Cooking time: *35 min*
Serves 4

— 12 crepes (see page 386)
— 3 tablespoons butter, plus extra for greasing
— 1 pound 2 ounces spinach
— 1 tablespoon olive oil
— scant 1 cup ricotta cheese
— 1 egg yolk
— 2 tablespoons grated Parmesan cheese

Prepare the crepes and let cool. Preheat the oven to 350°F. Grease an ovenproof dish with butter. Cook the spinach in just the water clinging to the leaves after washing for 5 minutes, then drain, squeeze out as much liquid as possible, and chop. Melt 2 tablespoons of the butter with the oil in a skillet, add the spinach, and cook over low heat, stirring frequently, for 5 minutes. Transfer to a bowl and combine with the ricotta and egg yolk. Spread the mixture on the crepes, fold in half, and arrange in the prepared dish. Sprinkle with the Parmesan and dot with the remaining butter. Bake for 15 minutes, then remove from the oven and let stand for a few minutes before serving.

CANNELLINI BEAN AND SPINACH SALAD WITH MUSTARD

INSALATA DI CANNELLINI E SPINACI ALLA SENAPE

Preparation time: *5 min*
Cooking time: *20 min*
Serves 4

— 2 tablespoons Dijon mustard
— 3 tablespoons red wine vinegar
— scant ½ cup olive oil
— 6 shallots, finely chopped
— 1¾ pounds canned cannellini beans, drained and rinsed
— 2 tablespoons chopped thyme
— 2 tablespoons chopped parsley
— 5⅓ cups chopped spinach
— salt and pepper

Combine the mustard and vinegar in a bowl and set aside. Reserve 2 tablespoons of the oil and heat the remainder in a wide pan. Add the shallots and cook over low heat, stirring occasionally, for 5 minutes, until softened and translucent. Stir in the cannellini beans and add the mustard-flavored vinegar and reserved olive oil. Season with salt and pepper and add the thyme, parsley, and spinach. Cook, stirring continuously, until the spinach has wilted, then remove from the heat. Serve immediately.

CONCHIGLIE WITH SPINACH

PHOTO PAGE 55

CONCHIGLIE CON GLI SPINACI

Preparation time: *20 min*
Cooking time: *20 min*
Serves 4

— 4 tablespoons butter
— 1 shallot, chopped
— 4⅔ cups chopped spinach
— 1 egg
— scant ½ cup ricotta cheese
— 12 ounces conchiglie
— salt and pepper

Melt the butter in a pan. Add the shallot and cook over low heat, stirring occasionally, for 5 minutes. Add the spinach and stir well, then season with salt, cover, and cook for a few minutes, until heated through. Be careful to remove the pan from the heat before the mixture dries out. Put the egg and ricotta into a tureen, season lightly with pepper, and beat until smooth and combined. Alternatively, you can replace the egg with ¼ cup of light cream. Cook the conchiglie in plenty of salted boiling water until al dente. Drain and stir into the ricotta mixture. Add the spinach mixture, toss lightly, and serve immediately.

SPINACH AND MUSHROOM SALAD

INSALATA DI SPINACI E FUNGHI

Preparation time: *15 min*
Serves 4

— 2 cups thinly sliced
  mushrooms
— juice of 1 lemon, strained
— 11 ounces spinach,
  coarse stalks removed
— ¼ cup pine nuts
— 4 tablespoons olive oil
— salt and pepper

Sprinkle the mushrooms with a little of the lemon juice and place in a salad bowl. Add the spinach and pine nuts. Whisk together the olive oil and remaining lemon juice in a bowl and season with salt and pepper. Pour the dressing over the salad, toss, and serve.

BAKED SPINACH MEDALLIONS

MEDAGLIONI DI SPINACI AL FORNO

Preparation time: *45 min*
Cooking time: *30 min*
Serves 6

— 1¾ pounds potatoes
— 2 eggs, lightly beaten
— 3 tablespoons all-purpose
   flour
— 3 tablespoons grated
   Parmesan cheese
— 2⅓ cups coarsely chopped
   baby spinach
— salt and pepper

Peel and dice the potatoes and steam until tender. Meanwhile, preheat the oven to 350°F. Line a large ovenproof dish with parchment paper. Remove the potatoes from the steamer and mash in a bowl. Add the eggs, flour, Parmesan, and spinach, and season with salt and pepper. Shape the mixture into 12 balls, then flatten these into medallions. Put the medallions into the prepared dish and bake for about 30 minutes, turning them over halfway through the cooking time. Remove from the oven and serve the medallions hot or lukewarm.

BAKED SPINACH WITH PECORINO

SPINACI AL FORNO CON PECORINO

Preparation time: *30 min*
Cooking time: *10 min*
Serves 4

— 2 tablespoons olive oil, plus
   extra for brushing
— 2¼ pounds spinach, coarse
   stalks removed
— 6 ripe tomatoes, chopped
— pinch of dried oregano
— 3 ounces sharp pecorino
   cheese, shaved into flakes
— 1 sprig thyme, chopped
— salt and pepper

Preheat the oven to 400°F. Brush an ovenproof dish with oil. Cook the spinach in just the water clinging to the leaves after washing for a few minutes, until wilted. Drain well, squeeze out the excess moisture, and put into the prepared dish. Combine the tomatoes, oil, and oregano in a bowl and season with salt and pepper, then spread the mixture over the spinach. Sprinkle with the pecorino flakes and thyme and bake for 10 minutes. Serve immediately.

SPINACH QUENELLES

QUENELLE DI SPINACI

Preparation time: *25 min*
Cooking time: *8–10 min*
Serves 4

— 3 tablespoons butter
— 3⅔ cups chopped spinach
— generous ½ cup chopped ham
— 1 sprig thyme, chopped
— ½ cup grated Gruyère cheese
— ½ cup olive oil
— salt

Melt the butter in a skillet. Add the spinach and ham and cook, stirring occasionally, for a few minutes. Season lightly with salt, sprinkle over the thyme and cheese, and remove the skillet from the heat. Shape the mixture into quenelles using 2 spoons. Heat the oil in a large skillet. Add the quenelles and cook over medium heat, turning occasionally, for 8–10 minutes. Remove with a slotted spoon and drain on paper towels. Transfer to a warm serving dish and serve immediately.

ZIMINO

ZIMINO

Preparation time: *25 min*
Cooking time: *45 min*
Serves 4–6

— ¼ cup dried mushrooms
— 1 pound 2 ounces Swiss chard
— 4 tablespoons olive oil
— 3 tomatoes, peeled and diced
— 1 onion, diced
— 1 carrot, diced
— 1 clove garlic, finely chopped
— 1 stalk celery, diced
— 1 sprig parsley, chopped
— salt and pepper

Put the mushrooms into a heatproof bowl, pour in hot water to cover, and let soak for 20 minutes, then drain and squeeze out the excess moisture. Meanwhile, remove and discard the stalks from the Swiss chard and chop the leaves. Heat the oil in a pan. Add the tomatoes, onion, carrot, garlic, and celery, and season with salt and pepper. Cook over low heat, stirring occasionally, for 15 minutes. Add 1–2 tablespoons of water if the mixture is becoming too dry. Stir in the Swiss chard leaves, mushrooms, and parsley, and simmer, stirring occasionally, for another 30 minutes. Salt cod is excellent cooked in this sauce.

SWISS CHARD RISOTTO

RISOTTO ALLA BIETOLA

Preparation time: *30 min*
Cooking time: *50 min*
Serves 4

— 11 ounces cuttlefish
— 4 tablespoons olive oil
— 1 pearl onion, finely chopped
— 1 clove garlic, finely chopped
— 1 pound 2 ounces Swiss chard,
  leaves chopped
— 1¼ cups risotto rice
— salt and pepper
— grated Parmesan cheese,
  to serve

To prepare the cuttlefish, cut off the tentacles just in front of the eyes and discard the beak from the center. Separate and skin the tentacles and pull the skin from the body. Cut along the back and remove and discard the cuttlebone. Carefully remove the ink sac and put into a bowl of water—you will need 3–4 sacs. Remove and discard the innards and the head. Chop the tentacles and bodies.

Heat the oil in a large pan. Add the cuttlefish and cook, stirring frequently, until lightly browned. Stir in the onion, garlic, and Swiss chard, cover, and cook, stirring occasionally, for 30 minutes. Meanwhile bring 5 cups of water to a boil in a pan, then reduce the heat and simmer. Add the rice to the cuttlefish mixture and stir in the reserved ink. Mix well, then pour in the hot water and cook, stirring frequently, for 15–20 minutes, until the rice is tender. Season with salt and pepper, sprinkle with the Parmesan, and serve immediately.

SWISS CHARD AU GRATIN

BIETOLE GRATINATE

Preparation time: *25 min*
Cooking time: *15 min*
Serves 4

— butter, for greasing
— 2¼ pounds Swiss chard
— 1 quantity béchamel sauce
  (see page 51)
— 1 cup grated Parmesan
  cheese
— salt

Preheat the oven to 350°F. Grease an ovenproof dish with butter. Separate the Swiss chard leaves from the stalks using kitchen scissors or a sharp knife. (Set the leaves aside to make soup.) Cook the stalks in lightly salted, boiling water for 10–15 minutes, until tender, then drain well and cut into small pieces. Make alternate layers of Swiss chard stalks, béchamel sauce, and Parmesan, ending with a layer of Parmesan in the prepared dish. Bake for about 15 minutes.

SWISS CHARD RISOTTO

SWISS CHARD AND ARTICHOKE PIE

TORTA DI BIETOLA E CARCIOFI

Preparation time: *1½ hours,*
plus 30 min resting
Cooking time: *40–45 min*
Serves 6

For the dough:
— 4½ cups All-purpose flour,
  plus extra for dusting
— ½ cup olive oil

For the filling:
— 1 pound 2 ounces Swiss chard,
  coarse stalks removed
— 2 slices white bread,
  crusts removed
— 4 tablespoons milk
— juice of 1 lemon, strained
— 12 globe artichokes
— 4 tablespoons olive oil
— 1 onion, thinly sliced
— generous 1 cup grated
  pecorino cheese
— ⅔ cup grated Parmesan
  cheese
— 1 tablespoon chopped
  marjoram
— butter, for greasing
— salt and pepper

To make the dough, sift the flour into a mound on a counter and make a well in the center. Add a pinch of salt, the oil, and 4 tablespoons of water to the well and gradually incorporate the flour into the liquid using your fingers. If necessary, add another 1–2 tablespoons water. Knead gently, then shape into a ball, wrap in plastic wrap, and let rest in the refrigerator for 30 minutes.

Meanwhile, bring a pan of salted water to a boil. Add the Swiss chard and cook for 10–15 minutes, until tender but still al dente. Drain, squeeze out the excess moisture, and chop. Tear the bread into pieces, put into a bowl, and pour in the milk. Let soak. Fill a bowl halfway with water and stir in the lemon juice. Trim the stems from the artichokes, remove the coarse leaves, and cut off the tips from the remaining leaves, then immediately add the artichokes to the acidulated water to prevent discoloration. Let soak for 10 minutes, then drain and chop. Heat the 4 tablespoons of oil in a skillet. Add the onion and artichokes and cook over low heat, stirring occasionally, for 5 minutes, until softened. Drain the bread and squeeze out the excess moisture, then add to the skillet with the Swiss chard, pecorino, and Parmesan. Mix well, season with salt and pepper, and sprinkle with the marjoram. Remove the skillet from the heat.

Preheat the oven to 400°F. Generously grease a 14 x 10-inch roasting pan with butter. Unwrap the dough and cut into 2 pieces, one slightly larger than the other. Roll out the larger piece on a lightly floured counter and carefully lift onto the bottom and partway up the sides of the prepared roasting pan. (It will be fragile and crumbly.) Spoon in the vegetable mixture. Roll out the second piece of dough and carefully lift it to cover the filling. Crimp the edges together well. Prick holes in a spiral pattern with the prongs of a fork all over the surface. Bake for 40–45 minutes, until golden brown. Served hot, warm, or cold.

SWISS CHARD WITH ANCHOVIES

BIETOLE CON LE ACCIUGHE

Preparation time: *30 min*
Cooking time: *20 min*
Serves 4

— 2¼ pounds Swiss chard
— 4 salted anchovies, heads
    removed, cleaned, and filleted,
    soaked in cold water for
    10 minutes and drained
— 2 tablespoons olive oil, plus
    extra for drizzling
— 1 clove garlic, chopped
— ½ cup grated Parmesan
    cheese
— salt and pepper

Separate the Swiss chard leaves from the stalks using kitchen scissors or a sharp knife. (Set the leaves aside to make soup.) Cut the stalks into 2-inch pieces and cook in lightly salted, boiling water for 10–15 minutes, until tender, then drain well. Meanwhile, chop the anchovies. Heat the olive oil in a skillet, add the garlic and anchovies, and cook over low heat, mashing with a wooden spoon until the anchovies have almost disintegrated. Add the Swiss chard stalks, increase the heat to high, and cook, stirring frequently, for a few minutes. Lower the heat to medium, season with salt and pepper, and drizzle with olive oil. Mix well and cook for another 10 minutes. Remove the skillet from the heat, sprinkle with the Parmesan, and serve.

GREEN CREAM SOUP

CREMA VERDE

Preparation time: *15 min*
Cooking time: *30 min*
Serves 4

— 2 tablespoons butter
— 2 leeks, white part only,
    thinly sliced
— 3 potatoes, diced
— 4¼ cups vegetable stock
— 4½ cups chopped watercress
— pinch freshly grated nutmeg
— ⅔ cup heavy cream
— salt and pepper
— buttered toasted croutons,
    to serve

Melt the butter in a pan, add the leeks, and cook over low heat, stirring occasionally, for 5 minutes, until softened. Add the potatoes, pour in the stock, and cook over low heat for 10 minutes. Add the watercress and nutmeg, season with salt and pepper, and cook for another 10 minutes. Transfer to a food processor and process to a puree. Pour into a pan, stir in the cream, and reheat briefly. Serve with toasted croutons lightly spread with butter.

SAUSAGE AND WILD CHICORY

SAUSAGE AND WILD CHICORY

SALSICCIA ALLA CICORIA

Preparation time: *10 min*
Cooking time: *7–8 min*
Serves 4

— 2 Italian sausages (salsiccia)
— 6⅔ cups croutons (about
    7 ounces)
— 7 ounces wild chicory
    or young dandelion leaves
— olive oil, for drizzling
— red wine vinegar, for drizzling
— salt and pepper

Put the sausages into a small pan, add 2 tablespoons of water, and poach gently for 7–8 minutes. Test whether the sausages are done by piercing with a fork; if the prongs come out shiny, they are ready. Remove from the pan and let stand until cool enough to handle. Meanwhile, put the croutons and wild chicory or dandelion leaves into a salad bowl. Peel off the sausage skins and crumble the meat into the salad. Season with salt and pepper, drizzle with oil and vinegar to taste, toss, and serve.

NETTLE SOUP

MINESTRA DI ORTICHE

Preparation time: *10 min*
Cooking time: *35–40 min*
Serves 4

— 1 pound 5 ounces fresh
    nettles
— 6¼ cups meat stock
— 3 tablespoons olive oil
— ⅓ cup diced pancetta
— 1 clove garlic, chopped
— 2 ripe tomatoes, peeled,
    seeded, and chopped
— scant ¾ cups long-grain rice
— salt

Wearing a pair of gloves, remove all the nettle leaves and strings that cling to the stems. Wash and drain well and chop coarsely. Put the stock in a pan and bring to a boil. Heat the oil in another pan, add the pancetta and garlic, and cook for 5 minutes. Add the tomatoes and cook for another 10 minutes, then season with salt and stir in the nettles. Cook for another few minutes, then pour in the stock, bring back to a boil, and add the rice. Cook for 15–20 minutes until the rice is tender. Ladle into a soup tureen and serve immediately.

NETTLE AND SPINACH RAVIOLI

PHOTO PAGE 65

RAVIOLI DI ORTICHE E SPINACI

Preparation time: *50 min,
plus 15 min resting*
Cooking time: *15 min*
Serves *4*

For the pasta dough:
— 1¾ cups all-purpose flour,
   plus extra for dusting
— 2 eggs

For the filling:
— 9 ounces very young
   nettle leaves
— 9 ounces spinach or
   Swiss chard, stalks removed
— scant 1 cup ricotta cheese
— 1 egg, lightly beaten
— 1 cup grated Parmesan
   cheese, plus extra to serve
— 1 teaspoon grated
   lemon rind
— pinch of marjoram
— pinch of freshly grated
   nutmeg
— pinch of ground cinnamon
   (optional)
— salt
— sauce of your choice, to serve

To make the pasta dough, sift the flour and a pinch of salt into a mound on a counter and make a well in the center. Break the eggs into the well and gradually incorporate the dry ingredients with your fingers. Knead well, shape the dough into a ball, cover, and let rest in a cool place for at least 15 minutes. Meanwhile, make the filling. Bring 2 pans of salted water to a boil. Add the nettle leaves to one pan and the spinach or Swiss chard leaves to the other. Cook for about 5 minutes, until tender, then drain and squeeze out any excess moisture. Chop all the leaves very finely and put them into a bowl. Stir in the ricotta, egg, Parmesan, lemon rind, marjoram, nutmeg, and cinnamon, if using, and season with salt. Roll out the pasta dough into a thin sheet on a lightly floured counter and cut into squares of your chosen size. Put a small quantity of filling in the center of each square, brush the edges with water, and fold over, enclosing the filling. Press the edges firmly together to seal well. Bring a large pan of salted water to a boil. Add the ravioli and cook for about 10 minutes, until tender. Drain and stir into your chosen sauce. Transfer to a warm serving dish and serve immediately, handing around more grated Parmesan separately.

WATERCRESS TARTINES

TARTINE AL CRESCIONE

Preparation time: *25 min*
Serves *4*

— 4 eggs, hard-cooked
— 4 tablespoons mayonnaise
— juice of 1 lemon, strained
— 1 bunch watercress,
   coarsely chopped
— 4–8 slices white bread,
   crusts removed
— salt and pepper

Shell and chop the eggs, then mix with the mayonnaise and lemon juice. Season with salt and pepper and stir in the watercress. Cut the slices of bread in half and spread with the mixture. Chill in the refrigerator until ready to serve.

NETTLE AND SPINACH RAVIOLI

NETTLE RISOTTO

RISOTTO ALLE ORTICHE

Preparation time: *10 min*
Cooking time: *35 min*
Serves 4

— 6 ¼ cups vegetable stock
— 2 tablespoons butter
— 3 tablespoons olive oil
— 11 ounces fresh young
    nettles, coarsely chopped
— 1 ¾ cups risotto rice
— 5 tablespoons dry white wine
— scant 1 cup light cream
— ½ cup grated Parmesan cheese
— salt and pepper

Pour the stock into a pan and bring to a boil. Meanwhile, melt the butter with the oil in another pan, add the nettles, and cook over low heat, stirring occasionally, for a few minutes. Stir in the rice and cook, stirring, until the grains are coated. Add the wine and cook until the alcohol has evaporated. Add a ladleful of the hot stock and cook, stirring, until absorbed. Continue adding the stock, a ladleful at a time, and stirring until each addition has been absorbed, for about 18–20 minutes. When the rice is almost tender, stir in the cream. When the rice is tender, remove the pan from the heat, stir in the Parmesan, taste, and season. Cover and let stand for 2 minutes before serving.

PUNTARELLE SALAD WITH ANCHOVY DRESSING

INSALATA DI PUNTARELLE ALLE ACCIUGHE

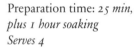

Preparation time: *25 min,*
plus 1 hour soaking
Serves 4

— 2 ¼ pounds puntarelle
    (Catalogna chicory),
    trimmed
— 3 canned anchovy fillets,
    drained and chopped
    or 3 ¼ inches anchovy paste
— 1 small clove garlic,
    finely chopped
— 2 tablespoons white
    wine vinegar
— 2 tablespoons olive oil

Cut the puntarelle into narrow strips, starting from the solid part of the base up to the extreme tips of the leaves. Put the strips into a bowl, pour in water to cover, and let soak for 1 hour, until the leaves curl up.

Meanwhile, make the dressing. Pound the anchovy fillets in a mortar until creamy, then add the garlic and pound until thoroughly combined. If using anchovy paste, pound the paste and garlic until thoroughly combined. Transfer to a bowl and stir in the vinegar, then whisk in the oil. Drain the puntarelle carefully, pat dry on a dish towel, and transfer to a salad bowl. Drizzle the dressing over and serve.

DANDELION WITH PARMESAN

CATALOGNA AL PARMIGIANO

Preparation time: *10 min*
Cooking time: *17 min*
Serves 4

— 1 pound 10 ounces Italian
   dandelion (cutting chicory)
   leaves, cut into strips
— 5 tablespoons butter
— 4 tablespoons Parmesan
   cheese, grated
— salt

Cook the dandelion strips in salted, boiling water for 15 minutes, then drain, squeeze out as much liquid as possible, chop coarsely, and place on a warm serving dish. Melt the butter in a small pan and, when it turns slightly golden in color, pour it over the dandelions. Sprinkle with the Parmesan and serve.

ESCAROLE STUFFED WITH OLIVES AND CAPERS

INDIVIA RIPIENA DI OLIVE E CAPPERI

Preparation time: *10 min*
Cooking time: *45 min*
Serves 4

— 1½ cloves garlic
— 2 heads escarole, trimmed
— 3 tablespoons olive oil,
   plus extra for brushing
— 1 cup fresh bread crumbs
— ¾ cup green olives,
   pitted and sliced
— 3 tablespoons capers, drained
   and rinsed
— 1 sprig parsley, chopped
— salt and pepper

Chop the whole garlic clove. Put the escarole heads, with some of the water from washing still clinging to their leaves, in a skillet with 2 tablespoons of the olive oil and the chopped garlic. Season with salt and pepper. Cover and cook over low heat for about 15 minutes.

Meanwhile, preheat the oven to 350°F. Brush an ovenproof dish with oil. Heat the remaining olive oil in a pan, add the bread crumbs and remaining garlic, and cook, stirring frequently, until the bread crumbs are golden. Remove and discard the garlic and stir in the olives, capers, and parsley. Gently open out the escarole leaves, stuff the heads with almost all the bread crumb mixture, and press back into their original shapes. Place in the prepared dish and sprinkle with the remaining bread crumbs. Bake for about 20 minutes.

ARTICHOKE AND MUSHROOM SALAD

INSALATA DI CARCIOFI E CHAMPIGNON

Preparation time: *30 min*
Serves 4

— 3 tender baby globe
    artichokes
— juice of 2 lemons, strained
— 2 cups sliced white
    mushrooms
— 4–5 tablespoons olive oil
— 3½ ounces Gruyère cheese
— salt and pepper

Remove the tough outer leaves of the artichokes. Slice the artichokes thinly, sprinkle with half of the lemon juice, and put into a salad bowl. Add the mushrooms and season with salt and pepper. Whisk together the remaining lemon juice and olive oil in a pitcher and pour the mixture over the salad. Toss well, sprinkle with the diced cheese, and serve.

ARTICHOKES AND OLIVES

CARCIOFI E OLIVE

Preparation time: *30 min*
Cooking time: *45 min*
Serves 4

— juice of 1 lemon, strained
— 8 globe artichokes
— olive oil
— 1 sprig thyme
— 1 bay leaf
— ½ onion, thinly sliced
    into rings
— 1¾ cups black olives,
    to serve
— salt and pepper

Fill a bowl halfway with water and stir in the lemon juice. Trim the artichoke stems, remove any coarse leaves and the chokes, and cut off the tips of the remaining leaves, then add the artichokes immediately to the acidulated water to prevent discoloration. Drain and pack them upright in a tall, narrow pan. Pour in water to come halfway up the artichokes, measuring how much you add. Then add half as much olive oil (so that the liquid comes three-quarters of the way up the artichokes). Season with salt and pepper and add the thyme, bay leaf, and onion rings. Cover and simmer for 45 minutes, until the artichokes are tender and almost all the water has been absorbed. Remove from the heat and let cool completely before serving with the olives.

ARTICHOKES WITH OLIVES AND LEMON

CARCIOFI ALLE OLIVE E LIMONE

Preparation time: *45 min*
Cooking time: *25 min*
Serves 6

— 2 lemons
— 12 globe artichokes
— 3–4 tablespoons olive oil
— 1¼ cups black olives,
   pitted
— 1 sprig thyme, finely
   chopped
— 2 cloves garlic, finely
   chopped
— salt and pepper

Squeeze the juice from one lemon and strain it into a bowl. Fill a bowl halfway with water and stir in half of the lemon juice. Trim the artichoke stems, remove any coarse leaves and the chokes, and cut off ½ inch from the tips of the remaining leaves, then immediately add the artichokes to the acidulated water to prevent discoloration. Heat the olive oil in a pan and drain and slice the artichokes. Add the artichokes, olives, thyme, and garlic to the pan and cook over low heat, stirring occasionally, for 5 minutes. Season with salt and pepper, pour in 1 cup water, and simmer for 10 minutes. Thinly slice the remaining lemon, add to the pan, and simmer for another 10 minutes. Remove from the heat and let cool slightly, then transfer to a serving plate and serve warm.

ARTICHOKES NAPOLETANA

CARCIOFI ALLA NAPOLETANA

Preparation time: *30 min*
Cooking time: *45 min*
Serves 4

— juice of ½ lemon, strained
— 8 globe artichokes
— 3–4 tablespoons olive oil
— 2 cloves garlic
— 1 tablespoon capers, drained
   and rinsed
— scant 1 cup green olives,
   pitted and chopped
— 1 tablespoon parsley, chopped
— 1 lemon, cut into wedges
— salt and pepper

Fill a bowl halfway with water and stir in the lemon juice. Trim the artichoke stems, remove any coarse leaves and the chokes, and cut off ½ inch from the tips of the remaining leaves, then immediately add the artichokes to the acidulated water to prevent discoloration. Let soak for 10 minutes, then drain and pat dry. Heat the olive oil in a pan, add the garlic, and cook for a few minutes until golden brown, then remove and discard. Cut the artichokes into wedges, add to the pan, and cook over high heat for 5 minutes, then add the capers and olives. Season with salt and pepper to taste and add ⅔ cup of warm water. Mix well, cover, and simmer for about 30 minutes, until tender. Remove the lid and boil off any excess liquid. Transfer the artichokes to a warm serving dish, sprinkle with the parsley, and garnish with the lemon wedges.

ARTICHOKE AND FENNEL FRITTERS

ARTICHOKE AND FENNEL FRITTERS

PHOTO PAGE 70

CARCIOFI E FIONOCCHI IN PASTELLA FRITTI

Preparation time: *15 min*
Cooking time: *10–20 min*
Serves 4

— 2 fennel bulbs, cut into
 wedges
— juice of ½ lemon, strained
— 4 globe artichokes
— olive oil, for deep-frying
— salt

For the batter:
— 1 egg
— 4 tablespoons milk
— ½ cup all-purpose flour
— salt

Bring a pan of salted water to a boil. Add the fennel wedges and simmer for 5 minutes, then drain. Fill a bowl halfway with water and stir in the lemon juice. Trim the artichoke stems, remove any coarse leaves and the chokes, and cut the artichokes into wedges, then add the wedges immediately to the acidulated water to prevent discoloration. To make the batter, combine the egg and milk in a bowl, then gradually beat in the flour and a pinch of salt, beating until smooth. Let stand for 5 minutes. Heat the oil in a deep-fryer or skillet to 350–375°F, or until a cube of day-old bread browns in 30 seconds. Drain the artichokes. Dip the vegetable wedges into the batter, a few at a time, and drain off the excess. Add to the hot oil and cook for 5–8 minutes, until golden brown. Remove with a slotted spoon and drain on paper towels. Keep warm while you cook the remaining vegetable wedges in the same way. Pile onto a serving dish, sprinkle with salt, and serve immediately.

JEWISH-STYLE ARTICHOKES

CARCIOFI ALLA GIUDIA

Preparation time: *3 min*
Cooking time: *25 min*
Serves 4

— 8 Roman (large globe)
 artichokes
— olive oil
— salt

Young, whole, round (if possible), thornless artichokes are required for this dish. Trim the artichoke stems, remove any coarse leaves and the chokes, and cut the artichokes into wedges, then add the wedges immediately to acidulated water to prevent discoloration. Fill a wide, deep, cast-iron skillet with enough olive oil to cover the artichokes halfway and heat gently. Open out the leaves slightly and place the artichokes upright in the oil. Cook over medium heat for 10–12 minutes, then increase the heat and turn the artichokes upside down. Cook for another 10 minutes, until they have turned golden brown and are crisp at the tips. Remove with a spatula, being careful not to break them. Serve immediately, sprinkled with a pinch of salt.

SORRENTINO ARTICHOKES

CARCIOFI ALLA SORRENTINA

Preparation time: *30 min*
Cooking time: *45 min*
Serves 4

— juice of 1 lemon, strained
— 4 large globe artichokes
— 5 ounces mozzarella cheese, diced
— ⅓ cup grated pecorino cheese
— 1 tablespoon chopped parsley
— 1 tablespoon fresh bread crumbs
— 1 egg, lightly beaten
— 4 canned anchovy fillets, drained and coarsely chopped
— olive oil, for drizzling
— salt and pepper

Fill a bowl halfway with water and stir in the lemon juice. Trim the artichoke stems, remove any coarse leaves and the chokes, and cut ½ inch from the tips of the remaining leaves, then add the artichokes immediately to the acidulated water to prevent discoloration. Combine the mozzarella, pecorino, parsley, bread crumbs, and egg in a bowl and season with salt and pepper. Drain the artichokes and open out the leaves slightly. Put a pinch of salt inside each artichoke, then fill them with the cheese mixture. Stand them upright, tightly packed, in a tall flameproof casserole. Pour in water to come halfway up the artichokes, add the anchovy fillets, drizzle with a little olive oil, and simmer for 30 minutes. Meanwhile, preheat the oven to 350°F. Transfer the casserole to the oven and bake for 15 minutes. Serve immediately.

ARTICHOKE SOUP WITH CHERVIL

CREMA DI CARCIOFI AL CERFOGLIO

Preparation time: *30 min*
Cooking time: *15–20 min*
Serves 4

— juice of 1 lemon, strained
— 6 globe artichokes
— 2 tablespoons butter
— 2 shallots, finely chopped
— 1 leek, sliced
— 1 cup milk
— 4¼ cups vegetable stock
— 1 sprig chervil, finely chopped
— dash Tabasco sauce
— salt
— thickly sliced white bread, toasted, to serve

Fill a bowl halfway with water and stir in half of the lemon juice. Trim the artichoke stems, remove any coarse leaves and the chokes, and cut the artichokes into quarters, then add the quarters immediately to the acidulated water to prevent discoloration. Bring a pan of salted water to a boil and stir in the remaining lemon juice. Add the artichokes and simmer for 15 minutes, then drain. Melt the butter in a large pan. Add the shallots, leek, and artichokes, and cook over low heat, stirring occasionally, for 5 minutes. Pour in the milk and stock and simmer for 10 minutes. Remove the pan from the heat and let cool slightly, then transfer the mixture to a food processor or blender and process until smooth. Return the soup to the pan, add the chervil and Tabasco sauce to taste, stir well, and heat through. Serve immediately with toasted bread.

ARTICHOKES STUFFED WITH RICOTTA & MUSHROOMS WITH SHALLOT SAUCE

CARCIOFI RIPIENI DI RICOTTA E FUNGHI
CON SALSA DI SCALOGNI

Preparation time: *50 min*
Cooking time: *1 hour*
Serves 4

— juice of 1 lemon, strained
— 4 globe artichokes

For the stuffing:
— 3 tablespoons olive oil
— 1 onion, finely chopped
— 1 clove garlic, finely
   chopped
— 1 sprig rosemary, finely
   chopped
— 9 ounces mushrooms
— scant 1 cup ricotta cheese
— salt and pepper

For the sauce:
— 4 tablespoons butter
— 3½ ounces shallots
— 1 tablespoon mild mustard
— scant ½ cup dry
   white wine
— 1 cup heavy cream

Fill a bowl halfway with water and stir in half of the lemon juice. Trim the artichoke stems and remove any coarse leaves and the chokes, then add the artichokes immediately to the acidulated water to prevent discoloration. Bring a pan of salted water to a boil and stir in the remaining lemon juice.

To make the stuffing, heat the oil in a pan. Add the onion, garlic, and rosemary, and cook over low heat, stirring occasionally, for 5 minutes. Increase the heat to medium, add the mushrooms, and cook, stirring frequently, for 5–8 minutes, until all the moisture they release has evaporated. Transfer the mixture to a bowl and stir and crush the mushrooms until they form a paste, then mix with the ricotta. Season with salt and pepper and set aside.

To make the sauce, melt the butter in a pan. Add the shallots and cook over low heat, stirring occasionally, for 5 minutes, until softened and translucent. Stir in the mustard and wine and cook, stirring continuously, until the alcohol has evaporated. Stir in the cream and cook, stirring, for a few minutes, until thickened. Remove from the heat and strain the sauce.

Fill the artichokes with the ricotta and mushroom mixture, and pour one or two teaspoons of sauce over each artichoke. Serve remaining sauce separately.

BRAISED ARTICHOKES

CARCIOFI STUFATI AL FORNO

Preparation time: *30 min*
Cooking time: *50 min*
Serves 4

— 2 cloves garlic, very finely
   chopped
— 1 onion, very finely chopped
— 1 sprig mint, finely chopped
— ½ sprig parsley, finely
   chopped
— juice of 1 lemon, strained
— 8 globe artichokes
— olive oil, for drizzling
— salt and pepper

Preheat the oven to 350°F. Put the garlic, onion, mint, and parsley in a bowl, season with salt and pepper, and mix well. Fill another bowl halfway with water and stir in the lemon juice. Trim and reserve the artichoke stems, remove any coarse leaves and the chokes, leaving only a layer surrounding the hearts, then add hearts immediately to the acidulated water to prevent discoloration. Peel the stems, cut into short lengths, and add to the bowl. Drain the artichokes and fill their centers with the garlic and onion mixture. Pour 1 cup of water into a casserole. Stand the artichokes upright and close together in the casserole and put the pieces of stem in the spaces between. Drizzle with olive oil, cover tightly, and bake for 50 minutes. Remove from the oven, transfer the artichokes to a serving dish, and serve hot or cold.

ARTICHOKES WITH OLIVE OIL AND GARLIC

PHOTO PAGE 75

CARCIOFI IN CASSERUOLA ALL'AGLIO E OLIO

Preparation time: *30 min*
Cooking time: *40 min*
Serves 4

— juice of 1 lemon, strained
— 8 globe artichokes
— olive oil
— 2 cloves garlic, peeled
— salt and pepper

Fill a bowl halfway with water and stir in the lemon juice. Trim the artichoke stems, remove any coarse leaves and the chokes, and cut off the tips of the remaining leaves, then add the artichokes immediately to the acidulated water to prevent discoloration. Drain and pack them tightly into a tall, narrow pan. Pour in water to come halfway up the artichokes, measuring how much you add. Then add half as much olive oil and the garlic, and season with salt and pepper. (The liquid should come three-quarters of the way up the artichokes.) Cover and cook over low heat for about 40 minutes, until the artichokes are tender and almost all the water has been absorbed. Remove from the heat and serve immediately.

ARTICHOKES WITH OLIVE OIL AND GARLIC

ARTICHOKES WITH PARMESAN

ARTICHOKES WITH PARMESAN

CARCIOFI AL PARMIGIANO

Preparation time: *35 min,*
plus 15 min soaking
Cooking time: *25 min*
Serves 4

— juice of 1 lemon, strained
— 8 globe artichokes
— 4 tablespoons olive oil
— ⅔ cup grated Parmesan
  cheese
— 1 tablespoon chopped parsley
— salt and pepper

Fill a bowl halfway with water and stir in the lemon juice. Trim the artichoke stems and remove any coarse outer leaves and the chokes, then add the artichokes immediately to the acidulated water to prevent discoloration. Let soak for 15 minutes, then drain and cut into thin slices. Heat the oil in a pan, add the artichokes, and cook over low heat, stirring and turning occasionally, for 15 minutes. Meanwhile, preheat the oven to 375°F. Lightly season the artichokes with salt and remove the pan from the heat. Transfer the artichokes to a casserole, sprinkle with the cheese and parsley, and season lightly with pepper. Bake for 10 minutes and serve immediately from the casserole.

BAKED ARTICHOKES WITH RICE

RISO AL FORNO AI CARCIOFI

Preparation time: *30 min*
Cooking time: *30 min*
Serves 4

— 5 tablespoons olive oil,
  plus extra for brushing
— juice of 1 lemon, strained
— 8 globe artichokes
— 1⅔ cups risotto rice
— 1 sprig parsley, finely
  chopped
— 1 small clove garlic,
  finely chopped
— 4¼ cups hot vegetable stock
— ⅓ cup grated pecorino
  cheese
— salt and pepper

Preheat the oven to 425°F. Brush the inside of a casserole with oil. Fill a bowl halfway with water and stir in the lemon juice. Trim the artichoke stems, remove any coarse leaves and the chokes, and slice thinly, then add the slices immediately to the acidulated water to prevent discoloration. Put the rice into the prepared casserole and sprinkle with the parsley and garlic. Drain the artichokes, add to the casserole, drizzle with the olive oil, and season lightly with salt. Add 3 ladles of the hot stock, sprinkle with the grated cheese, and bake for about 30 minutes, checking frequently to see if more stock is needed and adding as required. Remove from the oven, season with a little pepper, and serve immediately.

ARTICHOKE FLAN

FLAN DI CARCIOFI

Preparation time: *30 min*
Cooking time: *45 min*
Serves 4

— juice of 1 lemon, strained
— 6 globe artichokes
— butter, for greasing
— 2 eggs
— ⅔ cup grated Parmesan
  cheese
— 1 quantity béchamel sauce
  (see page 51)
— ¼ cup fine bread crumbs
— salt and pepper

Fill a bowl halfway with water and stir in half of the lemon juice. Trim off the stems and remove the artichoke leaves and the chokes, then immediately put the hearts in the acidulated water to prevent discoloration. Bring a pan of salted water to a boil and stir in the remaining lemon juice. Drain the artichoke hearts, add to the pan, cover, and simmer for 15 minutes.

Preheat the oven to 350°F. Grease a 9-inch cake pan with butter. Drain the artichoke hearts, chop, and let cool slightly. Lightly beat the eggs with the grated cheese in a bowl and gently stir in the artichoke hearts, then stir the mixture into the béchamel sauce and season with salt and pepper. Pour the mixture into the prepared pan and sprinkle with the bread crumbs. Bake for about 45 minutes, until set. Remove the pan from the oven and serve immediately.

ARTICHOKE AND HAM SALAD WITH MAYONNAISE

INSALATA DI CARCIOFI CON MAIONESE
AL PROSCIUTTO COTTO

Preparation time: *30 min*
Serves 4

— 6 tender baby globe
  artichokes
— juice of 1 lemon, strained
— 2½ ounces lean ham,
  trimmed of fat
— ½ cup mayonnaise
— 3½ ounces fontina cheese,
  cut into thin strips

Trim the stems and remove the tough outer leaves from the artichokes, then slice the artichokes thinly. Sprinkle with the lemon juice and put into a salad bowl. Chop the ham and combine with the mayonnaise in a bowl. Add the strips of cheese to the artichokes, then add the ham mixture. Mix gently and serve.

ARTICHOKE LASAGNETTE

LASAGNETTE AI CARCIOFI

Preparation time: *15 min*
Cooking time: *15 min*
Serves *4*

— juice of ½ lemon, strained
— 4 globe artichokes
— 4 tablespoons olive oil
— ½ onion, thinly sliced
— 10 ounces lasagnette
  (small lasagna noodles)
— 5 ounces cooked ham,
  cut into strips
— ⅔ cup grated Parmesan
  cheese
— salt and pepper

Fill a bowl halfway with water and stir in the lemon juice. Trim the artichoke stems, remove any coarse leaves and the chokes, and cut the artichokes into slices, then add the slices immediately to the acidulated water to prevent discoloration. Heat the olive oil in a skillet. Drain the artichokes, add them to the skillet with the onion, cover, and cook over low heat, stirring occasionally, for 15 minutes, until tender. Meanwhile, bring a large pan of salted water to a boil. Add the pasta, bring back to a boil, and cook for about 10 minutes, until tender but still al dente. When the artichokes are cooked, stir in the ham and cook for 2 minutes, then remove the skillet from the heat. Drain the lasagnette and turn into a serving dish. Add the artichoke mixture, toss lightly, sprinkle with the grated cheese, and serve immediately.

ARTICHOKE AND BEAN SOUP

CREMA DI CARCIOFI E FAGIOLI

Preparation time: *1 hour 20 min,*
plus overnight soaking
Cooking time: *50 min*
Serves *4*

— ¾ cup dried cannellini
  beans, soaked overnight
  in cold water and drained
— juice of 1 lemon, strained
— 4 globe artichokes
— 4¼ cups vegetable stock
— 2 tablespoons butter
— 1 tablespoon olive oil
— 1 onion, finely chopped
— 2 egg yolks
— 2 tablespoons heavy cream
— thick slices fried bread,
  to serve
— salt

Put the beans into a pan, pour in water to cover, and bring to a boil. Reduce the heat and simmer for 1 hour. Fill a bowl halfway with water and stir in the lemon juice. Trim the artichoke stems, remove any coarse leaves and the chokes, and thinly slice the artichokes, then add the slices immediately to the acidulated water. Pour the stock into a pan and heat gently. Melt the butter with the oil in a large pan. Add the onion and cook over low heat, stirring occasionally, for 5 minutes, until softened. Drain the beans, add them to the pan, and cook, stirring continuously, for a few minutes. Drain the artichoke slices and add them to the pan with the hot stock. Cover and simmer for 30 minutes. Remove the pan from the heat and let cool slightly, then ladle the mixture into a blender and blend until smooth. Pour into a clean pan and heat gently, but do not let the soup boil. Beat the egg yolks with the cream in a bowl, then stir into the soup and heat through without boiling. Serve immediately with slices of fried bread.

ARTICHOKE HEART TARTE TATIN

TARTE TATIN AI CARCIOFI

Preparation time: *50 min*
Cooking time: *30 min*
Serves 6

— 6–8 artichoke hearts
— 2 tablespoons olive oil
— 1 clove garlic, finely chopped
— 3 tomatoes, diced
— 1 bulb fennel, diced
— 2 shallots, diced
— 1–2 tablespoons tapenade
— ⅔ cup grated Parmesan
  cheese
— 9 ounces puff pastry dough,
  thawed if frozen
— all-purpose flour, for dusting
— salt and pepper

Bring a pan of lightly salted water to a boil. Add the artichoke hearts and simmer for 10 minutes, then remove with a slotted spoon. Heat the oil in a pan. Add the garlic, tomatoes, fennel, and shallots, season with salt and pepper, and cook over low heat, stirring occasionally, for 20 minutes. Meanwhile, preheat the oven to 350°F. Put the artichoke hearts in a tart pan and spread the tapenade over, then sprinkle with an even layer of the vegetables and the grated cheese. Roll out the pastry dough on a lightly floured counter, cut out a round slightly larger than the tart pan, and place over the vegetables, tucking in the edge. Bake for about 30 minutes, until the pastry has risen and is golden brown. Remove the pan from the oven, invert the tart onto a warm serving plate, and serve immediately.

ARTICHOKE AND MOZZARELLA PIE

Preparation time: *40 min*
Cooking time: *55–60 min*
Serves 4

— juice of 1 lemon, strained
— 3 globe artichokes
— butter, for greasing
— 11 ounces puff pastry dough,
  thawed if frozen
— all-purpose flour, for dusting
— 5 ounces mozzarella
  cheese
— 2 eggs
— generous 1 cup grated
  Parmesan cheese
— 1 clove garlic, finely chopped
— 1 sprig parsley, finely
  chopped
— olive oil, for drizzling
— salt and pepper

Fill a bowl halfway with water and stir in half of the lemon juice. Trim the artichoke stems, remove any coarse leaves and the chokes, and cut the artichokes into wedges, then add the wedges immediately to the acidulated water to prevent discoloration. Bring a pan of salted water to a boil and add the remaining lemon juice. Drain the artichokes, add them to the pan, and simmer for 10–15 minutes.

Meanwhile, preheat the oven to 350°F. Grease a 9-inch tart pan with butter. Roll out the dough on a lightly floured counter and use to line the prepared pan. Chill while preparing the filling. Dice half of the mozzarella. Beat the eggs with the Parmesan, garlic, parsley, and diced mozzarella in a bowl. Bake the unfilled pie shell for 15–20 minutes. Slice the remaining mozzarella and spread out the slices in the pie shell. Drain the artichokes, spread out in the pie shell, and ladle the egg mixture over. Season with salt and pepper, drizzle with a little olive oil, and bake for 40 minutes, until golden and just set. Serve hot, warm, or cold.

ARTICHOKE HEART RING WITH HAM

ANELLO DI CARCIOFI AL PROSCIUTTO COTTO

Preparation time: *45 min*
Cooking time: *45 min*
Serves 6–8

— 25 artichoke hearts
— 2 tablespoons butter, plus extra for greasing
— generous 1 cup grated Parmesan cheese
— 7–8 ounces thinly sliced ham
— 3½ ounces processed cheese slices
— salt and pepper
— buttered young, green peas, to serve (optional)

Bring a pan of lightly salted water to a boil. Cut the artichoke hearts into quarters or 6 segments, add them to the pan, and blanch for a few minutes, then drain. Melt the butter in a pan. Add the artichoke hearts and cook over low heat, occasionally stirring gently, for 10 minutes. Lightly season the artichoke hearts with salt and cook for another 5 minutes. Sprinkle with the grated cheese and season with pepper and more salt, if necessary. Remove the pan from the heat. Meanwhile, preheat the oven to 375°F. Grease a 6¼-cup ring mold with butter. Line the prepared ring mold with the ham, letting the slices overhang the rim. Make alternate layers of the artichoke heart mixture and the processed cheese slices, then fold over the overhanging ham. Put the mold in a roasting pan and pour in hot water to come about halfway up the side. Bake for about 45 minutes, until set. Remove from the oven, turn out onto a warm serving dish, surround with buttered young, green peas, if you like, and serve immediately.

TUSCAN-STYLE EGG AND ARTICHOKE TART

TORTA DI UOVA E CARCIOFI ALLA TOSCANA

Preparation time: *30 min*
Cooking time: *15 min*
Serves 4

— 4 globe artichokes
— all-purpose flour, for dusting
— olive oil, for frying
— butter, for greasing
— 6 eggs
— 1 sprig marjoram or parsley, chopped
— salt and pepper

Trim the artichoke stems, remove any coarse leaves and the chokes, and cut the artichokes into quarters, then dust with flour. Heat enough olive oil in a pan for frying. Add the artichokes and cook over low heat, turning occasionally, for 8 minutes. Preheat the oven to 350°F. Grease a casserole with butter. Remove the artichokes with a slotted spoon and drain on paper towels. Beat the eggs with the marjoram or parsley in a bowl with a fork and season with salt and pepper. Put the artichokes in the prepared casserole, season lightly with salt, and pour the egg mixture over. Bake for 15 minutes, until risen, crisp, and golden brown. Remove from the oven and serve immediately.

ARTICHOKE AND ZUCCHINI STRUDEL

PHOTO PAGE 83

STRUDEL DI CARCIOFI E ZUCCHINE

Preparation time: *40 min*
Cooking time: *1 hour*
Serves *6*

— juice of ½ lemon, strained
— 4 globe artichokes
— 4 tablespoons olive oil
— 2 cloves garlic, peeled
— 2 zucchini, diced
— scant ½ cup vegetable stock
— pinch of ground mace
  (optional)
— scant 1 cup ricotta cheese
— 9 ounces puff pastry dough,
  thawed if frozen
— all-purpose flour, for dusting
— 1 egg, lightly beaten
— 1 tablespoon sesame seeds
— salt and pepper

For the sauce:
— 2 tablespoons dried
  mushrooms
— 2¼ cups vegetable stock
— 2 tablespoons butter
— ¼ cup all-purpose flour
— ¼ cup chopped parsley
— salt and pepper

Fill a bowl halfway with water and stir in the lemon juice. Trim the artichoke stems, remove any coarse leaves and the chokes, and cut the artichokes into thin slices, then add the slices immediately to the acidulated water to prevent discoloration. Heat the oil in a large pan. Add the garlic cloves and cook over low heat, stirring frequently, for a few minutes, until golden. Remove and discard. Drain the artichokes and add to the pan.

Increase the heat to high and cook, stirring occasionally, for 5 minutes. Add the zucchini, stock, and mace, if using, season with salt and pepper, and cook, stirring occasionally, for 10 minutes.

Meanwhile, remove the pan from the heat and stir in the ricotta. Preheat the oven to 375°F. Line a large baking sheet with parchment paper. Roll out the dough into a large rectangle on a lightly floured counter. Spoon the vegetable and ricotta mixture on top, spreading it evenly and leaving a 3-inch margin at the shorter ends. Fold the ends over the filling, then roll up from a long side. Brush the top with the beaten egg, sprinkle over the sesame seeds, and make diagonal incisions in the dough with a small knife. Carefully transfer the strudel to the prepared baking sheet and bake for 20 minutes. Remove from the oven and let cool.

Meanwhile make the sauce. Put the mushrooms into a heatproof bowl, pour in warm water to cover, and let soak for 30 minutes, then drain, squeeze out the excess moisture, and chop. Pour the stock into a pan and bring to a boil. Meanwhile, melt the butter in another pan. Stir in the flour and cook, stirring continuously, for 2 minutes. Gradually add the hot stock, a little at a time, stirring continuously. Add the mushrooms and cook, stirring with a whisk, for about 20 minutes. Season with salt and pepper, and stir in the parsley. Remove the pan from the heat. Slice the strudel and put the slices on individual serving plates. Pour 1–2 tablespoons of the hot sauce next to each slice and serve immediately.

ARTICHOKE AND ZUCCHINI STRUDEL

LIMA BEAN AND ARTICHOKE STEW

LIMA BEAN AND ARTICHOKE STEW

GUAZZETTO DI FAGIOLI E CARCIOFI

Preparation time: *40 min*
Cooking time: *15 min*
Serves 6

— 2 ripe tomatoes, peeled,
   seeded, and chopped
— 1 scallion, coarsely
   chopped
— 1 small celery heart,
   blanched and sliced
— juice of 1 lemon, strained
— 2 globe artichokes
— 2 tablespoons olive oil,
   plus extra for drizzling
— 1 clove garlic
— 1 sprig parsley, chopped
— 9 ounces canned lima
   beans, drained and rinsed
— salt and pepper

Put the tomatoes, scallion, and celery into a blender or food processor, season with salt and pepper, and process until thoroughly combined. Pour the mixture into a small pan and simmer, stirring occasionally, for 10 minutes. Keep the sauce warm.

Meanwhile, fill a bowl halfway with water and stir in the lemon juice. Trim the artichoke stems, remove any coarse leaves and the chokes, and cut off ½ inch from the tips of the remaining leaves, then add the artichokes immediately to the acidulated water to prevent discoloration. Heat the oil in a pan. Add the garlic clove and cook over low heat, stirring occasionally, for a few minutes, until lightly browned, then remove and discard. Drain the artichokes, add to the pan along with the parsley, season with salt and pepper, and sprinkle with 1 tablespoon of water. Simmer for 10 minutes, then stir in the beans and heat through.

To serve, spoon 2 tablespoons of the tomato sauce onto each of 6 individual plates and top with the beans and artichokes. Drizzle with a little oil and serve.

ASPARAGUS IN BATTER

Preparation time: *20 min,
plus 1 hour resting*
Cooking time: *5 min*
Serves *4*

For the batter:
— 2¼ cups all-purpose flour
— 1 tablespoon olive oil
— 2 tablespoons beer
— 1 egg white
— salt

— 2¼ pounds asparagus,
    trimmed
— olive oil, for frying
— salt

To make the batter, sift the flour with a pinch of salt into a bowl. Beat in just enough water to make a fairly thick mixture, then stir in the oil and beer to make a smooth batter. Cover and let rest for 1 hour. Meanwhile, cut the asparagus stems into short lengths. Bring a pan of lightly salted water to a boil. Add the asparagus and simmer for 15 minutes, or until tender. Drain and set aside. In a grease-free bowl, whisk the egg white to stiff peaks, then gently fold into the batter. Pour the olive oil for frying into a skillet to a depth of about ½ inch and heat. Dip the pieces of asparagus in the batter, making sure that they are coated all over. Add to the pan and cook until golden. Remove with a slotted spoon, drain on paper towels and serve immediately.

ASPARAGUS AND HERB SALAD

Preparation time: *30 min*
Cooking time: *20 min*
Serves *4*

— 16 green asparagus spears,
    trimmed
— 2 tomatoes, peeled, seeded,
    and diced
— 1 bunch basil, finely
    chopped
— 2 bunches chervil, finely
    chopped
— 2 avocados
— juice of 1 lemon
— 1 shallot, finely chopped
— 1 teaspoon capers
— 4 tablespoons olive oil
— 2 tablespoons apple vinegar
— salt and pepper

Trim the asparagus spears to the same length and tie in a bundle with kitchen string. Bring a tall pan of lightly salted water to a boil. Add the asparagus, standing the bundle upright with the tips protruding above the water level. Cover and simmer for 15 minutes, or until tender. Lift out the asparagus and drain on paper towels, then let cool. Put the tomatoes, basil, and chervil into a salad bowl. Peel, halve, and pit the avocados, then dice. Toss with the lemon juice in a bowl to prevent discoloration. Cut the asparagus spears into ¾-inch lengths, combine with the shallot and capers, and add to the salad bowl. Add the avocado and stir gently. Season with salt and pepper, drizzle with the oil and vinegar, toss gently, and serve.

ASPARAGUS AND PANCETTA RISOTTO

Preparation time: *20 min*
Cooking time: *30 min*
Serves 4

— 5 ounces asparagus
— 5 cups vegetable stock
— 3 tablespoons butter
— 2 tablespoons olive oil
— 1 onion, chopped
— 2 ounces pancetta or bacon, finely chopped
— 1½ cups risotto rice
— ¼ cup Cointreau
— ½ cup grated Parmesan cheese
— 2 tablespoons chopped parsley
— salt and pepper

Trim the asparagus spears to the same length and tie in a bundle with kitchen string. Bring a tall pan of lightly salted water to a boil. Add the asparagus, standing the bundle upright with the tips protruding above the water level. Cover and simmer for 15 minutes, or until tender. Lift out the asparagus and drain on paper towels. Cut off the tips and set aside, then slice the stalks. Pour the stock into a pan and bring to a boil.

Meanwhile, melt half of the butter with the oil in a pan. Add the onion and pancetta or bacon and cook over low heat, stirring occasionally, for 5 minutes. Add the asparagus slices and cook briefly, then stir in the rice. Cook, stirring continuously, for 1–2 minutes, until all the grains are coated with oil.

Drizzle the Cointreau over the rice and cook until the alcohol has evaporated. Add a ladleful of the hot stock and cook, stirring continuously, until it has been absorbed. Continue to add the hot stock, a ladleful at a time, stirring continuously until each addition has been absorbed, for about 20 minutes.

Remove the pan from the heat and stir in the remaining butter and the grated cheese. Season with pepper and add the reserved asparagus tips. Transfer to a warm serving dish, sprinkle with the chopped parsley, and serve.

QUAIL EGGS AND ASPARAGUS

QUAIL EGGS AND ASPARAGUS

PHOTO PAGE 88

OVETTI NEL NIDO

Preparation time: 20 *min*
Cooking time: 25 *min*
Serves 8

— 1 hard-cooked egg
— ⅔ cup olive oil
— 10 green olives, pitted
— 1 tablespoon white wine
— 1 tablespoon white
    wine vinegar
— 1 tablespoon chopped
    parsley
— 1 tablespoon chopped
    marjoram
— 2¼ pounds asparagus,
    trimmed
— 16 quail eggs
— 1 lettuce heart, shredded
— salt and pepper

Shell the hard-cooked egg, then halve and scoop out the yolk into a bowl. Add the olive oil, olives, wine, and vinegar, season with salt and pepper, pour in 3 tablespoons water, and blend with a fork until thoroughly combined. Sprinkle over the parsley and marjoram and set the sauce aside. Trim the asparagus spears to the same length and tie in a bundle with kitchen string. Bring a tall pan of lightly salted water to a boil. Add the asparagus, standing the bundle upright with the tips protruding above the water level. Cover and simmer for 15 minutes, or until tender. Lift out the asparagus and drain on paper towels. Put the quail eggs into a pan of cold water, bring to a boil, and boil for 4 minutes. Remove from the heat, drain off the hot water, cover with cold water, and let cool. When cold, carefully shell and cut the eggs in half. Make a bed of lettuce in the center of a serving plate. Place the halved quail eggs on top. Slice the asparagus spears lengthwise and arrange them around the sides to resemble a nest. Pour over the sauce and serve.

ASPARAGUS AND MASCARPONE VELOUTÉ

VELLUTATA DI ASPARAGI AL MASCARPONE

Preparation time: 25 *min*
Cooking time: 20 *min*
Serves 4

— 1 cup heavy cream
— scant 1 cup mascarpone
    cheese
— 14 ounces asparagus
— 4¼ cups vegetable stock
— salt and pepper

Combine the cream and mascarpone in a bowl. Cut off the asparagus tips and set aside. Chop the stalks, put into a pan, and pour in the stock. Bring to a boil, then reduce the heat and simmer for 15 minutes or until tender. Remove the pan from the heat and let cool slightly, then ladle into a blender or food processor and process until smooth. Return the soup to the pan and bring to a simmer. Stir in the mascarpone cream and season with salt and pepper. Reserve a few asparagus tips for the garnish and stir the remainder into the pan. Simmer very gently for another 5 minutes. Remove the pan from the heat and pour the soup into a warm tureen or individual bowls. Garnish with the reserved asparagus tips and serve immediately.

ASPARAGUS IN LEMON BUTTER

PHOTO PAGE 90

ASPARAGI AL BURRO PROFUMATO DI LIMONE

Preparation time: 30 *min*
Cooking time: 25 *min*
Serves 4

— 2 ¼ pounds asparagus
— 6 tablespoons butter
— juice of ½ lemon, strained
— salt

Trim the asparagus spears to the same length and tie in a bundle with kitchen string. Bring a tall pan of lightly salted water to a boil. Add the asparagus, standing the bundle upright with the tips protruding above the water level. Cover and simmer for 15 minutes, or until tender. Lift out the asparagus and drain on paper towels, then cut the string and put the spears on a serving plate. Season lightly with salt. Melt the butter in a heatproof bowl set over a pan of barely simmering water. Stir in the lemon juice, then remove from the heat and pour the flavored butter carefully over the asparagus. Serve immediately.

ASPARAGUS IN MUSTARD SAUCE

ASPARAGI LESSATI IN SALSA ALLA SENAPE

Preparation time: 40 *min*
Cooking time: 20 *min*
Serves 4

— 2 ¼ pounds asparagus,
   trimmed
— 3 canned anchovies, drained
   and rinsed
— 1 tablespoon capers, drained,
   rinsed, and finely chopped
— 1 small bunch parsley,
   finely chopped
— ⅔ cup olive oil
— 4 tablespoons white
   wine vinegar
— ½ tablespoon Dijon mustard
— salt

Trim the asparagus spears to the same length and tie in a bundle with kitchen string. Bring a tall pan of lightly salted water to a boil. Add the asparagus, standing the bundle upright with the tips protruding above the water level. Cover and simmer for 15 minutes, or until tender. Lift out the asparagus and drain on paper towels. Cut the string and put the asparagus spears on a serving plate with the tips pointing in the same direction. Let cool completely.

To make the sauce, put the anchovies, capers, and parsley in a bowl. Pour in the oil and vinegar, add the mustard, and mix carefully. Pour the sauce over the asparagus and serve.

WHITE BEAN AND ASPARAGUS SALAD

PHOTO PAGE 93

INSALATA DI FAGIOLI E ASPARAGINA

Preparation time: *20 min*
Cooking time: *10 min*
Serves 6–8

— 1 bunch thin young
  asparagus
— 9 ounces canned lima
  beans, drained and rinsed
— 5 tablespoons olive oil
— juice of ½ lemon, strained
— 1 bunch parsley, finely
  chopped
— salt and freshly ground
  white pepper

Trim the asparagus spears to the same length and tie in a bundle with kitchen string. Bring a tall pan of lightly salted water to a boil. Add the asparagus, standing the bundle upright with the tips protruding above the water level. Cover and simmer for 10 minutes or until tender. Do not overcook. Lift out the asparagus and drain on paper towels. Put the beans into a serving dish. Whisk together the oil, lemon juice, and parsley in a bowl and season with salt and white pepper. Drizzle the dressing over the beans, put the asparagus on top, toss gently, and serve.

ROASTED ASPARAGUS, ZUCCHINI, AND RED ONION SALAD

INSALATA AL FORNO DI ASPARAGI, ZUCCHINE
E CIPOLLA ROSSA

Preparation time: *30 min*
Cooking time: *30 min*
Serves 6

— 5 tablespoons olive oil
— 1 red onion, very thinly
  sliced
— 1 chile, seeded and cut
  into strips
— 2 zucchini, diced
— 1 pound 2 ounces asparagus
  tips
— 2 tablespoons soy sauce
— 2 tablespoons honey
— salt and pepper

Preheat the oven to 350°F. Pour 2 tablespoons of the oil into a large ovenproof dish. Add the onion and chile, toss to coat, and roast for 20 minutes. Remove the dish from the oven and add the zucchini and asparagus tips, then toss gently, return to the oven, and roast for another 8–10 minutes. Whisk together the soy sauce, honey, and the remaining oil in a bowl and season with pepper. Remove the vegetables from the oven, pour the soy dressing over, and toss lightly.

WHITE BEAN AND ASPARAGUS SALAD

PARMESAN ASPARAGUS

ASPARAGI ALLA PARMIGIANA

Preparation time: *5 min*
Cooking time: *15 min*
Serves 4

— 2¼ pounds asparagus,
  spears trimmed
— 1 cup grated Parmesan
  cheese
— 2 tablespoons butter
— salt

Cook the asparagus in salted, boiling water for 15 minutes or until tender. Drain and pat dry gently. Arrange on a warm serving dish with the tips pointing inward. Sprinkle with the Parmesan. Melt the butter, season with a little salt, and pour onto the asparagus. Serve immediately.

VALLE D'AOSTA ASPARAGUS

ASPARAGI ALLA VALDOSTANA

Preparation time: *5 min*
Cooking time: *20–25 min*
Serves 4

— butter, for greasing
— 2¼ pounds asparagus,
  spears trimmed
— 2 slices cooked ham,
  cut into strips
— 4 ounces fontina
  cheese, sliced
— 2 eggs
— 2 tablespoons grated
  Parmesan cheese
— salt and pepper

Preheat the oven to 350°F. Grease an ovenproof dish with butter. Cook the asparagus in salted, boiling water for 10 minutes or until tender. Drain and place in the prepared dish, then top with the ham and fontina. Beat the eggs with the Parmesan, season with salt and pepper, and pour over the asparagus. Bake for 15–20 minutes, until the Parmesan has melted and the eggs have set. Serve immediately.

FAVA BEAN SOUP

ZUPPA DI FAVE

Preparation time: *25 min*
Cooking time: *35 min*
Serves 4

— 2 tablespoons olive oil
— 1 carrot, chopped
— ½ stalk celery, chopped
— 1 clove garlic, finely chopped
— ½ onion, chopped
— scant ½ cup dry
  white wine
— 2 tablespoons pureed
  canned tomatoes
— 2¾ cups shelled fava beans
— 2¼ cups beef stock
— salt and pepper
— grated Parmesan cheese,
  to serve
— small toasted bread slices,
  to serve
— chopped basil, to garnish

Heat the oil in a pan. Add the carrot, celery, garlic, and onion and cook over low heat, stirring occasionally, for 2 minutes. Pour in the wine and cook until the alcohol has evaporated. Stir in the tomatoes, season with salt and pepper, and simmer for 15 minutes. Meanwhile, pop the fava beans out of their skins between your finger and thumb. Add the beans and stock to the pan and simmer over low heat for 15 minutes. Sprinkle the cheese over the slices of toast and place in 4 soup bowls. Ladle the soup over, garnish with chopped basil, and serve immediately.

FAVA BEANS AND MINT

FAVE E MENTA

Preparation time: *15 min*
Cooking time: *30 min*
Serves 6

— 3 tablespoons butter
— ⅓ cup all-purpose flour
— 1 onion, finely chopped
— 1 sprig mint, chopped
— ¼ teaspoon coriander seeds,
  lightly crushed
— 3 cups vegetable stock
— 1¾ pounds fava beans,
  shelled
— salt and pepper

Melt the butter in a pan. Stir in the flour and cook, stirring continuously, for 2 minutes, until lightly browned. Add the onion, mint, and coriander seeds and pour in the stock. Bring to a boil, then add the beans, reduce the heat, and simmer for 30 minutes. Season with salt and pepper, and serve immediately.

FRESH FAVA BEAN PUREE

PURÉ DI FAVE FRESCHE

Preparation time: *35 min*
Cooking time: *10–15 min*
Serves 4

— 6½ pounds fava beans, shelled
— 2 small potatoes, diced
— scant ½ cup vegetable stock
— olive oil, for drizzling
— salt and pepper

Soak the beans in cold water for 30 minutes, then drain, peel, and put into a pan. Pour in just enough water to cover and bring to a boil over low heat. As soon as the water begins to boil, remove the pan from the heat, drain the beans, return to the pan, and mash. Season with salt, add the potatoes and stock, and cook for 10–15 minutes, until soft and creamy. Remove the pan from the heat, drizzle generously with olive oil, and season to taste with salt and pepper. Serve hot or cold.

FAVA BEAN AND PEA RISOTTO

RISOTTO CON FAVE E PISELLI

Preparation time: *20 min*
Cooking time: *45 min*
Serves 4

— scant 1½ cups shelled fava beans
— 1¾ cups shelled peas
— 1½ cups risotto rice
— 1 pound 2 ounces tomatoes, peeled, seeded, and coarsely chopped
— 2 tablespoons olive oil
— 1 onion, finely chopped
— 1 sprig mint, finely chopped
— 1 sprig marjoram, finely chopped
— 1 sprig thyme, finely chopped
— 1 sprig basil, finely chopped
— 2 tablespoons butter
— ½ cup grated Parmesan cheese
— salt and pepper

Pop the fava beans out of their skins between your finger and thumb. Bring a pan of lightly salted water to a boil. Add the beans and peas and cook until tender. Drain and set aside. Bring a large pan of salted water to a boil. Add the rice and cook, stirring frequently, for 20–25 minutes, until tender. Meanwhile, put the tomatoes into a blender or food processor and process to a pulp. Heat the oil in a large pan, add the onion, herbs, and tomato pulp, season with salt and pepper and bring to a boil. Reduce the heat, add the peas and fava beans, and cook for a few minutes. Drain the rice and turn it into the sauce. Beat in the butter and sprinkle with the cheese. Serve immediately.

FAVA BEANS WITH HAM

FAVE AL PROSCIUTTO

Preparation time: *20 min*
Cooking time: *25 min*
Serves 4

— 4½ pounds fava beans,
  shelled
— 3 tablespoons butter
— generous ½ cup diced,
  cooked ham
— 1 onion, chopped
— 1 carrot, chopped
— scant 1 cup meat stock
— 1 sprig parsley, chopped
— salt and pepper

Put the beans in a pan, add cold water to cover, bring to a boil, and cook for 10 minutes or until tender. Meanwhile, melt half of the butter in another pan, add the ham, onion, and carrot, and cook, stirring occasionally, for 5 minutes. Drain the beans and add to the ham mixture, then pour in the stock and season with salt and pepper. Simmer until the sauce is very thick, then stir in the remaining butter, transfer to a warm serving dish, and sprinkle with the parsley.

PIEDMONTESE FAVA BEANS

FAVE ALLA PIEMONTESE

Preparation time: *5 min*
Cooking time: *15 min*
Serves 4

— 4½ pounds fava beans,
  shelled
— scant 1 cup heavy cream
— 2 ounces fontina cheese,
  sliced
— salt

Cook the beans in salted, boiling water for 10 minutes, or until tender, then drain and turn into a skillet. Stir in the cream and simmer gently for about 10 minutes, until thickened. Stir in the fontina and cook until it is just starting to melt.

FAVA BEANS WITH CHEESE WAFERS

FAVE CON CIALDE DI FORMAGGIO

Preparation time: *20 min*
Cooking time: *40 min*
Serves 4

— melted butter, for brushing
— 1 cup grated Parmesan
  cheese
— scant 1½ cups shelled
  fava beans
— 4–5 plum tomatoes,
  seeded and cut lengthwise
  into small strips
— olive oil, for drizzling
— salt

To make the wafers, brush a small nonstick skillet with butter and heat over medium heat. Put 1½ tablespoons of grated cheese in the center and spread out with a spatula into a 4-inch round. When the cheese has set and turned slightly golden, remove with a spatula and lay on a cutting board. Make 7 more wafers in this way and let cool. Pop the beans out of their skins by squeezing gently between your finger and thumb. Put the beans and tomatoes into a bowl, drizzle with oil, and season with salt. Put a cheese wafer on each of 4 individual serving plates, divide the bean mixture among them, top with a second wafer, and serve. This can be served with prosciutto.

FRITEDDA

PHOTO PAGE 99

FRITEDDA

Preparation time: *30 min*
Cooking time: *40 min*
Serves 8

— juice of 1 lemon, strained
— 8 globe artichokes
— scant ½ cup olive oil
— 1 large onion, thinly sliced
— 3¼ pounds fava
  beans, shelled
— 3¼ pounds peas, shelled
— 3 tablespoons white
  wine vinegar
— 1 teaspoon sugar
— salt and pepper

Fill a bowl halfway with water and stir in the lemon juice. Trim the artichoke stems, remove any coarse leaves and the chokes, and cut the artichokes into wedges, then add the wedges immediately to the acidulated water to prevent discoloration. Heat 2 tablespoons of the oil in a large pan. Add the onion and cook over low heat, stirring occasionally, for 5 minutes, until softened and translucent. Drain the artichokes, add to the pan, and cook, stirring occasionally, for a few minutes, then stir in the fava beans. Drizzle with a little hot water and simmer for 10 minutes. Stir in the peas and simmer for another 20 minutes. Combine the vinegar and sugar in a bowl. Season the vegetables with salt and pepper, sprinkle with the vinegar mixture, increase the heat to high, and cook until evaporated. Transfer to a serving plate and let cool completely before serving.

PEA AND LETTUCE SOUP

ZUPPA DI PISELLI CON LATTUGA

Preparation time: *40 min*
Cooking time: *30 min*
Serves *4*

— 2 small lettuces, shredded
— 3 potatoes, peeled and diced
— 3 large scallions, thinly sliced
— 2¼ cups shelled peas
— 1 small bunch mixed herbs,
  such as parsley, fennel,
  and sage
— 3 tablespoons butter
— 1 sprig parsley, finely
  chopped
— salt and pepper

Put the lettuce, potatoes, scallions, peas, bunch of herbs, and half of the butter into a large pan, pour in 3 cups of water, and season with salt and pepper. Cover and cook over medium heat, stirring occasionally, for 30 minutes. Remove and discard the bunch of herbs and pour the soup into a soup tureen. Stir in the remaining butter and the parsley and serve immediately.

BROTH WITH PEAS AND PASTA

QUADRUCCI E PISELLI IN BRODO

Preparation time: *15 min*
Cooking time: *25 min*
Serves *4*

— 1 small onion, finely
  chopped
— 2 ounces prosciutto,
  finely chopped
— 2 tablespoons butter
— 2¾ cups shelled peas
— 1 teaspoon tomato paste
— 5 cups chicken stock
— 7 ounces fresh or dried
  quadrucci (flat, square-
  shaped pasta)
— salt and pepper
— grated Parmesan cheese,
  to serve

Put the onion, ham, and butter into a pan and cook over low heat, stirring occasionally, for 5 minutes, until the onion is softened and translucent. Stir in the peas and cook for 1 minute. Mix the tomato paste with 1 tablespoon of water in a small bowl and stir into the pan. Season the peas with salt and pepper, cover, and cook until they are tender. Pour in the stock and bring to a boil. Add the pasta and cook for 5–6 minutes. Remove from the heat, ladle into warm serving bowls, and serve immediately, handing around the grated Parmesan separately.

PEA TIMBALE

TORTINO DI PISELLI

Preparation time: *15 min*
Cooking time: *55 min*
Serves 6

— 3 tablespoons olive oil
— 2 large scallions, white
parts only, thinly sliced
— 4½ cups shelled peas
— butter, for greasing
— 6 tablespoons fine fresh
bread crumbs
— 3 eggs
— scant 1 cup grated pecorino
cheese
— 1 sprig mint, torn into
small pieces
— salt and pepper

Heat the oil in a skillet. Add the scallions and cook over low heat, stirring occasionally, for about 10 minutes, until very soft but not colored. Stir in the peas and cook for a few minutes, then pour in scant ½ cup of water, add a pinch of salt, and stir again. Cook over medium heat for about 15 minutes, until the peas are tender and the liquid has evaporated. Remove the skillet from the heat and let cool. Meanwhile, preheat the oven to 350°F. Grease an 8½-inch cake pan with butter and coat with the bread crumbs. Beat together the eggs, pecorino, and mint leaves in a bowl and season with salt and pepper. Stir in the peas and pour the mixture into the prepared pan. Bake for 30 minutes. Remove from the oven and let stand for a few minutes, then turn out onto a warm serving plate, and serve immediately.

RICE AND PEAS

RISI E BISI

Preparation time: *10 min*
Cooking time: *35 min*
Serves 4

— 5 cups meat stock
— 3 tablespoons olive oil
— 4 tablespoons butter
— 1 onion, chopped
— 1 clove garlic
— 1 stalk celery, chopped
— 2¼ cups shelled peas
— 1 cup risotto rice
— ⅓ cup grated Parmesan
cheese
— salt

Pour the stock into a pan and bring to a boil. Heat the oil and half of the butter in another pan, add the onion, garlic, and celery, and cook over low heat, stirring occasionally, for 5 minutes. Remove and discard the garlic. Add the peas followed by the rice. Stir for about 1 minute, then stir in a ladleful of the stock. Cook, adding the stock a ladleful at a time, for about 20 minutes or until the rice is tender and all the stock has been used. Season with salt to taste, stir in the remaining butter and the Parmesan, ladle into a soup tureen, and serve.

GARDEN VEGETABLE AND GOAT CHEESE PIE

TORTA DI RICOTTA, CAPRINI E VERDURE DELL'ORTO

Preparation time: *35 min, plus 30 min resting*
Cooking time: *50 min*
Serves 8

For the pastry dough:
— 3¼ cups all-purpose flour, plus extra for dusting
— generous ¾ cup (1⅝ sticks) butter, softened, plus extra for greasing
— 1 egg
— 2 tablespoons milk
— salt

For the filling:
— ¾ cup shelled peas
— 2 small zucchini, diced
— 1½ cups very fresh ricotta cheese
— 8 ounces goat cheese
— scant 1 cup heavy cream
— pinch freshly grated nutmeg
— 2 eggs, separated
— salt and pepper

To make the dough, sift the flour with a pinch of salt into a mound on a pastry board or counter and make a well in the center. Put the butter, egg, and milk into the well and mix with your fingers, gradually incorporating the dry ingredients, adding a little more milk if necessary. Shape the dough into a ball and divide into 2 flat rounds, 1 being slightly larger. Wrap in plastic wrap and let rest in the refrigerator for 30 minutes.

Meanwhile, make the filling. Bring a pan of salted water to a boil. Add the peas and zucchini, and cook for 8–10 minutes, until tender but still crisp, then drain well. Combine the ricotta, goat cheese, and cream in a bowl until blended. Add the vegetables and nutmeg. Beat the egg whites, then add to the cheese mixture. Season with salt and pepper.

Preheat the oven to 350°F. Grease a pie dish with butter and dust with flour. Roll out the larger piece of dough on a lightly floured counter and use to line the prepared pie dish. Spoon in the filling and smooth the top. Roll out the remaining dough and lift on top of the pie, pressing the edges to seal. Lightly beat the egg yolks with a tablespoon of water and brush the glaze over the surface of the pie. Put the dish on a baking sheet and bake for 50 minutes, until golden brown. Remove the pie from the oven and serve immediately.

PEA PUREE AU GRATIN

PURÈ DI PISELLI IN GRATIN

Preparation time: *1¼ hours,*
plus 1–2 hours soaking
Cooking time: *15 min*
Serves 4

— scant 2 cups dried peas,
   soaked in cold water to cover
   for 1–2 hours and drained
— 2 tablespoons butter, plus
   extra for greasing
— salt and pepper

For the cheese sauce:
— 2 tablespoons butter
— ¼ cup all-purpose flour
— 1 cup milk
— pinch of freshly grated
   nutmeg
— ½ cup grated Parmesan
   cheese

Put the peas into a pan, pour in 2¼ cups of water, and bring to a boil. Reduce the heat to very low, cover the pan, and cook for 30–40 minutes, until the peas are tender and have absorbed all the water. Transfer to a food processor and process to a puree. Stir in the butter and season with salt and pepper to taste. Preheat the oven to 400°F. Grease an ovenproof dish with butter.

To make the cheese sauce, melt the butter in a small pan. Beat in the flour with a balloon whisk. Pour in all the milk at once and continue whisking until the sauce starts to boil. Season with salt and a pinch of nutmeg, reduce the heat to as low as possible, and cook, stirring continuously, for 15 minutes, until thickened. Remove from the heat and stir in the grated cheese. Spoon the pea puree into the prepared dish, cover with the cheese sauce, and bake for about 15 minutes, until the top is golden brown. Serve immediately.

SAUTÉED PEAS WITH TOMATO

PISELLI IN TEGAME AL POMODORO

Preparation time: *15 min*
Cooking time: *15 min*
Serves 6–8

— 2 tablespoons olive oil
— 1 large scallion, very
   finely chopped
— 3½ cups shelled peas
— 1¾ cups pureed canned
   tomatoes
— ½ teaspoon sugar
— 1 sprig fresh basil
— salt and pepper

Heat the oil in a skillet. Add the scallion and cook over low heat, stirring occasionally, for 4–5 minutes, until softened and translucent. Increase the heat to medium, add the peas, tomatoes, and sugar, and season with salt and pepper. Bring to a boil, reduce the heat to as low as possible, cover, and simmer, shaking the pan occasionally, for 10–12 minutes, until the peas are tender. Tear the basil leaves into the pan, stir, and transfer to a warm serving dish.

PEAS WITH PANCETTA

PISELLI ALLA PANCETTA

Preparation time: *5 min*
Cooking time: *20 min*
Serves 4

— 3½ cups shelled peas
— 3 tablespoons butter
— 3½ ounces smoked
   pancetta, cut into strips
— salt

Cook the peas in salted, boiling water for 10–15 minutes or until tender, then drain well. Melt the butter in a pan over very low heat, add the pancetta, and cook until golden brown and tender. Add the peas and cook, stirring occasionally, for 5 minutes. Transfer to a warm serving dish.

SAVORY PEA LOAF WITH BELL PEPPERS AND TOMATOES

GATEAU DI PISELLI CON PEPERONI E DADINI DI POMODORI

Preparation time: *1 hour*
Cooking time: *20–25 min*
Serves 4

— butter, for greasing
— 3½ cups shelled peas
— scant ½ cup ricotta cheese
— 2 eggs, separated
— 1⅔ cups grated Parmesan
   cheese
— salt and pepper

For the sauce:
— 3 tablespoons olive oil
— 4–5 ripe plum tomatoes,
   peeled, seeded, and diced
— 4–5 basil leaves, torn
— salt and pepper

To garnish:
— ¼ red bell pepper, seeded
   and cut into thin strips
— ¼ yellow bell pepper, seeded
   and cut into thin strips

Preheat the oven to 350°F. Grease a loaf pan with butter. Bring a pan of salted water to a boil. Add the peas, bring back to a boil, and cook for 10–15 minutes or until tender. Meanwhile, make the sauce. Heat the oil in a pan. Add the tomatoes and cook over high heat, shaking the pan occasionally, for 3–4 minutes. Season with salt and pepper, stir in the basil, remove from the heat, and set aside. Drain the peas, turn into a food processor or blender, and process to a puree. Scrape the puree into a bowl, stir in the ricotta, egg yolks, and grated cheese, and season with salt and pepper. In a grease-free bowl, whisk the egg whites to stiff peaks, then fold into the pea mixture.

Spoon the mixture into the prepared loaf pan and stand it in a roasting pan. Pour in hot water to come about halfway up the sides and bake for 20–25 minutes, until set. Remove from the oven and let the pan cool slightly. Gently reheat the tomato sauce. Turn out the pea loaf onto a warm serving plate and garnish with the red and yellow bell pepper strips in a lattice pattern. Spoon the hot tomato sauce around the loaf and serve immediately.

PEA AND POTATO TIMBALES WITH PESTO

PEA AND POTATO TIMBALES WITH PESTO

PHOTO PAGE 106

SFORMATINI DI PISELLI E PATATE AL PESTO

Preparation time: *50 min*
Cooking time: *30 min*
Serves 6–8

— 1 pound 5 ounces potatoes
— 1¼ cups shelled peas
— butter, for greasing
— ½ cup grated pecorino
  cheese
— ½ cup grated Parmesan
  cheese
— 3 eggs, lightly beaten
— scant ½ cup quantity Pesto
  (see page 159)
— salt and pepper

Bring a large pan of salted water to a boil. Add the unpeeled potatoes and bring back to a boil, then reduce the heat and cook for 30 minutes. Meanwhile, bring another pan of salted water to a boil, add the peas, bring back to a boil and cook for 10 minutes or until tender, then drain and set aside.

Preheat the oven to 325°F. Grease 6–8 ramekins with butter. Drain the potatoes and, when cool enough to handle, peel. Mash the potatoes in a large mixing bowl. Stir in the pecorino, Parmesan, eggs, and a pinch each of salt and pepper. Finally, stir in the peas.

Divide the mixture among the prepared ramekins and stand them on a baking sheet. Bake for about 30 minutes. Remove from the oven and let cool slightly before turning out onto individual serving plates. Top each timbale with 1 tablespoon of the pesto and serve immediately.

PEAS WITH MINT

PISELLI ALLA MENTA

Preparation time: *5 min*
Cooking time: *20–25 min*
Serves 4

— 3½ cups shelled peas
— ½ teaspoon sugar
— 10 mint leaves
— 4 tablespoons butter
— salt and pepper

Cook the peas in salted, boiling water with the sugar and 5 of the mint leaves until tender. Drain and discard the mint. Melt the butter in a pan, add the peas, stir well, and cook over low heat for 5 minutes. Season with salt and pepper to taste, add the remaining mint leaves, and serve.

SAVORY PEA PUDDING

SFORMATO DI PISELLI

Preparation time: *10 min*
Cooking time: *20 min*
Serves 6

— butter, for greasing
— 3½ cups cooked peas
— scant ½ cup fresh
   cream cheese
— 3 egg yolks, plus 1 egg white
— 2⅓ cups grated Parmesan
   cheese
— salt and pepper
— strips of Sweet and Sour
   Bell Peppers (see page 221),
   to serve
— diced raw tomatoes or
   zucchini, to serve

Preheat the oven to 400°F. Grease a ovenproof dish with butter. Put the peas, cream cheese, egg yolks, and egg white in a food processor, season with salt and pepper, and process to a puree. Scrape the puree into a bowl and stir in the Parmesan, then spoon the mixture into the prepared dish. Put the dish into a roasting pan and pour in hot water to come about halfway up the side. Bake for 20 minutes. Remove from the oven and let stand for a few minutes before turning out onto a warm serving plate. Garnish with the strips of bell pepper and diced tomatoes or zucchini, and serve.

CREAMY RADISHES

RAVANELLI CREMOSO

Preparation time: *15 min*
Cooking time: *5 min*
Serves 4

— 1½ pounds radishes,
   trimmed and halved
— 3 tablespoons butter
— 2 tablespoons heavy cream
— salt and pepper

Bring a pan of salted water to a boil, add the radishes, and parboil for 10 minutes, then drain. Melt the butter in a pan, pour in the cream, and add the radishes. Cook over low heat for 5 minutes, until the radishes are tender and the cream has thickened. Season to taste with salt and pepper. Serve immediately.

RADISH SALAD WITH YOGURT

RAVANELLI IN INSALATA CON LO YOGURT

Preparation time: *10 min*
Serves 4

— 2 large white radishes,
   thinly sliced
— 1 green apple
— 4 tablespoons plain yogurt
— salt and freshly ground
   white pepper

Put the radishes in a salad bowl, sprinkle with a pinch of salt, stir, and let stand for 10 minutes. Peel and core the apple and cut into wedges. Using a very sharp knife, cut the wedges into wafer-thin slices and add to the radishes. Mix together the yogurt and a pinch of pepper in a bowl, add to the salad, toss, and serve.

RADISH SALAD WITH OLIVES

RAVANELLI IN INSALATA CON LE OLIVE

PHOTO PAGE 110

Preparation time: *10 min*
Serves 4

— 6 red radishes, trimmed
— juice of 1 lemon, strained
— 3½ ounces mâche
   (corn salad)
— 10 black olives, pitted
— olive oil, for drizzling
— salt

Cut the radishes into very thin horizontal slices, put in a salad bowl, and sprinkle with the lemon juice. Add the mâche and olives, drizzle with olive oil, and season with salt to taste. Mix gently and let stand for 10 minutes before serving.

RADISH SALAD WITH OLIVES (PAGE 109)

AVOCADO SALAD WITH OLIVES

INSALATA DI AVOCADO CON OLIVE

Preparation time: *20 min*
Serves 4

— 2 firm ripe avocados
— juice of 1 lemon
— 1 grapefruit
— 1 onion
— ½ cup black olives, pitted
— olive oil, for drizzling
— salt and pepper

Peel and halve the avocados, and remove and discard the pits. Dice the flesh, put into a bowl, and sprinkle with the lemon juice to prevent discoloration. Peel the grapefruit and remove all traces of the bitter white pith. Using a small, sharp knife, cut between the membranes and add the segments to the bowl. Add the onion and olives, drizzle with olive oil, and season with salt and pepper. Mix gently and serve.

AVOCADO AND YOGURT SOUP

ZUPPA DI AVOCADO E YOGURT

Preparation time: *35 min,*
plus 1 hour chilling
Serves 4

— 4 avocados
— juice of 1 lemon, strained
— ½ cup plain yogurt
— 3 cups vegetable
    stock
— salt and pepper
— chopped chives, to garnish

Peel and halve the avocados, and remove and discard the pits. Coarsely dice the flesh, put it into a shallow dish, and sprinkle over the lemon juice to prevent discoloration. Pour in the yogurt and mix gently. Transfer the mixture to a blender, add the stock, and process several times until smooth, scraping down the inside of the goblet. Pour the soup into a tureen, season with salt and pepper, cover tightly with plastic wrap, and chill in the refrigerator for 1 hour. Stir the soup, sprinkle with the chives, and serve.

AVOCADO AND GORGONZOLA CREAM PASTA SALAD

INSALATA DI MEZZI RIGATONI ALL'AVOCADO E CREMA DI GORGONZOLA

Preparation time: *20 min*
Cooking time: *12 min*
Serves 4

— 2½ ounces Gorgonzola
    cheese, diced
— 3 tablespoons butter, diced
— generous 1 cup cream cheese
— 2 avocados
— 7 ounces rigatoni pasta
— salt and pepper

Put the Gorgonzola and butter in a bowl and let soften at room temperature, then beat in the cream cheese until smooth. Season with salt and pepper. Peel and halve the avocados, and remove and discard the pits. Dice the flesh and add to the cream. Bring a large pan of salted water to a boil. Add the pasta, bring back to a boil, and cook for 10 minutes, or according to package directions, until tender but still al dente. Drain and refresh. Turn into a salad bowl, add the cream, toss well, and serve.

AVOCADO AND ASPARAGUS

Preparation time: *20 min, plus 1 hour chilling*
Cooking time: *15–20 min*
Serves 4

— 1 carrot, diced
— 2 stalks green celery, diced
— 12 olives, pitted
— 1 tablespoon capers in vinegar, drained and chopped
— 1 shallot, chopped
— 1 teaspoon dried thyme
— 1 teaspoon curry powder
— pinch of ground nutmeg
— 7 ounces thick green asparagus, trimmed
— 7 ounces avocados
— 1 tablespoon olive oil
— salt

Put the carrot and celery in a bowl, season lightly with salt, cover with plastic wrap, and chill in the refrigerator for 1 hour. Stir in the olives, capers, and shallot, sprinkle over the dried thyme, curry powder, and nutmeg, and season with salt. Trim the asparagus spears to the same length and tie in a bundle with kitchen string. Bring a tall pan of lightly salted water to a boil and have ready a bowl of ice water. Add the bundle of asparagus to the pan, standing it upright with the tips protruding above the water level. Cover and simmer for 15 minutes, or until tender. Lift out the asparagus and plunge into the ice water. Drain well and remove the string.

Cut off the asparagus tips and set aside. Chop the stalks and add to the vegetable mixture. Peel and halve the avocados, and remove and discard the pits. Dice the flesh and add to the vegetable mixture. Pour the oil over the salad, mix well, and transfer to a serving dish. Garnish with the asparagus tips and serve.

AVOCADO, YOGURT, AND HONEY CREAM

PHOTO PAGE 113

CREMA DI YOGURT AL MIELE E AVOCADO

Preparation time: *25 min*
Cooking time: *10 min*
Serves 4

— scant 1 cup shelled hazelnuts
— 1 cup plain yogurt
— ¼ cup honey
— 1 avocado

Preheat the oven to 325°F. Spread out the hazelnuts on a baking sheet and toast in the oven for 10 minutes. Remove from the oven and turn onto a clean dish towel. Rub off the skins with the dish towel, then put the hazelnuts into a food processor and chop finely. Combine the yogurt and honey in a bowl. Peel and halve the avocados, and remove and discard the pits. Dice the flesh immediately and add it to the yogurt mixture to prevent discoloration. Stir gently. Transfer to a glass bowl and sprinkle with the chopped hazelnuts. Chill until serving.

AVOCADO, YOGURT, AND HONEY CREAM

OLD-FASHIONED ONION TART

OLD-FASHIONED ONION TART

PHOTO PAGE 114

TORTA DI CIPOLLE ALL'ANTICA

Preparation time: *20 min*
Cooking time: *1 hour 15 min*
Serves 6

— 4 tablespoons butter, plus
  extra for greasing
— all-purpose flour, for dusting
— 1 cup golden raisins
— 1 cup dry white wine
— 7 ounces basic pie dough,
  thawed if frozen
— 2¼ pounds onions,
  thinly sliced
— marrow from 2 beef
  bones, diced
— pinch of sugar
— salt and pepper

Preheat the oven to 325°F. Grease an 8-inch tart or quiche pan with butter and sprinkle with flour, tipping the pan to coat. Put the golden raisins in a bowl, pour over the wine, and set aside to soak. Roll out the basic pie dough on a lightly floured counter and line the prepared pan, trimming the edges. Reserve the trimmings. Prick the bottom all over with a fork. Line with parchment paper, fill with pie weights, and bake for 15 minutes. Remove the pie shell and increase the oven temperature to 350°F. Meanwhile, melt the butter in a skillet, add the onions, and cook over low heat, stirring occasionally, for 10 minutes or until golden brown. Stir in the beef marrow, the golden raisins with the wine, and a pinch of sugar, season with salt and pepper, and cook until the wine has evaporated. Remove the parchment and beans from the pie shell, pour in the onion mixture, and spread evenly. Roll out the trimmings, cut into thin strips, brush the ends with water, and arrange in a lattice over the top of the tart. Bake for 30 minutes. Serve warm, cut into slices.

ONION AND RICE MOLD

SFORMATO DI RISO E CIPOLLA

Preparation time: *30 min*
Cooking time: *20 min*
Serves 4

— 4 tablespoons olive oil
— 1 pound white onions,
  very thinly sliced
— 1⅔ cups long-grain rice
— pat of butter, plus extra
  for greasing
— salt and pepper

Heat the olive oil in a large skillet. Add the onions and cook over low heat, stirring for 10 minutes, until very soft but not colored. Season with salt and pepper and remove from the heat. Bring a large pan of salted water to a boil. Add the rice and cook for 15–20 minutes, until tender. Preheat the oven to 350°F. Grease an ovenproof mold with butter. Drain the rice and stir in a pat of butter. Make a layer of rice in the prepared mold and cover with a layer of onion. Continue making alternate layers until all the ingredients have been used. Put the mold onto a baking sheet and bake for 20 minutes. Remove from the oven and let stand for 10 minutes. Turn out onto a plate and serve immediately.

CHEESE AND ONION QUICHE

QUICHE DI CIPOLLE E FORMAGGIO

Preparation time: *20 min*
Cooking time: *1 hour 20 min*
Serves *4*

— 2 tablespoons butter
— 12 ounces onions,
    thinly sliced
— all-purpose flour, for dusting
— 1 egg, plus 1 egg yolk
— ½ cup milk
— 12 ounces puff pastry dough,
    thawed if frozen
— ⅔ cups grated Gruyère
    cheese
— 1 tablespoon finely chopped
    parsley
— salt and pepper

Melt the butter in a pan. Add the onions and cook over low heat, stirring occasionally, for 20 minutes, until they are softened and translucent. Sprinkle with a pinch of salt, remove from the heat, and let cool. Preheat the oven to 400°F. Dust a 9-inch tart or quiche pan with flour. Using a balloon whisk, beat together the egg, egg yolk, and milk in a bowl and season with salt and pepper. Roll out the dough on a lightly floured counter and use to line the prepared pan. Prick and bake the unfilled pie shell for 15 minutes, remove from the oven, and reduce the oven temperature to 325°F. Sprinkle half of the Gruyère cheese over the bottom of the pie shell, spread out the onions on top of the cheese, and pour the egg mixture over. Sprinkle with the remaining Gruyère. Put the pan on a baking sheet and bake for 40 minutes, until set and golden. Remove from the oven, sprinkle with the parsley, and serve.

RED ONIONS WITH PISTACHIO NUTS

PHOTO PAGE 117

CIPOLLE DI TROPEA AL SALE CON PISTACCHI

Preparation time: *30 min*
Cooking time: *1 hour*
Serves *6*

— 6 large red onions
— 2¼–3¼ pounds coarse
    sea salt
— 3 tablespoons shelled
    pistachio nuts, coarsely
    chopped
— olive oil, for drizzling
— white wine vinegar,
    for drizzling
— salt and pepper

Preheat the oven to 425°F. Put the unpeeled onions into a deep ovenproof dish and cover completely with coarse salt. Bake for 1 hour. Remove the dish from the oven, lift out the onions with a slotted spoon, and brush off all traces of salt, then peel. Slice them vertically into wedges and arrange in a serving dish. Sprinkle the onions with the pistachios, season with salt and pepper, and drizzle with the oil and a little vinegar. This vegetable dish goes very well with burrata and mozzarella cheeses.

RED ONIONS WITH PISTACHIO NUTS

ONION GRATIN

Preparation time: *15 min*
Cooking time: *45 min*
Serves 6

— olive oil, for brushing
   and drizzling
— 6 white onions, peeled and
   halved horizontally
— 3 eggs
— scant ½ cup milk
— scant ½ cup heavy cream
— 2 tablespoons chopped basil
— ⅔ cup grated Parmesan
   cheese
— salt and pepper

Preheat the oven to 400°F. Line an ovenproof dish with aluminum foil and brush with oil. Put the onions into the prepared dish, drizzle with oil, and season lightly with pepper. Bake for 15 minutes.

Meanwhile, lightly beat together the eggs, milk, cream, and basil in a bowl and season with salt and pepper. Remove the dish from the oven and pour the egg mixture over the onions. Sprinkle with the cheese, return to the oven, and bake for another 30 minutes. Serve immediately.

BRAISED SCALLIONS

PHOTO PAGE 118

Preparation time: *15 min*
Cooking time: *30 min*
Serves 4

— 2 tablespoons butter
— 2 tablespoons finely chopped
   mixed herbs, such as thyme,
   marjoram, and sage
— 1 pound 2 ounces large
   scallions, thickly sliced
— 2 ounces pancetta or bacon,
   cut into thin strips
— salt and pepper

Melt the butter with the herbs in a pan. Add the scallions and cook over low heat, stirring continuously, for 10 minutes. Add the pancetta and cook, stirring occasionally, for another 10 minutes. Add 2 tablespoons of hot water and simmer for 10 minutes, until the scallions are tender and all the liquid has evaporated. Season with salt and pepper and serve immediately.

ONION FOCACCIA

PHOTO PAGE 121

FOCACCIA DI CIPOLLE

Preparation time: *20 min,*
plus 2 hours rising
Cooking time: *30 min*
Serves 4

— 1 cup lukewarm milk
— 1 teaspoon sugar
— 2 teaspoons active dry yeast
— 2¼ cups all-purpose flour
— 1 egg
— 4 tablespoons butter, plus
  extra for greasing
— 2 large onions, finely
  chopped
— 2 sprigs parsley, finely
  chopped
— olive oil
— salt

Pour half of the milk into a bowl and stir in the sugar. Sprinkle the yeast over the surface and let stand for 10–15 minutes, until frothy. Stir well to a smooth paste. Mix the yeast with enough flour to make a small ball of soft dough about the size of a bread roll. Cover and let rise at warm room temperature for about 1 hour. Sift the remaining flour and a pinch of salt into a mound on a counter and make a well in the center. Break the egg into the well, add the dough, and combine with the flour, adding enough milk to form a soft dough. Shape into a ball, cover, and let rise for 1 hour. Meanwhile, melt the butter in a pan. Add the onions and cook over low heat, stirring occasionally, for 8–10 minutes, until very soft but not colored. Season with salt, stir in the parsley, and remove the pan from the heat. Preheat the oven to 350°F. Grease the bottom of an 8-inch shallow cake pan with butter. Reserve a few spoons of the onion mixture and add the remainder to the dough, working it in briefly by hand. Shape the dough into a round and put it into the pan. Spread the remaining onion mixture over the top, cover with aluminum foil, and bake for 30 minutes. Remove from the oven, turn out, and serve hot.

SUCCULENT ROASTED ONIONS

CIPOLLE SAPORITE AL FORNO

Preparation time: *20 min*
Cooking time: *30–35 min*
Serves 4

— 4 onions, peeled
— 1 egg, lightly beaten
— scant 1 cup Parmesan grated
  cheese
— 1 tablespoon fresh
  bread crumbs
— 8 black olives, pitted and
  coarsely chopped
— olive oil, for drizzling
— salt and pepper

Preheat the oven to 350°F. Bring a large pan of lightly salted water to a boil. Add the onions and parboil for 5 minutes, then drain. Using a teaspoon, scoop out some of the flesh from their centers to allow room for a little stuffing. Combine the egg, cheese, bread crumbs, and olives in a bowl and season with salt and pepper. Fill the onions with the mixture. Stand the onions upright in an ovenproof dish, drizzle with oil, and roast for 30–35 minutes, until browned. Remove from the oven and serve.

ONION FOCACCIA

BELGIAN ENDIVE WITH CRAB

BELGIAN ENDIVE WITH CRAB

INDIVIA BELGA AI GRANCHIO

Preparation time: *15 min*
Serves 4

— 1–2 heads Belgian endive
— 1 cup mayonnaise
— 9 ounces canned crabmeat,
  drained
— 2 tablespoons heavy cream
— 2 tablespoons ketchup
— ½ teaspoon Worcestershire
  sauce
— brandy, for drizzling

Separate the Belgian endive into individual leaves and
arrange in concentric circles on a serving dish, using the
smaller leaves for the inner circles. Combine the mayonnaise
and crabmeat in a bowl, gently stir in the cream, ketchup,
and Worcestershire sauce, and drizzle with the brandy. Mix
gently. Put 1 tablespoon of the mixture into the concave part
of each Belgian endive leaf and serve.

BELGIAN ENDIVE AND BACON SALAD

INSALATA DI INDIVIA BELGA E BACON

Preparation time: *10 min*
Cooking time: *6–8 min*
Serves 6

— 1 pound 5 ounces Belgian
  endive
— 1 onion, sliced
— 1 tablespoon white wine
  vinegar
— 2 tablespoons olive oil
— 3½ ounces bacon, cut
  into strips
— salt

Separate the Belgian endive into leaves and put in a salad
bowl with the onion slices. Stir a pinch of salt into the
vinegar in a small bowl, then sprinkle over the salad.

Heat the oil in a skillet. Add the bacon and cook over
medium-low heat, stirring occasionally, for 4–6 minutes.
Add the bacon to the salad, toss well, and serve immediately.

BELGIAN ENDIVE

BELGIAN ENDIVE GRATIN

BELGA BRASATA GRATINATA IN FORNO

Preparation time: 25 *min*
Cooking time: 45 *min*
Serves 4

— 10 heads Belgian endive,
   coarse leaves and cores
   removed
— 4 tablespoons butter, plus
   extra for greasing
— juice of ½ lemon, strained
— 5 ounces, ham thinly
   sliced
— ½ quantity béchamel
   sauce (see page 51)
— salt and pepper

Put the Belgian endive into a flameproof casserole, add the butter, and season with salt and pepper. Pour in just enough water to cover and sprinkle with the lemon juice. Cover and cook over medium heat for 30 minutes, adding a little more hot water if necessary. Remove from the heat, transfer the Belgian endive to a dish, and let cool. Preheat the oven to 350°F. Grease a shallow ovenproof dish with butter. Cut the slices of ham in half. Wrap each Belgian endive head in half of a slice of ham and put into the prepared dish. Spoon the béchamel sauce over the ham and Belgian endive bundles, and bake for 15 minutes, until the surface is lightly browned. Serve immediately.

BELGIAN ENDIVE WITH VEGETABLES

BELGA RIPIENA DI VERDURINE

Preparation time: 20 *min*
Serves 6

— 2 carrots, julienned
— 1 stalk celery, julienned
— 1 onion, julienned
— 3½ ounces spinach,
   coarse stalks removed,
   sliced into ¾–1¼-inch strips
— 2 heads Belgian endive, cored
   and divided into 24 leaves

For the dressing:
— scant 1 cup heavy cream
— white wine vinegar
— pinch of ground pink
   pepper
— salt

Divide the carrots, celery, onion, and spinach among the Belgian endive leaves and arrange on a serving plate.

For the dressing, lightly beat the cream in a bowl and sprinkle with a little vinegar, pink pepper, and salt. Divide the dressing among the Belgian endive "boats" and serve.

BELGIAN ENDIVE AND CHERVIL SALAD

Preparation time: *25 min*
Serves 4

— 2 oranges
— 3 heads Belgian endive, cut
   into thin strips
— 12 walnut halves

For the vinaigrette:
— 1 tablespoon white wine
   vinegar
— 5 tablespoons olive oil
— 1 shallot, finely chopped
— 3 tablespoons chopped
   chervil
— salt and pepper

Peel the oranges, removing all traces of the bitter white pith, then cut into segments between the membranes, holding the fruit over a plate to catch the juice.

To make the vinaigrette, whisk together the vinegar and oil in a salad bowl. Add the shallot and chervil, stir in the reserved orange juice, and season with salt and pepper. Just before serving, toss the Belgian endive in the vinaigrette, arrange on a serving plate, and garnish with the walnut halves and the orange segments.

BELGIAN ENDIVE SALAD WITH CAPER DRESSING

Preparation time: *15 min*
Serves 4

— 3 tablespoons salted capers,
   rinsed
— 1 large sprig parsley, chopped
— 1 small clove garlic
— 1 canned anchovy fillet,
   drained
— 5 green olives, pitted
— 4 tablespoons olive oil
— 4 heads Belgian endive,
   thinly sliced
— pepper

Put the capers, parsley, garlic, anchovy, olives, and oil in a blender, season with pepper, and process to a paste. Divide the Belgian endive slices among 4 individual plates and top with a tablespoon of the caper dressing.

BELGIAN ENDIVE RISOTTO

RISO E CICORIA

Preparation time: *40 min*
Cooking time: *35 min*
Serves *4*

— 1 pound 2 ounces Belgian
   endive, trimmed and halved
— 5 cups vegetable stock
— 4 tablespoons butter
— 1 onion, finely chopped
— 1 stalk celery, finely chopped
— 1 clove garlic, finely chopped
— 2 ripe tomatoes, peeled,
   seeded and chopped
— 1½ cups risotto rice
— ⅔ cup grated pecorino
   cheese
— 1 sprig parsley, chopped
— salt and pepper

Bring a pan of salted water to a boil. Add the Belgian endive and cook for 15 minutes, then drain and cut into strips. Pour the stock into a pan and bring to a boil. Meanwhile, melt half of the butter in another pan. Add the onion, celery, and garlic, and cook over low heat, stirring occasionally, for 5 minutes. Add the tomatoes, season with salt and pepper, and cook over low heat, stirring occasionally, for 10 minutes. Add the Belgian endive and cook for a few minutes, then stir in the rice. Add a ladleful of the hot stock and cook, stirring continuously, until absorbed. Continue to add the hot stock, a ladleful at a time, stirring continuously until each addition has been absorbed before adding the next, about 20 minutes. Remove from the heat, add the remaining butter, sprinkle with the grated cheese and chopped parsley, and serve.

BELGIAN ENDIVE AND WATERCRESS WITH ORANGE

CICORIA E CRESCIONE ALL'ARANCIA E MELA

PHOTO PAGE 127

Preparation time: *25 min*
Serves *4–6*

— 2 heads Belgian endive
— 1 orange
— 1 green apple
— 1 bunch watercress,
   cut into sprigs
— 4 tablespoons olive oil
— 1 tablespoon walnut oil
— juice of ½ lemon, strained
— pepper

Separate the Belgian endive into leaves. Peel the orange, removing all traces of the bitter white pith, and cut into segments between the membranes. Peel and core the apple, cut into rounds, and then cut these in half. Arrange the Belgian endive, orange segments, apple slices, and watercress sprigs decoratively on a serving platter. Whisk together the olive oil, walnut oil, lemon juice, and a pinch of pepper in a bowl. Drizzle the dressing over the salad, let rest for 5 minutes, and then serve.

BELGIAN ENDIVE AND WATERCRESS WITH ORANGE

HERBS

ARUGULA

GREEN BEANS

EGGPLANTS

ZUCCHINI

CUCUMBERS

TOMATOES

BELL PEPPERS

FENNEL

CORN

SUMMER

SUMMER

If green is the dominant color of the spring vegetable garden, the entire color spectrum is on display in summer, when the longer days and warmer temperatures encourage vegetables to flourish. Whether in your own garden or at your local market, the abundance of summer produce is the highlight of the growing year. Juicy, ripe tomatoes, sweet bell peppers, and tender eggplants are all integral ingredients in Italian home cooking, and they will not taste as delicious at any other time of year.

The choices for dinner in the summer garden are almost endless, and Italian cooks have many inventive ways of cooking with the best summer produce. Cold Cucumber Cream Soup (see page 201) or Spicy Tomato Granita (page 211) make refreshing appetizers for dining al fresco. The very best tomatoes are delicious simply dressed in a salad with olive oil and salt, but they can also be stuffed and baked, made into soups, or combined with mozzarella and basil in a torte or salad. Bell peppers can be combined with eggs, olives, capers, and anchovies, stuffed, or used in risotto. Young zucchini can be added to flans or made into pesto with almonds and mint, while their flowers are widely used in salads, or stuffed and served as a first course. Although vegetables are generally prepared in savory dishes, they can also be used to make unconventional desserts such as Basil Sherbet (see page 167).

The key to maintaining the summer garden is to stay on top of weeding, watering, and staking. Most varieties of tomato need supporting to keep the fruit off the ground to avoid rotting, while large eggplant and pepper plants also benefit from being propped up. With summer storms and the heavy weight of ripening fruit, these plants can tumble over by midsummer. Corn rows need hilling (mounding up soil around the young plant) so that the mature plants do not blow over. Potatoes also need hilling to increase yields and produce larger tubers later in the summer.

Harvesting summer vegetables is a pleasure. Make sure you have a good-size harvesting basket or trug, because it will fill quickly when summer vegetables are ready. Even if the salad drawer in your refrigerator is already full of home-grown produce, it is important to keep picking summer vegetables as they mature. For many vegetables, the more you pick, the more they produce. If you let zucchini, beans, cucumbers, and bell peppers become oversized, the plants will stop producing more fruit. Consider freezing, canning, or pickling your excess vegetables, or give them away to friends and family. Regular harvesting will allow, you to enjoy your vegetables until the first frost.

HERBS

Herbs play a vital role in adding depth of flavor, aroma, and color to Italian food. Flat-leaf parsley, also known as Italian parsley, is the most popular herb in the Italian kitchen. It complements a wide range of other ingredients and features prominently in pastas and sauces. However, bay, rosemary, thyme, basil, sage, marjoram, or oregano are just as important.

Basil and tomato, pork and sage, and potatoes and rosemary are all classic partners. Marjoram or oregano enhance flavorful tomato sauces for pizzas and pastas. Fresh herbs are included in salads and some, such as parsley, may be fried to make an attractive garnish. Strongly aromatic herbs are also used to flavor desserts.

Look for lively, blemish-free bunches of herbs with vibrant color. To store, wrap them in damp paper towels, put into a plastic bag, and keep in the salad drawer of the refrigerator for a few days—although they are always best used as fresh as possible. Most fresh herbs are chopped before being added to dishes to release aromas and oils, but delicate leaves, such as basil, are better torn into pieces by hand.

IN THE GARDEN Growing herbs is especially rewarding for gardeners with limited space. The most common Italian herbs love full sun and warm, well-drained soil that has not been heavily fertilized. Begin harvesting as soon as leaves are large enough to eat, picking them in the morning for best flavor. Use fresh herbs immediately or dry stems by hanging them up in an airy, warm room for winter use.

HERB RECIPES ON PAGES 158–167

ARUGULA
RUCOLA

Peppery leaves that resemble dandelion leaves, arugula has a spicy and slightly bitter flavor that is often used to liven up mixed salad greens. In Italy, it is traditionally served with carpaccio, but it also complements cheese, eggs, fish, and shellfish. It may be made into a spicy tasting pesto, added to risotto at the last minute, or cooked quickly in oil and stirred into pasta. Wild arugula with Parmesan and balsamic vinegar is a simple but very tasty salad, ideal as an appetizer or as a side dish.

Arugula is less bitter when young. When buying, choose fresh baby leaves that are spotless and firm, and avoid leaves with holes, tears, and yellowing edges, signs that greens are past their prime. To store, seal in a tightly sealed bag and keep in the refrigerator for a few days.

IN THE GARDEN As part of the mustard family, this spicy herb grows quickly in cool weather. Once the weather warms, the flavor quickly becomes hot and peppery. Wild arugula has an even more pungent taste. Plant arugula seeds in the late winter or spring and again in fall. Sow seeds 1 inch apart in rows 1 foot apart. Once seedlings are growing, thin them to 6 inches apart. For a continual harvest, sow crops every few weeks in the spring and fall. Start harvesting 1 month after sowing. Snip off young leaves when they are 2 inches long. Alternatively, wait a few weeks and remove the whole plant by cutting it back to the ground or pulling it out. After cutting, plants will regrow and can be harvested again as long as the weather stays cool.

ARUGULA RECIPES ON PAGES 168–171

GREEN BEANS

One of the most convenient and adaptable vegetables, green beans are available all year round. Both green and yellow beans are popular in Italy and often paired with cream and Parmesan, baked in tomato sauce, or cooked in butter with garlic and anchovies. Green beans have an affinity with basil and are delicious served with pesto.

Check for freshness by snapping a bean; it should snap easily and be fresh and juicy. Whatever the variety, the beans should be crisp, bright in color, and firm. Unwashed fresh bean pods can be stored in a plastic bag in the refrigerator salad drawer for up to 7 days.

To prepare, simply trim and either leave whole or cut larger beans into short lengths. Cook, uncovered, in salted boiling water for 5–10 minutes, until tender-crisp, then drain. If serving the beans in a salad, refresh under cold water to stop any additional cooking unless the recipe recommends otherwise.

IN THE GARDEN Green beans are one of the easiest vegetables to grow. Sow seeds 3 inches apart in rows 2 feet apart in spring when all danger of frost has passed. Most varieties mature 2 months after sowing. Harvest when the pods are 6 inches long and before the bean seeds inside them begin to form. Modern varieties tend to produce most of their beans within 1–2 weeks. Pick regularly, daily if possible, to ensure longer cropping.

GREEN BEAN RECIPES ON PAGES 172–180

EGGPLANTS

MELANZANE

Subtle and mildly earthy in flavor, the eggplant is prized for its meatiness, softening to a silky smooth texture when cooked. Favorite dishes include caponata, risotto, terrines, pies, and fritters. This robust vegetable also has a notable affinity with tomatoes and cheese as in Italian classics, such as Eggplant Parmigiana (see page 184) and Eggplant and Ricotta Lasagne (see page 188).

When buying eggplants, look for firm, glossy, blemish-free skin and a fresh-looking green stalk. The vegetable should feel heavy for its size. Store in the salad drawer of the refrigerator. Salting eggplants prior to cooking is not essential but it does help to reduce the quantity of oil soaked up during frying.

IN THE GARDEN Plant young plants in fertile, well-drained, compost-enhanced soil after all danger of frost has passed. Most varieties grow to 2–3 feet tall and wide, making a beautiful ornamental plant with edible eggplants. In cool climates, cover the ground with sheets of black plastic to absorb heat, conserve moisture, and prevent weeds from growing. Apply a balanced fertilizer monthly and keep well watered. Dull, soft skin is a sign of over maturity and bitter flavor. Press the skin with your finger and if it bounces back, the fruits are ripe.

EGGPLANT RECIPES ON PAGES 181–188

ZUCCHINI
ZUCCHINI

Zucchini are baby squash that have not yet developed the seeds, fibers, and watery flesh of the mature vegetables and have a delicate flavor. The green and yellow varieties are most commonly available. From Roasted Zucchini, Potatoes, and Tomatoes (see page 196) to a Ricotta, Zucchini, and Zucchini Flower Flan (see page 193) to Roman-Style Crispy Fried Zucchini (see page 195), the versatility of the zucchini makes it immensely popular.

Look for firm, shiny, smooth vegetables and store in the salad drawer of the refrigerator for up to 2 days. Simply trim the ends, except for tiny ones, then slice or dice according to the recipe. Zucchini flowers, which can be deep-fried, stuffed and fried, or baked, are harder to find but may be available at some grocery stores.

IN THE GARDEN Sow seeds in spring in compost-enhanced soil after all danger of frost has passed. In regions with cool summers, lay sheets of black plastic over the bed, and sow seeds through holes cut into the plastic to encourage faster growth. Sow 2 seeds per hole, spaced 2–3 feet apart in rows 5 feet apart. Thin to the strongest seedling per hole. Zucchini have separate male and female flowers, so they need bees to pollinate them. Improperly pollinated vegetables will rot at the tip and drop off the plant. Zucchini taste best when harvested at 6 inches long. The more you pick, the more the plant will produce. If you miss a large zucchini, harvest it immediately to encourage more to set.

ZUCCHINI RECIPES ON PAGES 189–198

CUCUMBERS

CETRIOLO

Crisp, cool, and refreshing, cucumber makes perfect salads, either in a creamy dressing, with a vinaigrette, or combined with other salad vegetables, such as tomatoes, bell peppers, and olives. It also goes well with cheese and eggs. Cucumber is rarely cooked in Italy, although sautéed gently in butter, it is delicious with fish. Small pickled cucumbers are used in vinegary sauces to serve with meat and as a garnish for cold dishes.

Look for firm cucumbers and avoid those that are yellow, blemished, or wrinkled. Store in the salad drawer of the refrigerator for up to 1 week. Peeling cucumber is a matter of taste, but if you don't, wash it thoroughly in case it has a wax coating. If you want to get rid of some of the high water content, halve the cucumber, scoop out the seeds, and slice thinly. Sprinkle with salt and let drain for 1 hour, then squeeze dry in a dish towel.

IN THE GARDEN Plant seeds or transplants 2 feet apart in compost-enhanced soil after all danger of frost has passed. Before planting in cool areas, cover the beds with sheets of black plastic to warm the soil and conserve water, and make holes in the plastic to plant the seedlings. Keep plants well watered to prevent the cucumbers from developing bitterness. Harvest pickling cucumbers when they are 3 inches long and slicing cucumbers when they are 6 inches long. The more you harvest, the more cucumbers will be produced. Oversized cucumbers have many seeds and may be bitter.

CUCUMBER RECIPES ON PAGES 199–202

TOMATOES
POMODORI

No other vegetable in Italian cuisine is as ubiquitous and revered as the tomato. Whether it is the modest cherry variety or succulent flavorsome plum tomatoes, this vegetable is quintessential to Italian cooking. Tomatoes go well with most ingredients, but classic partnerships are with basil, cheese, particularly mozzarella, and onion. Classics include Tomato Bruschetta (see page 206), Buffalo Milk Mozzarella Caprese Salad (see page 211), and Tuscan Tomato Soup (see page 209), and tomatoes can be made into flans, sauces, gratins, and risotto.

Look for smooth, unblemished skins and fresh-looking green tops. Unripe tomatoes will ripen in a paper bag in the salad drawer of the refrigerator and overripe tomatoes, providing they have no signs of mold, are perfect for soups. Tomatoes are best stored in a bowl at room temperature. To peel, cut a cross in the tops and put them in a heatproof bowl. Pour in boiling water and let stand for 1 minute, then drain and peel off the skins with a sharp knife. To seed, cut in half and scoop out the seeds with a teaspoon.

IN THE GARDEN Tomatoes grow best in full sun on well-drained, fertile soil. Grow a mix of bush varieties for small spaces and containers and large varieties for the vegetable patch. Cover the ground with sheets of plastic or with straw to conserve soil moisture and deter weeds. Larger growing varieties need tomato cages, stakes, or trellises to keep the tomatoes off the ground. Harvest when the tomatoes turn their mature color. If picked when they are beginning to show color, tomatoes will continue to mature off the vine when stored in a warm room out of the sun.

TOMATO RECIPES ON PAGES 202–219

BELL PEPPERS

PEPERONI

To distinguish these peppers, which include bell peppers, from chiles, they are often called sweet peppers. Red are sweeter than green because they are riper. Yellow and orange bell peppers are slightly less sweet than red, while black varieties are more pungent. In Italy, smaller, slim, pointed green sweet peppers from Lombardy are the most highly valued. Bell peppers feature in many salads and they can also be sautéed, roasted, and combined with other vegetables. Stuffed with meat, vegetables, or a rice mixture, they may be fried or baked. Bell peppers complement eggs and tomatoes, and are perfect with pasta.

Choose plump, glossy specimens with no wrinkles or blemishes. Store in the salad drawer of the refrigerator for a few days. To prepare, remove the stems, seeds, and membranes. If the bell peppers are to be sliced or diced, just halve them first; but if they are to be stuffed, slice off the tops and cut out the seeds and membranes, leaving the "shells" intact.

To peel bell peppers, either roast in a preheated oven, 350°F, or under the broiler, until the skins are charred and blistered. Transfer to a plastic bag and tie the top. When they are cool enough to handle, peel off the skins.

IN THE GARDEN Plant seedlings in compost-enhanced soil after all danger of frost has passed. In areas with cool summers, lay sheets of black plastic on the beds to heat the soil first. Space the plants 18 inches apart, planting through holes made into the plastic. Keep well watered and feed monthly. Start harvesting a few peppers when they reach full size but are still green to encourage cropping. They take an additional 2–4 weeks beyond the full-size green stage to reach their mature color.

BELL PEPPER RECIPES ON PAGES 220–227

FENNEL
FINOCCHIO

Fennel bulbs, known as Florence fennel, have a strong anise seed flavor and aroma with a hint of sweetness. Fennel adds a wonderful crispness to salads and pairs nicely with other crunchy ingredients, such as celery and apple, or citrus fruits, such as grapefruit, while tasting delicious simply dressed with olive oil, lemon juice, and salt. Fennel is also good braised, fried in egg and bread crumbs, in gratins, and in risotto.

Look for well-rounded bulbs without blemishes and with their fronds intact. Store in the salad drawer of the refrigerator for 2–3 days. The fronds can be used for garnishes or for flavoring stock. Remove and discard the core and the first layer of the bulb, unless it is very young and tender, then slice thinly. Use immediately or put it into a bowl of acidulated water to avoid discoloration.

IN THE GARDEN Sow seeds in spring around the last frost date. Create a well-drained, raised bed on sandy loam soil and sow seeds 4 inches apart. Thin to 8 inches apart when the plants are 4 inches high. For best bulb production, mulch with straw once the plants are established to keep the soil cool and moist. When the bulb is 2 inches wide, mound soil around the base of the plant to blanch it, because this produces a milder flavor. Harvest bulbs when they are 3 inches wide. Fennel grows best in cool weather and takes more than 2 months to mature. If grown during periods of hot weather or watered inadequately, it will bolt.

FENNEL RECIPES ON PAGES 229–234

CORN

MAIS

Sweet and juicy when really fresh, corncobs are excellent boiled in unsalted water for 10–15 minutes and served with melted butter, but they are even more delicious when roasted or cooked on the barbecue to enhance their sweetness. Look for plump cobs with tightly packed, juicy kernels. If still in the husk, this should be pale green and the silk (the soft filamentous threads) should be golden brown, fine, untangled, and smooth. Because the sugar begins to turn to starch as soon as the cobs are picked, they should be cooked as soon after purchase as possible. Before cooking, strip away the husks. To use the kernels, cut downward from top to bottom with a sharp knife.

Corn is a popular addition to salads because it goes well both with other sweet ingredients, such as apple, and with contrasting flavors, such as the mild bitterness of radicchio. Canned corn kernels are often used in place of fresh because they are so convenient.

IN THE GARDEN To extend the harvest season grow early, mid, and late season varieties. Sow seeds in warm, fertile soil 8 inches apart in rows 2 feet apart after all danger of frost has passed. Apply a high-nitrogen fertilizer when the corn is knee high and when ears begin to form. When the silks turn brown, squeeze the ear tips. If they feel firm, peel back the husk and pinch some kernels. If a milky white liquid squirts out, they are ready to harvest.

CORN RECIPES ON PAGES 235–239

BASIL BUTTER

BURRO AL BASILICO

Preparation time: *10 min*
Serves 4

— 7 tablespoons butter, diced
— 1 large bunch basil leaves,
  torn into pieces
— 2–3 tablespoons lemon juice,
  strained
— salt and pepper

Put the butter in the top of a double boiler or in a heatproof bowl and melt over barely simmering water. Remove from the heat, whisk in the basil and lemon juice, and season with salt and pepper. Good with fish or shellfish.

PARSLEY BUTTER

BURRO AL PREZZEMOLO

Preparation time: *10 min*
Serves 4

— 7 tablespoons butter, softened
— 1 tablespoon chopped
  parsley
— 1 tablespoon lemon juice
— salt and freshly ground white
  pepper

Beat the butter in a bowl with a wooden spoon, then beat in the parsley, lemon juice, and a pinch each of salt and white pepper until thoroughly combined. Chill in the refrigerator until required. It is excellent served cold on hot steaks.

SAGE BUTTER

BURRO ALLA SALVIA

Preparation time: *10 min*
Cooking time: *5 min*
Serves 4

— 7 tablespoons butter
— 15 sage leaves
— salt

Melt the butter in a small pan over low heat. As soon as it starts to color, add the sage leaves and season with salt. When the leaves are crisp, remove the pan from the heat and serve the butter immediately. Good with boiled rice, broiled meat, or ravioli.

PESTO

PESTO

Preparation time: *15 min*
Serves 4

— 25 basil leaves
— scant ½ cup extra virgin
   olive oil
— ⅓ cup pine nuts
— ⅓ cup grated Parmesan
   cheese
— ⅓ cup grated pecorino
   cheese
— salt

Put the basil leaves in a food processor with the olive oil,
pine nuts, and a pinch of salt. Process briefly at medium
speed. Add the grated cheeses and process again.
Delicious with asparagus, egg dishes, spaghetti, or gnocchi.

BASIL MAYONNAISE

MAIONESE AL BASILICO

Preparation time: *5 min*
Serves 4

For mayonnaise:
— 2 egg yolks
— scant 1 cup sunflower
   or mild olive oil
— 2 tablespoons lemon juice
   or white wine vinegar

— 10 basil leaves
— salt and pepper

Put the egg yolks in a bowl and season with salt and pepper.
Add the oil, a drop at a time, beating continuously with
a small whisk or wooden spoon. As soon as the mixture
thickens, beat in a drop of lemon juice or vinegar. Continue
adding the oil and lemon juice or vinegar alternately in
a thin steady stream until the ingredients are thoroughly
blended.

Tear the basil leaves into pieces and gently stir them into
mayonnaise in a bowl. Season to taste with salt and pepper.
Store in the refrigerator until required.

ROSEMARY FOCACCIA

ROSEMARY FOCACCIA

PHOTO PAGE 160

FOCACCIA AL ROSMARINO

Preparation time: *35 min,*
plus 1 hour rising
Cooking time: *50 min*
Serves 6–8

— 2 tablespoons olive oil,
  plus extra for brushing
— ½ ounce fresh yeast or 2
  teaspoons dried yeast or 1½
  teaspoons active dry yeast
— 1 cup lukewarm milk
— 1 teaspoon superfine sugar
— 3½ cups strong white bread
  or all-purpose flour, plus
  extra for dusting
— 2 teaspoons salt
— 2 sprigs rosemary, coarsely
  chopped
— coarse sea salt

Brush a large baking sheet with oil or line with parchment paper. If using fresh yeast, put it into a bowl with the warm milk and mash well with a fork to make a smooth paste. If using dried yeast, dissolve the sugar in the warm milk in a bowl, sprinkle the yeast over the surface, and let stand for 10–15 minutes, until frothy. Stir well to make a smooth paste. (If using active dry yeast, add to the flour in the bowl.) Sift together the flour and salt into a bowl. Stir in your chosen yeast and add the sugar (if not using dried yeast), rosemary, and oil. Add the warm milk if using active dry yeast. Mix well, turn out onto a lightly floured counter, and knead for 10 minutes or until smooth and elastic.

Roll out to a 9-inch round and carefully place on the prepared baking sheet. Using your fingertip, make 10 dimples in the surface of the dough and insert 2–3 grains of coarse salt in each. Brush with the oil and let rise in a warm place for 1 hour. Meanwhile, preheat the oven to 400°F. Bake the loaf for 30 minutes, until deep golden brown. Remove from the oven, transfer to a wire rack to cool slightly, and serve warm.

DEEP-FRIED SAGE PUFFS

STUZZICHINI DI SALVIA

Preparation time: *25 min*
Cooking time: *10 min.*
plus 1 hour resting
Serves 4

— 4½ cups all-purpose flour,
  plus extra for dusting
— 10 sage leaves
— ¼ cup dry white wine
— 1 egg yolk
— scant 1 cup sunflower
  or mild olive oil
— salt

Sift together the flour and a pinch of salt into a mound on a counter, stir in the sage, and make a well in the center. Add the wine, egg yolk, and 2 tablespoons of the oil and gradually incorporate the dry ingredients with your fingertips, adding enough water to make a smooth dough. Shape into a ball, cover with plastic wrap, and refrigerate for 1 hour. Roll out the dough on a lightly floured counter to ⅛-inch thick and stamp out rounds with a fluted cookie cutter. Let stand for 20 minutes. Heat the oil in a skillet. Add the dough in batches and cook until golden brown. Remove with a slotted spoon, drain on paper towels, and keep warm while you cook the remaining batches. Serve immediately.

OMELET WITH AROMATIC HERBS

PHOTO PAGE 163

OMELETTE ALLE ERBE AROMATICHE

Preparation time: *10 min*
Cooking time: *10 min*
Serves 4

— 6 eggs
— 1 tablespoon finely
  chopped parsley
— 1 tablespoon finely
  chopped chives
— 1 tablespoon finely
  chopped tarragon
— 1 tablespoon finely
  chopped chervil
— 2 tablespoons butter
— salt and pepper

Lightly beat the eggs with 1 tablespoon water in a bowl, season with salt and pepper, and stir in the herbs. Melt the butter in a skillet over medium-high heat. Pour in the egg mixture and tilt and rotate the skillet to spread the mixture evenly. Cook for 10 seconds, then lift the cooked bottom with a spatula to let the uncooked egg run underneath. Continue cooking in this way until the omelet is just set underneath but the top is still soft and creamy. Loosen the edge with a spatula, tilt the skillet so that the omelet folds over itself, and slide it onto a serving plate. Serve immediately.

LEMON AND BASIL RISOTTO

RISOTTO AL LIMONE E BASILICO

Preparation time: *15 min*
Cooking time: *25 min*
Serves 4

— 4¼ cups vegetable stock
— 2 tablespoons olive oil,
  plus extra for drizzling
— ½ onion, finely chopped
— 1 shallot, finely chopped
— 1⅔ cups risotto rice
— scant 1 cup dry white wine
— ½ teaspoon grated lemon
  rind
— 2 tablespoons butter
— juice of 1 lemon, strained
— 6 fresh basil leaves, chopped
— salt and pepper

Pour the stock into a pan and bring to a boil. Meanwhile, heat the oil in a large pan. Add the onion and shallot and cook over low heat, stirring occasionally, for 5 minutes, until softened and translucent. Stir in the rice and cook, stirring, for 1 minute, until all the grains are coated in oil. Add the wine and cook until the alcohol has evaporated, then season with salt. Add a ladleful of the hot stock and cook, stirring continuously, until it has been absorbed. Continue to add the hot stock, a ladleful at a time, stirring continuously until each addition has been absorbed before adding the next, for about 20 minutes. About 5 minutes before the end of the cooking time, stir in the lemon rind. When the rice is tender and creamy, remove the pan from the heat, add the butter, drizzle with olive oil and the lemon juice, add a pinch of pepper and the chopped basil, and stir. Let stand for 1 minute, then transfer to a warm serving dish and serve immediately.

OMELET WITH AROMATIC HERBS

HERB SANDWICH

PHOTO PAGE 165

ERBAZZONE

Preparation time: *50 min*
Cooking time: *25 min*
Serves 6

— 3 ¼ pounds Catalogna
   lettuce or dandelion leaves
— 2 tablespoons olive oil,
   plus extra for brushing
— 2 shallots, very thinly sliced
— 2 cloves garlic, finely
   chopped
— 1 cup grated Parmesan
   cheese
— 1 quantity of bread dough
   (about 14 ounces)
— all-purpose flour, for dusting
— salt and pepper

Bring a pan of water to a boil. Add the lettuce or dandelion leaves and simmer for 5–6 minutes, then drain and chop. Heat the oil in a skillet. Add the shallots, season with pepper, and cook over low heat, stirring occasionally, for about 8 minutes, until lightly golden. Add the greens and garlic, and season with salt and a little more pepper. Cook, stirring occasionally, for another 20 minutes. Meanwhile, preheat the oven to 400°F. Sprinkle the Parmesan over a baking sheet. Halve the bread dough and pat out into 2 rounds on a lightly floured counter. Put one round on the prepared baking sheet. Season with pepper, spoon the lettuce mixture evenly over it, and cover with the second round of dough. Seal the edges with your fingertips, prick the surface with a fork, and brush with oil. Bake for 25 minutes. Remove from the oven and let rest for 5 minutes before serving.

VEAL NOISETTES WITH BUTTER, SAGE, AND ROSEMARY

NODINI AL BURRO, SALVIA E ROSMARINO

Preparation time: *20 min*
Cooking time: *40 min*
Serves 4

— 1 ¼–2 cups beef stock
— 4 veal noisettes
— 6 tablespoons butter
— 2 sprigs rosemary,
   finely chopped
— 8 sage leaves
— scant ½ cup white
   wine
— salt and pepper

Pour the stock into a pan and bring to a boil. Meanwhile, flatten the noisettes slightly with a meat mallet or the side of a rolling pin. Put into a flameproof casserole and dot with the butter. Sprinkle with the rosemary and sage, and cook over medium heat for 4 minutes, until the undersides are browned. Turn over and cook for another 4 minutes. Season with salt and pepper, sprinkle over the wine, and cook until the alcohol has evaporated. Reduce the heat to low, pour 2 ladles of the hot stock over the noisettes, cover, and simmer, adding more stock as necessary, for 30 minutes, until the noisettes are tender and the stock is nut brown in color and reduced.

HERB AND BELL PEPPER ROULADE

ROTELLINE DI ERBETTE AI PEPERONI

Preparation time: *50 min,*
plus 2 *hours chilling*
Cooking time: *30 min*
Serves 6

— butter, for greasing
— 1 pound 2 ounces mixed
   herbs
— 3 basil leaves
— 3–4 eggs, separated
— 2 tablespoons milk
— ⅓ cup grated Parmesan
   cheese
— 1 teaspoon lemon juice
— salt

For the filling:
— 2 large red bell peppers,
   halved and seeded
— scant ½ cup cream cheese
— salt and pepper

Preheat the oven to 375°F. Line a rectangular baking sheet with parchment paper and grease with butter. Bring a pan of salted water to a boil. Add the mixed herbs and simmer for 15 minutes, then drain and squeeze out the excess moisture. Put them into a food processor, add the basil leaves, and process briefly. Add the egg yolks, milk, and Parmesan and process until just combined. Transfer to a bowl. In a grease-free bowl, whisk the egg whites with the lemon juice to stiff peaks and fold into the mixture. Pour the mixture onto the prepared baking sheet and bake for 15 minutes. Remove from the oven, invert the baking sheet onto a dish towel, and roll up the herb roulade in the dish towel. Let cool.

Meanwhile, increase the oven temperature to 400°F. Put the bell peppers, skin side up, on a baking sheet and roast for 10–15 minutes, until charred and blistered. Remove from the oven and, using tongs, transfer to a plastic bag, seal the top, and let stand until cool enough to handle. Remove the bell peppers from the bag, peel off the skins, and coarsely chop the flesh. Put the chopped peppers into a food processor with the cream cheese and process until smooth and combined. Gently unroll the roulade, remove the dish towel, and spread the bell pepper mixture over the roulade. Roll up again, this time, without the dish towel, wrap in aluminum foil, and chill in the refrigerator for at least 2 hours.

To serve, remove the roulade from the refrigerator, discard the aluminum foil, and cut into ½-inch slices.

MINT ICE CREAM

Preparation time: *25 min,
plus 3–4 hours freezing*
Serves 4

— 2 cups very finely chopped
 mint leaves, plus extra to
 decorate
— scant ½ cup superfine sugar
— 2½ ounces semisweet
 chocolate, broken into pieces
— 2 egg yolks
— scant 1 cup heavy cream,
 plus extra to decorate

Combine the mint leaves and sugar in a food processor or blender and process until very fine. Put the chocolate in a heatproof bowl set over a pan of barely simmering water, not letting the bottom of the bowl touch the surface of the water, and heat, stirring occasionally, until melted. Remove the bowl from the heat and let cool slightly. Stir in the egg yolks, mixing until thoroughly combined. Whisk the cream until stiff peaks form, then gently stir into mint mixture. Lightly fold the cream and mint mixture into the melted chocolate. Rinse a freezerproof mold or bowl with water, then pour in the mint mixture. Freeze for 3–4 hours, until set. Turn out onto a serving dish, decorate with whipped cream and mint leaves, and serve.

BASIL SHERBET

Preparation time: *30 min,
plus 45 min freezing*
Serves 4

— 16 basil leaves, plus extra
 to decorate
— generous 2 cups dry
 sparkling wine
— ½ cup confectioners' sugar
— juice of 1 lemon, strained
— 4 egg whites

Put the basil leaves, wine, sugar, and lemon juice in a food processor or blender and process at high speed for 1 minute, then transfer the mixture to a bowl. In a grease-free bowl, whisk the egg whites to stiff peaks and carefully fold into the wine mixture. Pour into a freezerproof container and freeze for about 45 minutes or until the mixture is grainy. Remove from the freezer and divide among 4 dessert glasses. Decorate with a few whole basil leaves and serve.

CANAPÉS WITH ARUGULA

CANAPÉ CASALINGHI ALLA RUCOLA

Preparation time: *10 min*
Cooking time: *12–15 min*
Serves 4

— olive oil, for brushing
  and drizzling
— 1 bunch arugula
— red wine vinegar,
  for drizzling
— 4 slices homemade or
  rustic bread
— 2 tablespoons milk,
  for sprinkling
— 4 anchovy fillets
— 4 slices mozzarella, fontina,
  or other melting cheese
— salt and pepper

Preheat the oven to 350°F. Brush a baking sheet with oil. Tear the arugula into pieces, put into a bowl, drizzle with oil and vinegar to taste, and season with salt and pepper. Put the slices of bread on the prepared baking sheet, sprinkle lightly with milk, and drizzle with oil. Bake for 10 minutes, until golden brown, then remove from the oven. Put an anchovy fillet in the middle of each slice and cover with a slice of cheese. Return to the oven and bake for a few minutes, until the cheese topping is golden brown. Transfer to a serving dish, garnish with the arugula, and serve immediately.

CREAM AND ARUGULA RISOTTO

RISOTTO CON PANNA E RUCOLA

Preparation time: *20 min*
Cooking time: *30 min*
Serves 4

— 6¼ cups vegetable stock
— 3 tablespoons butter
— 1 onion, finely chopped
— 1¾ cups risotto rice
— 5 tablespoons dry white
  wine
— ⅓ cup grated Parmesan
  cheese, plus extra to serve
— ¾ cup light cream
— small bunch arugula,
  chopped
— salt and pepper

Pour the stock into a pan and bring to a boil. Meanwhile, melt the butter in another pan, add the onion, and cook over low heat, stirring occasionally, for 5 minutes. Stir in the rice and cook, stirring, until the grains are coated in butter. Pour in the wine and cook until the alcohol has evaporated. Add a ladleful of the hot stock and cook, stirring, until it has been absorbed. Continue adding the stock, a ladleful at a time, stirring until each addition has been absorbed, about 20 minutes. Just before the rice is tender, stir in the Parmesan and cream, sprinkle with the arugula, and season with salt and pepper to taste. Transfer to a warm serving dish and serve with extra Parmesan.

ARUGULA, ROBIOLA, RICOTTA, AND MASCARPONE RAVIOLI

Preparation time: *1 hour 10 min, plus 2 hours resting*
Cooking time: *50 min*
Serves 6

For the pasta dough:
— 1½ cups all-purpose flour, plus extra for dusting
— ¾ cup semolina flour
— 2 eggs
— salt

For the filling:
— ⅔ cup arugula
— 1½ tablespoons butter
— 2 tablespoons chopped shallot
— ½ clove garlic
— ⅓ cup ricotta cheese
— 3 ounces robiola cheese
— 2½ tablespoons mascarpone cheese
— pinch of fresh bread crumbs
— 1–2 tablespoons vegetable stock (optional)
— salt and pepper

For the cream:
— 5 tablespoons milk
— 1½ tablespoons butter
— pinch of freshly grated nutmeg
— 5 tablespoons all-purpose flour, sifted
— ½ cup grated Parmesan cheese
— salt and pepper

For the sauce:
— 2 tablespoons olive oil
— ¾ cup shredded arugula
— 1 clove garlic, very finely chopped
— 2 tablespoons butter
— 5 ounces tomatoes, peeled, seeded, and diced
— salt and pepper

To make the pasta dough, sift the flours and a pinch of salt into a mound on a counter and make a well in the center. Break the eggs into the well and gradually incorporate the dry ingredients with your fingers. Knead thoroughly, then shape into a ball, cover, and let rest for 2 hours. Meanwhile, make the filling. Put the arugula into a small pan with just the water clinging to its leaves after washing, and cook over low heat, turning occasionally, for 5 minutes. Drain, squeeze out the excess liquid, and chop. Melt the butter in a shallow pan. Add the shallot and garlic and cook over low heat, stirring occasionally, for 5 minutes, removing and discarding the garlic when it has turned golden brown. Stir in the arugula and ricotta, remove the pan from the heat, and let cool. Stir in the robiola, mascarpone, and bread crumbs and add the stock if the mixture is too stiff. Season with salt and pepper and mix well.

To make the cream, pour the milk into a pan, add the butter and nutmeg, season with salt and pepper, and bring just to a boil. Immediately add the sifted flour and stir vigorously. Cook, stirring continuously, for a few minutes until thickened, then stir in the cooled filling and Parmesan. Remove the pan from the heat and let cool. Add another pinch of bread crumbs if the mixture is too runny.

Roll out the pasta dough on a lightly floured counter into a thin sheet. Put small mounds of the filling in even rows over one-half of the pasta sheet. Fold over the other half of the sheet and press around the filling with your fingers to seal. Cut out the ravioli and press the edges together firmly. Cook the ravioli in plenty of salted boiling water until it rises to the surface and is al dente, then drain.

To make the sauce, heat the oil in a shallow pan. Add the arugula and garlic and cook, stirring continuously, for 1 minute. Add the butter and the ravioli and toss gently. Add the tomatoes and heat through for a few seconds. Transfer the ravioli to a warm serving dish and serve immediately.

ARUGULA AND TALEGGIO PIE

ARUGULA AND TALEGGIO PIE

PHOTO PAGE 170

TORTA ALLA RUCOLA E TALEGGIO

Preparation time: *15 min*
Cooking time: *1 hour, plus*
1 hour resting
Serves 6

— 1¾ cups all-purpose flour,
   plus extra for dusting
— 1 tablespoon poppy seeds
— 1 tablespoon chopped
   marjoram
— 7 tablespoons butter,
   chilled and diced,
   plus extra for greasing

For the filling:
— 1½ cups arugula
— 1⅓ cups cream cheese
— 7 ounces Taleggio
   cheese, diced
— 2 tablespoons bread crumbs
— 2 eggs
— salt and pepper

Sift the flour with a pinch of salt into a mound on a counter, sprinkle with the poppy seeds and marjoram, and rub in the butter with your fingertips. Add enough cold water to make a soft dough, then shape into a ball, cover with plastic wrap, and let rest for 1 hour.

Preheat the oven to 350°F. Grease an 8-inch tart or quiche pan with butter. Parboil the arugula for a few minutes in salted water, then drain, squeezing out as much liquid as possible. Put the arugula in a food processor with both cheeses, the bread crumbs, and eggs. Process at low speed, then season with salt and pepper. Roll out the dough on a lightly floured counter, and line the prepared pan. Trim the edges and reserve the trimmings. Fill with the arugula and cheese mixture. Roll out the trimmings, cut into thin strips, brush the ends with water, and arrange in a lattice over the top of the pie. Bake for about 40 minutes.

ARUGULA AND VEAL

RUCOLA E VITELLO

Preparation time: *15 min*
Serves 4

— ¾ cup arugula
— 11 ounces cold roasted veal,
   thinly sliced
— 3½ ounces good-quality
   slicing cheese, thinly sliced
— 3 tablespoons olive oil
— juice of 1 lemon, strained
— salt and pepper

Tear or cut half the arugula into fairly small pieces, making a bed of arugula on a serving dish. Cut the veal slices into strips ½-inch wide and put them on the bed of arugula. Cover with the cheese slices and arrange the whole arugula leaves around the edge. Whisk together the oil and lemon juice in a bowl and season with salt and pepper. Sprinkle the dressing over the salad and let stand for a few minutes before serving.

SAUTÉED GREEN BEANS

FAGIOLINI IN PADELLA

Preparation time: *15 min*
Cooking time: *20 min*
Serves 4

— 4 cups trimmed green beans
— 4 tablespoons olive oil
— 1 clove garlic
— 1 tablespoon finely chopped
  parsley
— salt and pepper

Bring a pan of lightly salted water to a boil. Add the beans and cook for 10 minutes. Meanwhile, heat the oil with the garlic clove over low heat. When the garlic is lightly browned, remove and discard. Drain the beans and add to the pan with a pinch of salt. Increase the heat to medium-high and cook, stirring frequently, for 5 minutes. Remove from the heat, season with pepper, and sprinkle with the parsley. Serve immediately.

GREEN BEANS WITH SMOKED PROVOLONE CHEESE

FAGIOLINI ALLA PROVOLA AFFUMICATA

Preparation time: *25 min*
Cooking time: *10 min*
Serves 4

— 4 cups trimmed green beans
— butter, for greasing
— 3 tablespoons olive oil
— 1½ ounces speck or other
  ham, cut into thin strips
— 2 eggs, lightly beaten
— ½ cup grated Parmesan
  cheese
— 3½ ounces smoked
  provolone or mozzarella
  cheese, thinly sliced
— salt and pepper

Bring a pan of salted water to a boil. Add the beans and cook for 10 minutes, then drain. Preheat the oven to 375°F. Grease an ovenproof dish with butter. Heat the oil and strips of speck in a pan, add the beans, and cook, stirring occasionally, for a few minutes. Remove from the heat and let cool slightly. Put the warm beans into the prepared dish. Combine the eggs and grated cheese, season with salt and pepper, and pour the mixture over the beans. Cover with the slices of smoked cheese and bake for 10 minutes, until the cheese topping has just started to brown. Remove from the oven and let stand for 10 minutes before serving.

GREEN BEANS WITH ANCHOVY CREAM

FAGIOLINI ALLA CREMA DI ACCIUGHE

Preparation time: *25 min*
Cooking time: *20 min*
Serves 6

— 1¾ pounds green
  beans, trimmed
— 2 tablespoons olive oil
— 4 canned anchovy fillets,
  drained and chopped
— 2 egg yolks
— 2 tablespoons heavy
  cream, whipped
— 2½ ounces robiola cheese
— salt and pepper

Bring a pan of salted water to a boil. Add the beans and cook for 8–10 minutes, until crisp-tender. Heat the oil in a skillet. Add the anchovies and cook over low heat, mashing them with a fork until they have disintegrated. Add the beans and cook, stirring frequently, for 5–8 minutes, until heated through. Remove the skillet from the heat. Put the egg yolks and cream into a pan and stir over very low heat until thoroughly combined. Stir in the cheese and heat gently until smoothly blended. Remove from the heat and season lightly with salt and pepper. Spoon the hot sauce onto each of 6 individual plates and top with the beans. Serve immediately.

GREEN BEANS WITH PESTO

FAGIOLINI AL PESTO

Preparation time: *10 min*
Cooking time: *10 min*
Serves 4

— 4 cups trimmed green beans
— 2 boiled potatoes, diced
— olive oil, for drizzling
— 2 tablespoons pesto
  (see page 159)
— salt and pepper

Boil the beans in salted water for 8 minutes, then drain. Put the beans and the diced potatoes into a salad bowl, season with salt and pepper, drizzle with olive oil, and toss. Add the pesto and toss again, then serve.

GREEN BEANS WITH GARLIC

FAGIOLINI ALL'AGLIO

Preparation time: *15 min*
Cooking time: *20 min*
Serves 6

— 1¾ pounds green
  beans, trimmed
— 4 tablespoons olive oil
— 2 cloves garlic
— salt and pepper

Bring a pan of salted water to a boil. Add the beans and simmer for 5 minutes, then drain. Heat the oil in a pan. Add the garlic and cook over low heat, stirring frequently, for a few minutes, until light golden brown. Remove and discard if you do not like a strong garlic taste, otherwise leave in the pan. Add the beans, cover, and cook over low heat, stirring occasionally, for 15 minutes. Season with salt and pepper, and remove from the heat. Remove and discard the garlic and transfer the beans to a warm serving dish. Serve immediately.

FRISÉE SALAD WITH GREEN BEANS AND RED CURRANTS

PHOTO PAGE 175

INSALATA RICCIA CON FAGIOLINI E RIBES

Preparation time: *20 min*
Cooking time: *10 min*
Serves 4

— 1⅓ cups trimmed green
  beans
— scant 1 cup red currants
— 5 tablespoons olive oil
— 5–6 small mint leaves,
  chopped
— 1 head frisée, chopped
— salt and pepper

Bring a pan of salted water to a boil. Add the beans and cook for 10 minutes, until tender but still al dente. Drain and let cool. Crush 2 tablespoons of the red currants in a bowl and strain the juice into another bowl. Discard the crushed currants. Add the oil and mint to the strained juice, season with salt and pepper, and beat with a fork until thoroughly combined. Cut the green beans into short lengths and put into a salad bowl. Add the frisée, pour in the red currant dressing, and toss lightly. Garnish with the remaining red currants and serve.

FRISÉE SALAD WITH GREEN BEANS AND RED CURRANTS

GREEN BEAN LOAF

PHOTO PAGE 176

POLPETTONI DI FAGIOLINI

Preparation time: *1 hour*
Cooking time: *50 min*
Serves 6

— 3 potatoes
— 2⅔ cups trimmed green
  beans
— 1 tablespoon olive oil,
  for brushing
— 4–5 tablespoons fresh
  bread crumbs
— 1 bread roll
— 4 tablespoons milk
— 1 teaspoon marjoram
— 2–3 eggs, lightly beaten
— ⅔ cup grated Parmesan
  cheese
— salt and pepper

Put the unpeeled potatoes into a pan, pour in water to cover, add a pinch of salt, and bring to a boil. Reduce the heat and simmer until tender. Drain, peel, and mash in a bowl, then stir until completely smooth. Bring a pan of salted water to a boil. Add the green beans and simmer for 10–15 minutes. Drain and let cool, then cut into small pieces. Preheat the oven to 350°F. Brush a loaf pan with oil and sprinkle with the bread crumbs. Meanwhile, pull off the crust from the bread roll, put the remaining roll into a bowl, add the milk, and let soak for 10 minutes. Drain and squeeze out any excess moisture. Add the soaked roll, green beans, marjoram, eggs, Parmesan, and olive oil to the potato, season with salt and pepper, and mix well. Spoon the mixture into the prepared pan and bake for 50 minutes. Remove from the oven and let rest for a few minutes, then turn out onto a warm serving plate. Serve immediately.

GREEN BEANS AND POTATOES

FAGIOLINI E PATATE

Preparation time: *30 min*
Cooking time: *40 min*
Serves 4

— 2⅔ cups trimmed green
  beans
— 3 tablespoons olive oil
— 1 clove garlic
— 1 onion, finely chopped
— 2–3 potatoes, thinly sliced
— 1 tablespoon chopped
  parsley
— salt and pepper

Bring a pan of salted water to a boil. Add the beans and cook for 8–10 minutes, then drain well and cut in half. Heat the oil in a pan. Add the garlic and cook over low heat, stirring frequently, for a few minutes, until lightly browned. Remove and discard. Add the onion and cook, stirring occasionally, for 5 minutes, until softened. Add the potatoes and cook, stirring occasionally, for another 30 minutes. Add the beans and cook, stirring occasionally, for 10 minutes. Season with salt and pepper and remove from the heat. Transfer to a warm serving dish, sprinkle with the parsley, and serve immediately.

GREEN BEAN GRATIN

TORTA DI FAGIOLINI

Preparation time: *35 min*
Cooking time: *40 min*
Serves 4

— butter, for greasing
— 4–5 tablespoons
  fresh bread crumbs
— 3 ½ cups trimmed green
  beans
— 1 tablespoon olive oil
— 1 shallot, finely chopped
— ½ quantity béchamel
  sauce (see page 51)
— 3 ½ ounces fontina
  cheese, grated
— 3 eggs
— 1 sprig parsley, finely
  chopped
— ⅔ cup grated Parmesan
  cheese
— salt and pepper

Preheat the oven to 350°F. Grease an ovenproof dish with butter and sprinkle with bread crumbs, tipping out any excess. Bring a pan of lightly salted water to a boil. Add the beans and cook for 8–10 minutes, then drain and cut into short lengths. Heat the oil in a pan. Add the shallot and cook over low heat, stirring occasionally, for 5 minutes, until softened. Stir in the beans and season with salt and pepper. Reheat the béchamel sauce in a small pan over very low heat. Remove from the heat and stir in the fontina cheese. Then add the eggs, 1 at a time, parsley, Parmesan, and the bean mixture, stirring well after each addition. Spoon the mixture into the prepared dish, cover with aluminum foil, and bake for 30 minutes. Remove the aluminum foil and bake for another 10 minutes.

GREEN AND YELLOW BEANS

PHOTO PAGE 179

FAGIOLINI VERDI E GIALLI

Preparation time: *10 min*
Cooking time: *35 min*
Serves 4

— 2 tablespoons butter
— 2 tablespoons olive oil
— 1 onion, sliced
— 2 tomatoes, peeled, seeded,
  and coarsely chopped
— 2⅔ cups trimmed green
  beans
— 2⅔ cups trimmed yellow
  beans
— 1 clove garlic, crushed
— 1 sprig parsley, chopped
— scant 1 cup dry white wine
— salt and pepper

Melt the butter with the oil in a pan. Add the onion and cook over low heat, stirring occasionally, for 5 minutes, until softened. Add the tomatoes, beans, garlic, and chopped parsley and stir well. Pour in the wine, season with salt and pepper, cover, and simmer for 30 minutes. Serve hot or cold.

GREEN BEANS WITH PARMESAN

FAGIOLINI AL PARMIGIANO

Preparation time: *5 min*
Cooking time: *30 min*
Serves 4

— butter, for greasing
— 1¾ pounds green beans,
  trimmed
— 3 eggs
— 5 tablespoons milk
— generous 1 cup grated
  Parmesan cheese
— salt and pepper

Preheat the oven to 350°F. Grease an ovenproof dish with butter. Cook the beans in salted, boiling water for 15 minutes, then drain and place in the prepared dish. Beat the eggs with the milk and Parmesan and season with salt and pepper. Pour the egg mixture over the beans and bake until just set. Serve immediately.

GREEN BEANS WITH TOMATO

FAGIOLINI AL POMODORO

Preparation time: *10 min*
Cooking time: *35 min*
Serves 4

— 4 cups trimmed green
  beans
— 2 tablespoons olive oil
— 1 onion, chopped
— 1 clove garlic
— 5 tomatoes, peeled, seeded,
  and chopped
— 6 green olives, pitted
  and quartered
— 6 fresh basil leaves, chopped
— salt and pepper

Cook the beans in salted, boiling water for 10 minutes. Meanwhile, heat the oil in another pan, add the onion and garlic, and cook over low heat, stirring occasionally, for 5 minutes. Drain the beans, add to the pan, and mix well. Stir in the tomatoes, season with salt and pepper, then remove and discard the garlic. Simmer over low heat for about 10 minutes, then stir in the olives and basil, and cook for another 5 minutes. Serve warm.

MARINATED EGGPLANT

MELANZANE MARINATE

Preparation time: *45 min,*
plus 6 hours marinating
Cooking time: *25 min*
Serves 4

— 1 large eggplant, cut into
¼-inch-thick slices
— ¾ cup olive oil
— 1 chile, seeded and
chopped
— 3 cloves garlic, finely
chopped
— 1 tablespoon capers, drained,
rinsed, and chopped
— 10 mint leaves, chopped
— salt and pepper

Put the eggplant slices in a colander, sprinkle with salt, and let drain for about 30 minutes. Heat a heavy, nonstick skillet. Rinse the eggplants, pat dry, and brush with some of the oil. Add the eggplant slices to the skillet, in batches if necessary, and cook over high heat until golden brown on both sides. Combine the chile, garlic, capers, and mint in a bowl and season with salt and pepper. Make a layer of eggplant slices in a salad bowl, sprinkle with a tablespoon of the chili dressing, and continue making layers until all the ingredients are used. Pour in the remaining olive oil and let marinate in a cool place for at least 6 hours.

GRANDMOTHER'S EGGPLANTS

MELANZANE DELLA NONNA

Preparation time: *15 min,*
plus 30 min draining
Cooking time: *25 min*
Serves 4

— 4 eggplants, halved
— 2 tablespoons olive oil
— 2 onions, thinly sliced
— 2 cloves garlic
— 5 tomatoes, peeled, seeded,
and diced
— 1 sprig parsley, chopped
— 1 tablespoon capers, drained,
rinsed, and chopped
— 1 tablespoon black olives,
pitted and sliced
— 1 tablespoon white wine
vinegar
— 1 teaspoon sugar
— salt and pepper

Scoop out and discard the central, seed-filled part of the eggplants and dice the remaining flesh. Place in a colander, sprinkle with salt, and let drain for 30 minutes, then rinse and pat dry with paper towels. Heat the oil in a skillet, add the onions and garlic, and cook for 1–2 minutes over low heat, until the garlic is light golden brown, then remove and discard. Add the eggplants to the skillet, mix well, then stir in the tomatoes and season with salt and pepper. Cook, stirring frequently, for 15 minutes. Add the parsley, capers, olives, vinegar, and sugar, and cook for another few minutes. Taste for the combination of sweet and sour. If the mixture is too sweet, add a little more vinegar; if it is too sour, add a pinch of sugar. After a few minutes, remove the skillet from the heat and transfer the eggplants to a warm serving dish.

EGGPLANT BALLS

PHOTO PAGE 182

POLPETTE DI MELANZANE

Preparation time: *40 min*
Cooking time: *30 min*
Serves 4

— ¾ eggplant, trimmed
— 6 basil leaves, chopped
— 1 clove garlic, chopped
— 7 slices day-old crusty
   whole wheat bread, diced
— ⅔ cup grated pecorino
   cheese
— 2 eggs, lightly beaten
— all-purpose flour, for dusting
— scant ½ cup olive oil
— salt and pepper
— fresh tomato sauce, to serve

Bring a pan of salted water to a boil. Add the eggplant and cook until very soft, then drain and chop. Put into a bowl, add the basil, garlic, bread, grated cheese, and eggs, season with salt and pepper, and mix gently to a soft dense mixture. With floured hands, scoop up small portions of the mixture and shape into ovals, then flatten slightly. Dust with flour. Heat the oil in a skillet. Add the eggplant balls, in batches, and cook over medium heat, turning occasionally, until golden brown. Remove with a slotted spoon and drain on paper towels. Serve hot or cold with a fresh tomato sauce on the side.

EGGPLANT AND PROVOLONE RISOTTO

RISOTTO ALLA PROVOLA E MELANZANE

Preparation time: *30 min*
Cooking time: *35 min*
Serves 4

— 4¼ cups vegetable stock
— scant ½ cup olive oil
— 1 eggplant, diced
— 1 onion, very thinly sliced
— scant 1 cup dry white wine
— 1½ cups risotto rice
— 7 ounces smoked
   provolone cheese, diced
— 2 tablespoons butter
— salt

Pour the stock into a pan and bring to a boil. Heat 5 tablespoons of the oil in a skillet. Add the eggplant and cook over medium-low heat, stirring frequently, for 10 minutes, until lightly browned. Remove with a slotted spoon and drain on paper towels. Meanwhile, heat the remaining oil in a large pan. Add the onion and cook over low heat, stirring occasionally, for 5 minutes, until softened. Pour in the wine and cook until the alcohol has evaporated. Stir in the rice and cook, stirring continuously, for 1–2 minutes, until translucent, then season with salt. Add a ladleful of the hot stock and cook, stirring continuously, until it has been absorbed. Continue to add the hot stock, a ladleful at a time, stirring continuously until each addition has been absorbed, for about 20 minutes. About 5 minutes from the end of the cooking time, add the cheese and eggplant. When the rice is tender and creamy, remove the pan from the heat. Stir in the butter, transfer to a warm serving dish, and serve.

EGGPLANT PARMIGIANA

PHOTO PAGE 185

PARMIGIANA DI MELANZANE

Preparation time: *40 min*
Cooking time: *30 min*
Serves 4

— 4 eggplants, sliced
  lengthwise
— all-purpose flour, for dusting
— 5–6 tablespoons olive oil,
  plus extra for drizzling
— 3 cups peeled, seeded, and
  chopped tomatoes
— 1 sprig basil
— generous 1 cup grated
  Parmesan cheese
— 9 ounces mozzarella
  cheese, sliced
— 2 eggs, lightly beaten
— salt

Season the eggplant slices with salt and dust with flour. Heat 2 tablespoons of the oil in a large skillet. Add the eggplant slices, in batches, and cook for 5 minutes on each side, until golden brown. Remove with a spatula and drain on paper towels. Cook the remaining batches in the same way, adding more oil as necessary. Meanwhile, put the tomatoes into a heavy pan, tear in the basil leaves, and simmer gently, stirring occasionally, for 15–20 minutes, until pulpy and thickened. Preheat the oven to 350°F. Spoon some of the tomato sauce over the bottom of an ovenproof dish and make a layer of eggplant slices on top. Sprinkle with a little Parmesan, top with some slices of mozzarella, and drizzle with a little beaten egg. Continue making layers in this way until all the ingredients have been used, ending with a layer of tomato sauce. Drizzle with olive oil and bake for 30 minutes.

EGGPLANTS BRAISED IN TOMATO SAUCE

MELANZANE BRASATE AL POMODORO

Preparation time: *45 min*
Cooking time: *20 min*
Serves 4

— 3 cups peeled, seeded, and
  diced tomatoes
— 1 onion, thinly sliced
— 7 canned anchovy fillets,
  drained and chopped
— 1 tablespoon chopped
  parsley
— 6–7 black olives, pitted
  and coarsely chopped
— 3 tablespoons olive oil, plus
  extra for drizzling
— pinch of sugar
— 2 eggplants, cut into
  ¼-inch slices widthwise
— 1 clove garlic, chopped
— salt and pepper

Preheat the oven to 350°F. Combine the tomatoes, onion, anchovies, parsley, and olives in a pan. Add the oil and garlic, season lightly with salt and pepper, and stir in the sugar. Cover and cook over low heat, stirring occasionally, for 10 minutes, until thickened. Meanwhile, heat a grill pan over medium-high heat. Add the slices of eggplant, in batches, and cook for 45–60 seconds on each side. Drizzle a little oil into an ovenproof dish and arrange overlapping eggplant slices inside. Pour the tomato sauce over them, drizzle with oil, and bake for 20 minutes. Remove from the oven and let cool to lukewarm before serving.

EGGPLANT PARMIGIANA

CREAMY EGGPLANT WITH YOGURT

CREAMY EGGPLANT WITH YOGURT

PHOTO PAGE 186

CREMA DI MELANZANE ALLO YOGURT

Preparation time: *15 min*
Cooking time: *20–25 min*
Serves 6

— 2 eggplants
— 1 small onion, chopped
— 4–5 mint leaves, chopped
— 1 cup olive oil
— 1 tablespoon white
   wine vinegar
— ⅔ cup Greek-style yogurt
— 4 tablespoons mayonnaise
— salt and pepper
— olives and dill pickles,
   to garnish (optional)

Preheat the oven to 350°F. Pierce the eggplants several times with the prongs of a fork, then place on a baking sheet and bake for 20–25 minutes. Remove from the oven and let cool, then peel off the skins. Put the flesh into a food processor or blender, add the onion and mint leaves, and season with salt and pepper. Process until smooth and combined. With the motor running, gradually add the oil through the feeder tube until completely incorporated, then add the vinegar. Scrape the mixture into a bowl and gently stir in the yogurt and mayonnaise. Transfer the mixture to a serving dish and garnish with olives and dill pickles, if you like. Serve immediately.

EGGPLANT FRITTERS

FIORE DI MELANZANE FRITTE

Preparation time: *15 min*
Cooking time: *15 min*
Serves 4

— 3 eggplants, peeled
   and sliced lengthwise
— 1 cup milk
— 3 tablespoons all-purpose
   flour
— scant 1 cup olive oil
— 1 small bunch parsley, cut
   into sprigs
— salt

Dip the eggplant slices in the milk and coat lightly with the flour. Heat the oil in a skillet. Add the eggplant slices, in batches, and cook over medium heat, turning occasionally, for 5–8 minutes, until golden on both sides. Remove with a slotted spoon and drain on paper towels. Arrange the slices in a flower shape on a warm serving plate and season with salt. Fry the parsley sprigs in the same pan of oil for a few minutes, then remove with a slotted spoon and use them as a garnish. Serve immediately.

EGGPLANT PIZZA

PIZZA ALLE MELANZANE

Preparation time: *20 min,*
plus 30 min draining
Cooking time: *30 min*
Serves 4

— 2 eggplants, thinly sliced
— olive oil, for brushing
  and drizzling
— 1 quantity pizza dough
  (about 1 pound 2 ounces)
— all-purpose flour, for dusting
— 7 ounces canned tomatoes,
  drained and chopped
— 5 ounces mozzarella cheese,
  cut into strips
— 4–5 basil leaves, chopped
— salt and pepper

Put the eggplant slices into a colander, sprinkling each layer with salt, and let drain for 30 minutes, then rinse and pat dry with paper towels. Preheat the oven to 425°F and brush a baking sheet with oil. Roll out the dough on a lightly floured counter to a ¾-inch-thick sheet and transfer to the prepared baking sheet. Cover with the eggplant slices, sprinkle with the tomatoes, and top with the strips of mozzarella. Season with salt and pepper, drizzle with oil, and sprinkle with the basil. Bake for 30 minutes and serve immediately.

EGGPLANT AND RICOTTA LASAGNE

LASAGNE CON MELANZANE E RICOTTA

Preparation time: *15 min,*
plus 1 hour draining
Cooking time: *40 min*
Serves 4

— 1 large eggplant, sliced
— butter, for greasing
— 9 ounces lasagna noodles,
  cooked according to the
  package directions
— ½ cup chopped pine nuts
— ⅔ cup crumbled ricotta
  cheese
— ½ cup concentrated tomato
  paste
— 12 basil leaves
— olive oil, for drizzling
— ⅔ cup grated Parmesan
  cheese
— salt

Place the eggplant slices in a colander, sprinkle with salt, and let drain for 1 hour. Rinse, pat dry, and cook under a preheated broiler until tender. Preheat the oven to 350°F. Grease an ovenproof dish with butter. Arrange a layer of lasagna noodles on the bottom of the prepared dish, place half of the eggplant slices on top, and sprinkle with half of the pine nuts, half of the ricotta, 4 tablespoons of the tomato paste, and six of the basil leaves. Drizzle with olive oil and repeat the layers. Sprinkle with the Parmesan, bake for about 40 minutes, and serve.

ZUCCHINI AND BEET CARPACCIO

CARPACCIO DI ZUCCHINE E BARBABIETOLE

Preparation time: *15 min,
plus 30 min chilling*
Cooking time: *5 min*
Serves 4

— 1¼ cups pine nuts
— scant ½ cup olive oil
— 1 teaspoon Dijon mustard
— juice of 1 lemon, strained
— 4 tender, small zucchini,
  cut lengthwise into strips
— 4 cooked beets, sliced
— 7 ounces smoked Scamorza
  or smoked mozzarella,
  thinly sliced
— salt and pepper

Toast the pine nuts in a nonstick skillet over low heat, stirring frequently, for a few minutes. Remove the skillet from the heat. Whisk together the oil, mustard, and lemon juice in a bowl, and season with salt and pepper. Arrange the zucchini strips in a lattice pattern on a serving plate or on 4 individual plates and sprinkle with the pine nuts. Drizzle with half of the dressing and chill in the refrigerator for 30 minutes. Put the beets and cheese on top of the zucchini, drizzle with the remaining dressing, and serve.

ZUCCHINI, GOAT CHEESE, AND BLACK OLIVE FRITTATA

FRITTATA DI ZUCCHINE AL CAPRINO E OLIVE NERE

Preparation time: *25 min*
Cooking time: *15 min*
Serves 4

— 2 tablespoons olive oil
— 3 cups thinly sliced zucchini
— 1 sprig thyme
— 5 eggs
— pinch of curry powder
— 1 cup grated Parmesan
  cheese
— 2 tablespoons chopped
  mixed parsley, chives, and
  chervil
— ½ cup black olives,
  pitted and halved
— 1 goat cheese, rind
  removed, crumbled
— 1¼ cups milk (optional)
— salt and pepper

Heat the oil in a skillet. Add the zucchini and thyme and cook over medium heat, stirring occasionally, until the liquid given off by the zucchini has evaporated. Season with salt and pepper, remove from the heat, and set aside. Beat the eggs with the curry powder in a bowl and season with salt and pepper. Stir in the grated cheese, mixed herbs, olives, and goat cheese. If the mixture is too thick, pour in just enough milk to loosen. Return the skillet with the zucchini to the heat and pour in the egg mixture. Cook, occasionally shaking the pan, for 5 minutes, until the eggs are lightly set, then remove from the heat. Slide the frittata onto a warm serving plate and serve immediately. Alternatively, transfer the frittata to a flameproof dish brushed with oil and put under a preheated broiler for about 2 minutes, until the top browns, then remove from the heat and serve.

ZUCCHINI SOUP

MINESTRA DI ZUCCHINE

Preparation time: *10 min*
Cooking time: *30 min*
Serves 4

— 3 tablespoons olive oil
— 6 zucchini, diced
— 3 eggs
— ½ cup grated Parmesan
  cheese
— 1 bunch basil, chopped
— salt and pepper

Heat the oil in a skillet. Add the zucchini and cook over low heat, stirring occasionally, for 5 minutes, until light golden brown. Pour in boiling water to cover and season with salt and pepper. Cover and simmer for 25 minutes, until tender. Beat the eggs with the cheese and basil in a bowl and season with salt and pepper. Remove the skillet from the heat and pour in the egg mixture. Stir, return to the heat, and bring back to a boil for a few minutes, then transfer to a warm soup tureen and serve immediately.

PHOTO PAGE 191

ZUCCHINI, BEANS, AND SHRIMP

FANTASIA DI ZUCCHINE, FAGIOLI E SCAMPI

Preparation time: *10 min*
Cooking time: *5 min*
Serves 4

— 2 zucchini
— 11 ounces canned
  cannellini beans,
  drained and rinsed
— 7 ounces peeled,
  cooked shrimp
— 4–6 tablespoons olive oil
— 1 tablespoon lemon juice
— 1 tablespoon white
  wine vinegar
— salt and freshly ground
  white pepper

Bring a pan of salted water to a boil, add the zucchini, and blanch for 5 minutes, then drain and cut into very thin slices. Put the slices into a salad bowl with the beans and shrimp. Drizzle generously with the olive oil, season with salt and pepper, and toss gently. Whisk together the lemon juice and vinegar in a bowl and sprinkle over the salad. Toss well and serve.

ZUCCHINI, BEANS, AND SHRIMP

ZUCCHINI TART

TORTA DI ZUCCHINE

Preparation time: *30 min*
Cooking time: *35 min*
Serves 4

— 1 tablespoon olive oil,
  plus extra for brushing
— 4–5 tablespoons fresh
  bread crumbs
— 1 onion, thinly sliced
— 2 zucchini, thinly sliced
— 1 tablespoon chopped
  parsley
— 6 eggs
— ⅓ cup grated Parmesan
  cheese
— 2 tablespoons milk
— salt and pepper

Preheat the oven to 350°F. Brush a deep pie dish with oil and coat the bottom with the bread crumbs. Heat the oil in a skillet. Add the onion and cook over low heat, stirring occasionally, for 5 minutes, until softened. Season with salt, add the zucchini and parsley, and cook, stirring occasionally, for 10 minutes. Remove the skillet from the heat. Beat the eggs in bowl, stir in the Parmesan and milk, and season with salt and pepper. Pour the eggs over the zucchini and mix well, then spoon the mixture into the prepared dish. Bake for about 20 minutes, until golden and set. Serve immediately.

FRIED ZUCCHINI FLOWERS

FIORI DI ZUCCHINE FRITTI

Preparation time: *10 min*
Cooking time: *1 hour 10 min*
Serves 4

— generous ¾ cup all-purpose
  flour
— 2 tablespoons olive oil
— 5 tablespoons dry white
  wine
— 1 egg, separated
— vegetable oil, for deep-frying
— 12 zucchini flowers,
  trimmed
— salt and pepper

Combine the flour, oil, wine, and egg yolk in a bowl and season with salt and pepper. Add ⅔–1 cup of warm water to make a fairly runny, smooth batter. Let stand for 1 hour. In a grease-free bowl, whisk the egg white and fold gently into the batter. Heat the oil for deep-frying in a large pan. Dip the flowers in the batter, shake off the excess, and fry in the hot oil until golden. Remove with a spatula and drain on paper towels. Sprinkle with salt and serve immediately.

STUFFED ZUCCHINI

ZUCCHINE RIPIENE

Preparation time: *1 hour*
Cooking time: *30 min*
Serves 4

— 6–7 zucchini,
   halved lengthwise
— scant 1 cup diced onions
— 1 tablespoon olive oil
— generous ½ cup finely
   chopped lean ham
— 2 tomatoes, peeled and diced
— butter, for greasing
— 2¾ cups diced white
   mushroom caps
— 1 egg, lightly beaten
— 3 tablespoons fresh
   bread crumbs
— ⅔ cup grated Parmesan cheese
— salt and pepper

Bring a pan of salted water to a boil. Add the zucchini and cook for 10 minutes, until just tender but still al dente. Drain well, scoop out some of the flesh with a teaspoon, and put them on a dish towel, cut side down, to drain. Meanwhile, bring a nonstick pan of salted water to a boil. Add the onion and cook until the water has completely evaporated, then stir in the oil. Add the ham and cook for a few minutes, then stir in the tomatoes and simmer, stirring occasionally, until nearly all their moisture has evaporated. Meanwhile, preheat the oven to 350°F. Grease an ovenproof dish with butter. Heat a heavy pan. Sprinkle in the mushrooms, cover, and cook over medium-high heat until the liquid they release has evaporated. Add the mushrooms to the ham mixture, stir gently, and cook for a few minutes. Remove from the heat and stir in the egg, bread crumbs, and Parmesan, then season with salt and pepper. Fill the zucchini with the mixture, put into the prepared dish, and bake for 30 minutes. Serve immediately.

RICOTTA, ZUCCHINI, AND ZUCCHINI FLOWER FLAN

GRAN FLAN DI RICOTTA, ZUCCHINE E FIORI DI ZUCCHINA

Preparation time: *20 min*
Cooking time: *15 min*
Serves 6

— butter, for greasing
— 2 eggs
— 1½ cups ricotta cheese
— ⅓ cup all-purpose flour
— 2½ cups diced zucchini
— 6 zucchini flowers, pistils
   removed
— salt

Preheat the oven to 400°F. Line a rectangular 8-inch cake pan with parchment paper and grease with butter. Beat the eggs in a bowl with a pinch of salt. Add the ricotta and beat until creamy and thoroughly combined. Sift the flour over the mixture and stir in, then add the zucchini. Cut the zucchini flowers into strips and gently stir into the ricotta mixture. Pour the mixture into the prepared pan, smooth the surface, and bake for 15 minutes, until golden and set. Remove from the oven and serve immediately.

LINGUINE WITH ZUCCHINI, ALMOND, AND MINT PESTO

LINGUINE WITH ZUCCHINI, ALMOND, AND MINT PESTO

PHOTO PAGE 194

LINGUINE AL PESTO DI ZUCCHINE, MANDORLE E MENTA

Preparation time: *40 min*
Cooking time: *40 min*
Serves 6

— 3 tablespoons olive oil
— ⅓ cup slivered almonds
— 2½ zucchini
— 18 mint leaves
— ½ clove garlic
— 2 tablespoons chopped
  parsley
— ½ cup chopped blanched
  almonds
— generous 1 cup grated
  Parmesan cheese
— ⅔ cup olive oil,
  plus extra for drizzling
— 1 pound 2 ounces linguine
— salt and pepper

Heat the oil in a small pan. Add the slivered almonds and cook, stirring frequently, for a few minutes, until browned. Remove from the heat. Halve the zucchini and scoop out the seeds and some of the flesh. Bring a pan of salted water to a boil. Add the zucchini and simmer for 8–10 minutes, until tender but still al dente. Remove with a slotted spoon, reserving the cooking water, and let cool. Put the zucchini, mint leaves, garlic, parsley, chopped almonds, and Parmesan into a food processor and process until thoroughly combined. With the motor running, gradually add the oil through the feeder tube. Season with salt and pepper. Bring the reserved cooking water to a boil in a large pan. Add the linguine, bring back to a boil, and cook for 8–10 minutes, or according to package directions, until tender but still al dente. Drain and transfer to a warm serving dish. Spoon the zucchini pesto over, drizzle with olive oil, season with pepper, and toss lightly. Garnish with the slivered almonds and serve immediately.

ROMAN-STYLE CRISPY FRIED ZUCCHINI

FILETTI DI ZUCCHINE FRITTI ALLA ROMANA

Preparation time: *20 min*
Cooking time: *5–10 min*
Serves 6

— 10 small zucchini
— all-purpose flour, for dusting
— ½ cup olive oil
— salt

This recipe's originality relies on the way in which the zucchini are sliced. Cut off both ends of each zucchini and slice them thinly lengthwise, then cut each slice into thin strips, only ⅛-inch wide. Put them into a bowl, sprinkle with salt, and let stand for about 15 minutes. Drain the zucchini and gently pat dry with a dish towel. Toss in the flour, shaking off any excess. Heat the oil in a wide skillet. Add the zucchini strips, in batches, and cook for a few minutes, until pale golden brown. Remove with a slotted spoon and drain on paper towels. Pile them up loosely in a pyramid shape on a warm serving plate and serve very hot.

ROASTED ZUCCHINI, POTATOES, AND TOMATOES

PHOTO PAGE 197

ZUCCHINE, PATATE E POMODORI AL FORNO

Preparation time: *20 min*
Cooking time: *1 hour*
Serves 4

— 4 potatoes, cut into chunks
— 1 onion, chopped
— 1 clove garlic
— olive oil, for drizzling
— 1 sprig rosemary, chopped
— 6 cups diced zucchini
— 1¾ cups coarsely chopped tomatoes
— salt and pepper

Preheat the oven to 375°F. Put the potatoes into an ovenproof dish, add the onion and garlic clove, and season with salt and pepper. Drizzle with the olive oil and sprinkle with the rosemary. Roast for 40 minutes, then remove from the oven but do not switch off. Remove and discard the garlic clove. Add the zucchini and tomatoes to the dish, lightly season with salt, and stir. Return the dish to the oven and roast for another 20 minutes, until the vegetables are tender. Serve immediately.

ZUCCHINI FLAN WITH TOMATO SAUCE

MINI FLAN DI ZUCCHINE CON SALSA AL POMODORO

Preparation time: *30 min*
Cooking time: *40 min*
Serves 4

— olive oil, for brushing
— 3 zucchini, very finely chopped
— ⅔ cup grated Parmesan cheese
— 5 tablespoons milk
— 4 teaspoons heavy cream
— 1 egg, beaten
— 6 basil leaves, finely chopped
— salt and pepper

For the tomato sauce:
— 2 firm ripe tomatoes, peeled, seeded, and quartered
— 1 tablespoon red wine vinegar
— 5 tablespoons olive oil
— salt

Brush 4 individual ramekins with oil. Sprinkle ½ teaspoon of salt over the zucchini and let drain for 30 minutes. Preheat the oven to 275°F. Place the zucchini on a clean dish towel and wring to remove any excess liquid. Combine the zucchini, Parmesan, milk, cream, egg, and basil in a bowl, and season with salt and pepper. Divide the mixture among the prepared ramekins and put them into a roasting pan. Pour in hot water to come about halfway up their sides and bake for 40 minutes. Remove from the oven, but let the ramekins stand in the hot water to keep warm.

To make the sauce, put the tomatoes, vinegar, and a pinch of salt into a food processor and process for 30 seconds. With the motor running, gradually add the oil through the feeder tube until the mixture is thick and creamy. Pour 2–3 tablespoons of the tomato sauce onto 4 individual plates and gently turn out the zucchini flans on top.

ROASTED ZUCCHINI, POTATOES, AND TOMATOES

ZUCCHINI WITH TOMATO, OREGANO, AND BASIL

PIZZAIOLA DI ZUCCHINE

Preparation time: *30 min, plus 3 hours drying*
Cooking time: *45 min*
Serves 6

— 3 ¼ pounds zucchini, thinly sliced
— all-purpose flour, for dusting
— 4 tablespoons olive oil
— 3 ½ cups peeled, seeded, and chopped tomatoes
— 1 sprig oregano, chopped
— 1 sprig basil, chopped
— salt and pepper

Spread out the zucchini slices on a dish towel and let dry out for at least 3 hours. Dust with flour and shake off any excess. Heat the oil in a large skillet. Add the zucchini, in batches, and cook for about 5 minutes on each side, until golden brown. Remove with a slotted spoon and drain on paper towels. Put the zucchini into a clean skillet, add the tomatoes, oregano, and basil, and cook over medium heat, shaking the skillet occasionally, for 5–10 minutes. Season to taste with salt and pepper, then remove from the heat and transfer the mixture to a serving dish. Serve hot or cold.

ZUCCHINI FLOWERS STUFFED WITH MOZZARELLA

FIORI DI ZUCCHINE RIPIENI DI MOZZARELLA

Preparation time: *20 min*
Cooking time: *15 min*
Serves 4

— 2 ½ ounces mozzarella cheese, cut into 12 pieces
— 6 canned anchovy fillets, drained and halved
— 12 zucchini flowers, pistils removed

For the batter:
— ½ cup all-purpose flour
— scant ½ cup lager
— 1 sprig marjoram, chopped
— vegetable oil, for deep-frying
— salt

Put a piece of mozzarella cheese and half an anchovy fillet into each zucchini flower. Gently twist the tips of the petals to close. To make the batter, sift the flour and a pinch of salt into a bowl, then beat in the lager and marjoram.

Heat the oil in a deep-fryer to 350–375°F or until a cube of day-old bread browns in 30 seconds. Quickly dip the stuffed zucchini flowers into the batter and drain off the excess. Add to the hot oil, in batches, and cook, turning gently, until golden brown. Remove with a spatula, drain on paper towels, and serve hot.

CUCUMBERS IN YOGURT

CETRIOLI ALLO YOGURT

Preparation time: *20 min*
Serves 4

— 4 small cucumbers,
  thinly sliced
— 1 iceberg lettuce, shredded
— 2 hard-cooked eggs, cut
  into wedges
— ⅔ cup plain yogurt
— 1–2 tablespoons lemon
  juice, strained
— salt and pepper

Put the cucumbers, lettuce, and wedges of hard-cooked eggs into a salad bowl. Combine the yogurt and lemon juice to taste in a small bowl and pour over the salad. Season with salt and pepper, toss lightly, and serve.

CUCUMBER WITH MUSTARD

CETRIOLI ALLA SENAPE

Preparation time: *15 min,
plus 30 min draining*
Serves 4

— 3 cucumbers, peeled and
  thinly sliced
— 1–2 tablespoons chopped
  chervil
— juice of 1 lemon, strained
— 1 teaspoon Dijon mustard
— 2–3 tablespoons olive oil
— salt and pepper

Put the cucumber slices into a fine strainer, sprinkle with salt, and let drain for 30 minutes. Rinse, pat dry with a dish towel, and transfer to a salad bowl. Sprinkle with the chervil. Whisk together the lemon juice, mustard, and oil in a bowl and season with salt and pepper. Drizzle the dressing over the cucumbers and toss lightly. Serve immediately.

COLD CUCUMBER CREAM SOUP

COLD CUCUMBER CREAM SOUP

CREMA FREDDA DI CETRIOLI

Preparation time: *15 min,*
plus 2 hours chilling
Cooking time: *25 min*
Serves 4

— 2¼ cups vegetable stock
— 3 tablespoons olive oil
— 1 onion, chopped
— 2¼ cups chopped cucumbers
— scant 1 cup diced potatoes
— ½ cup chopped lettuce
— 6 fresh mint leaves,
    plus extra to garnish
— ¼ cup heavy cream
— salt and pepper

Pour the stock into a pan and bring to a boil. Heat the oil in another pan, add the onion, and cook over low heat, stirring occasionally, for 5 minutes, until softened. Add the cucumber, potatoes, lettuce, and mint, and cook for another 5 minutes. Season with salt and pepper to taste, pour in the hot stock, and cook for about 15 minutes. Transfer to a food processor and process to a puree. Pour into a pan and reheat. Stir in the cream and heat for another 5 minutes. Remove from the heat, let cool to room temperature, then chill in the refrigerator for several hours. To serve, pour into a soup tureen and garnish with mint leaves.

RICE SALAD WITH CUCUMBER AND GRAPES IN AROMATIC OIL

RISO FREDDO CON CETRIOLI E UVA ALL'OLIO AROMATICO

Preparation time: *25 min*
Cooking time: *15 min*
Serves 4

— 1½ cups long-grain rice
— 3 tablespoons golden raisins
— 6 tablespoons olive oil,
    plus extra for drizzling
— 2 tablespoons balsamic
    vinegar
— 3 tablespoons finely
    chopped parsley
— 2 tablespoons finely
    chopped basil
— 2⅓ cups thinly sliced fennel
— 1 small onion, thinly sliced
— 2 cups thinly sliced cucumber
— ⅔ cup halved seedless black
    grapes
— ½ cup chopped, shelled
    walnuts
— salt and pepper

Bring a large pan of salted water to a boil. Add the rice and cook for about 15 minutes, until tender. Meanwhile, put the golden raisins into a heatproof bowl, pour in water to cover, and let soak for 15 minutes. Drain the rice and refresh under cold running water, then transfer to a salad bowl. Drizzle with a little oil and set aside in a cool place. Drain the golden raisins. Whisk together the oil, vinegar, parsley, and basil in a bowl and season with salt and pepper. Add the fennel, onion, cucumber, grapes, walnuts, and golden raisins to the rice and mix well. Pour the dressing over the salad, mix again, and serve.

CUCUMBER SALAD

PHOTO PAGE 203

CETRIOLI IN INSALATA

Preparation time: *15 min, plus*
1 hour draining and standing
Serves 4

— 2 cucumbers
— 2 sprigs thyme, chopped
— ¾ teaspoon sugar
— olive oil, for drizzling
— salt and freshly ground
   white pepper

Peel the cucumbers, slice thinly, and put into a colander, then sprinkle each layer with salt and let drain for 30 minutes. Rinse the cucumber slices and pat dry with paper towels. Put them into a bowl, sprinkle with the thyme, sugar, and a pinch of salt, and let stand for 30 minutes. Stir the salad, drizzle with the oil, and check the seasoning, adding more salt, if necessary, and white pepper. Serve immediately.

CHERRY TOMATOES STUFFED WITH SAFFRON RICE

POMODORINI RIPIENI DI RISO PILAF ALLO ZAFFERANO

Preparation time: *15 min*
Cooking time: *25 min*
Serves 4

— 1 cup vegetable stock
— 1 pinch saffron threads
— 2 tablespoons butter
— ½ onion, finely chopped
— scant 1 cup risotto rice
— 12 cherry tomatoes
— 1 tablespoon olive oil,
   plus extra for drizzling
— 1 zucchini, diced
— 2 tablespoons finely
   chopped parsley, to garnish
— salt and pepper
— parsley sprigs, to garnish
— thin zucchini strips,
   to garnish (optional)

Preheat the oven to 350°F. Put 1 tablespoon of the stock into a small bowl and add the saffron. Melt the butter in a fairly shallow flameproof casserole. Add the onion and cook over low heat, stirring occasionally, for 5 minutes, until softened and translucent. Stir in the rice and a pinch of salt, and cook, stirring continuously, until all the grains are coated in butter. Pour in the remaining stock and bring to a boil, stirring, then stir in the saffron mixture. Cover, transfer the casserole to the oven, and cook for 18–20 minutes without lifting the lid or stirring. Remove the rice from the oven and let cool.

Meanwhile, cut out the core from each tomato, removing the central flesh and the seeds. Sprinkle a little salt inside each one, turn upside down on a layer of paper towels, and let drain. Heat the oil in a skillet. Add the zucchini and cook over low heat, stirring frequently, for 10 minutes, until lightly browned. Season lightly with salt and remove from the heat. Combine the rice, zucchini, and parsley in a bowl, drizzle with a little oil, and season with salt and pepper. Stir gently and fill the tomatoes with the mixture without pressing it down into them. Transfer the tomatoes to a serving plate, garnish with parsley sprigs and some thin strips of zucchini, if using, and serve.

MEDITERRANEAN STUFFED TOMATOES

MEDITERRANEAN STUFFED TOMATOES

PHOTO PAGE 204

POMODORI FARCITI ALLA MEDITERRANEA

Preparation time: *30 min,*
plus 1 hour draining
Cooking time: *20 min*
Serves 6

— 6 tomatoes
— 2 tablespoons olive oil
— ½ red onion, finely chopped
— 1 red bell pepper, seeded and cut into ¼-inch dice
— 1 yellow bell pepper, seeded and cut into ¼-inch dice
— 1 eggplant, cut into ¼-inch dice
— 1 zucchini, cut into ¼-inch dice
— pinch of sugar
— 2 tablespoons apple vinegar
— salt and pepper

For the pesto:
— 5 sprigs basil
— ⅔ cup olive oil
— scant 1 cup grated Parmesan cheese
— 1 clove garlic

Slice the tops off the tomatoes and use a teaspoon to scoop out the seeds and as much flesh as possible without piercing the "shells." Sprinkle a little salt inside each tomato, turn upside down on a layer of paper towels, and let drain for 1 hour. Meanwhile, heat the oil in a pan. Add the onion and cook over low heat, stirring occasionally, for 5 minutes, until softened. Add the bell peppers and cook for 2 minutes, then add the eggplant and cook for another 5 minutes, and, finally, add the zucchini and cook for another 5 minutes. Season with salt and pepper, and add the sugar. Increase the heat to high, sprinkle the vegetables with the vinegar, and cook for another 5 minutes, until all the moisture from the vegetables has evaporated. Remove from the heat and let cool completely. Stuff the tomatoes with the vegetable mixture.

To make the pesto, put all the ingredients into a food processor or blender and process until thoroughly combined, scraping down the sides once or twice. Put the tomatoes on a serving dish and spoon a tablespoon of the pesto over each. Keep in a cool place until ready to serve.

TOMATOES WITH CRESCENZA

POMODORI ALLA CRESCENZA

Preparation time: *20 min,*
plus 1 hour chilling
Serves 4

— 12 round cherry tomatoes
— 1¾ cups grated crescenza or taleggio cheese
— 3 dill pickles, drained and chopped
— olive oil, for drizzling
— salt and pepper

Cut off the tops of the cherry tomatoes and scoop out the flesh with a small spoon without piercing the "shells." Combine the cheese and dill pickles in a bowl, season with salt and pepper, and drizzle with a little oil. Fill the cherry tomatoes with the cheese mixture, put them on a serving plate, and chill in the refrigerator for 1 hour before serving.

TOMATO BRUSCHETTA

PHOTO PAGE 207

BRUSCHETTA AL POMODORO

Preparation time: *10 min*
Serves 4

— 8 slices rustic bread
— 4 cloves garlic
— 6–8 ripe plum tomatoes,
   diced
— extra virgin olive oil,
   for drizzling
— salt and pepper

Toast the slices of bread on both sides under the broiler or on a barbecue. Rub them with garlic while still hot and put back under the broiler for a moment. Arrange the tomatoes on the bread. Season with salt and pepper and drizzle with olive oil.

TOMATO, MOZZARELLA, AND BASIL FLAN

TORTA AL POMODORO, MOZZARELLA E BASILICO

Preparation time: *30 min,*
plus 20 min resting
Cooking time: *50 min*
Serves 6–8

For the dough:
— 2¼ cups all-purpose flour,
   plus extra for dusting
— generous ½ cup (1⅛ sticks)
   butter, cut into small pieces
— 1 tablespoon fresh rosemary
   leaves, finely chopped
— salt

For the filling:
— 4 tomatoes, peeled, seeded,
   and cut into quarters
— 7 ounces mozzarella
   cheese, cut into small cubes
— 8 canned anchovy fillets,
   drained and halved
   lengthwise
— 6 black olives, pitted and
   halved
— 2 tablespoons Parmesan
   cheese, grated
— 1 sprig parsley, finely
   chopped
— 1 sprig basil, finely chopped
— olive oil, for drizzling

To make the dough, sift the flour into a bowl and cut in the butter and rosemary with 2 knives. Rub in the butter with your fingertips until the mixture resembles fresh bread crumbs. Stir in 4–5 tablespoons of ice water, then bring together with your fingertips. Knead very briefly, shape into a ball, cover with plastic wrap, and let rest for 20 minutes.

Preheat the oven to 375°F. Line a 9-inch tart pan with parchment paper. Roll out the pastry dough on a lightly floured counter and use to line the prepared pan. Line the pie shell with aluminum foil and pie weights and bake for 15 minutes. Remove the aluminum foil and pie weights and bake for another 10 minutes. Put the tomatoes in the pie shell and cover with the mozzarella. Arrange the anchovies in a lattice on top, with the olives placed between them. Sprinkle with the Parmesan cheese, parsley, and basil, drizzle with olive oil, and put the pan on a baking sheet. Bake for 30–40 minutes, until golden. Remove from the oven and serve immediately.

TOMATO BRUSCHETTA

TOMATO AND BASIL TARTAR

TARTARE DI POMODORI AL BASILICO

Preparation time: *15 min,*
plus 30 min draining
Serves 4

— 16 cherry tomatoes, halved
   and seeded
— 11 ounces firm, fresh
   white cheese, diced
— 16 black olives, pitted
— 1 small bunch basil,
   leaves torn into small pieces
— olive oil, for drizzling
— salt

Cut the tomatoes into small pieces and put them into a colander. Sprinkle with salt and let drain for 30 minutes. Put the tomatoes into a salad bowl and add the cheese, olives, and basil. Drizzle with oil, sprinkle with a pinch of salt, and stir. Keep cool until ready to serve.

TUSCAN TOMATO SOUP

PAPPA COL POMODORO

Preparation time: *30 min*
Cooking time: *1¼ hours*
Serves 4

— generous 1¾ cups peeled,
   seeded, and chopped ripe
   tomatoes
— 1 stalk celery, finely chopped
— 1 clove garlic, finely chopped
— 1 tablespoon olive oil
— 2 slices day-old rustic bread,
   cut into small cubes
— 4 basil leaves, torn into
   small pieces
— ⅔ cup grated Parmesan
   cheese
— salt and pepper

Put the tomatoes, celery, garlic, and olive oil into a large pan, season with salt and pepper, and pour in 5 cups of water. Bring to a boil, then reduce the heat and simmer for 1 hour. Turn off the heat and let the soup stand. About 30 minutes before serving, reheat the soup, add the diced bread, and simmer gently. Ladle into warm soup bowls, sprinkle with the basil leaves and grated cheese, and serve immediately.

BUFFALO MILK MOZZARELLA CAPRESE SALAD

SPICY TOMATO GRANITA

GRANITA PICCANTE DI POMODORO

Preparation time: *15 min,
plus 30 min freezing*
Cooking time: *3 min*
Serves *4*

— ¼ cup superfine sugar
— 2¼ cups tomato juice
— juice of ½ lemon, strained
— dash Tabasco sauce (optional)
— salt and pepper
— fresh mint leaves, to garnish
— 1 lemon, thinly sliced,
  to garnish

Pour scant 1 cup of water into a small pan, stir in the sugar, and bring to a boil, stirring until the sugar has dissolved. Boil, without stirring, for 2–3 minutes, until syrupy, then remove from the heat and pour into a large bowl. Stir in the tomato juice, lemon juice, and Tabasco to taste, if using, and season with salt and pepper. Stir well and pour the mixture into an ice-cream maker. Freeze according to the manufacturer's directions. This will take about 30 minutes. Spoon the granita into 4 glasses and garnish with small mint leaves and slices of lemon. Serve immediately.

BUFFALO MILK MOZZARELLA CAPRESE SALAD

CAPRESE DI MOZZARELLA DI BUFALA

PHOTO PAGE 210

Preparation time: *10 min*
Serves *4*

— 11 ounces buffalo milk
  mozzarella cheese
— 3–4 tomatoes, peeled and
  sliced
— basil leaves
— olive oil, for drizzling
— salt

Drain the mozzarella and cut into ⅛-inch-thick slices. Arrange the mozzarella and tomato slices alternately in concentric rings on a serving dish. Sprinkle with the basil leaves, drizzle with olive oil, and season with salt. Keep in a cool place until ready to serve.

SPAGHETTI AMATRICIANA

SPAGHETTI ALL'AMATRICIANA

Preparation time: *10 min*
Cooking time: *50 min*
Serves 4

— olive oil, for brushing
— 3½ ounces pancetta, diced
— 1 onion, thinly sliced
— 3 cups peeled, seeded,
    and diced tomatoes
— 1 chile, seeded and chopped
— 12 ounces spaghetti
— salt and pepper

Brush a flameproof casserole with oil, add the pancetta, and cook over low heat until the fat runs. Add the onion and cook, stirring occasionally, for 10 minutes, until lightly browned. Add the tomatoes and chile, season with salt and pepper, cover, and cook for about 40 minutes, adding a little warm water if necessary. Cook the spaghetti in a large pan of salted, boiling water until al dente, then drain and toss with the sauce in a warm serving dish.

MARINATED CHERRY TOMATO SALAD

PHOTO PAGE 213

INSALATA DI POMODORINI MARINATI

Preparation time: *15 min,*
plus 2 hours chilling
Serves 4

— 1⅓ cups halved cherry
    tomatoes
— 1 heart celery, thinly sliced
— 5–6 tablespoons olive oil
— 1 canned anchovy fillet,
    drained and finely chopped
— 1 teaspoon lemon juice
— 1 strip finely pared lemon
    rind
— 1 sprig oregano, chopped,
    or 1 teaspoon dried oregano
— 1 clove garlic, thinly sliced
— salt and pepper

Put the tomatoes into a large bowl and add the celery heart. Pour the oil into another bowl, add the anchovy fillet, lemon juice, lemon rind, oregano, and garlic, and season with salt and pepper. Whisk together with a fork, then pour the dressing over the tomato salad. Stir, cover with plastic wrap, and chill in the refrigerator for at least 2 hours before serving. This makes an enjoyable salad to serve with tuna carpaccio.

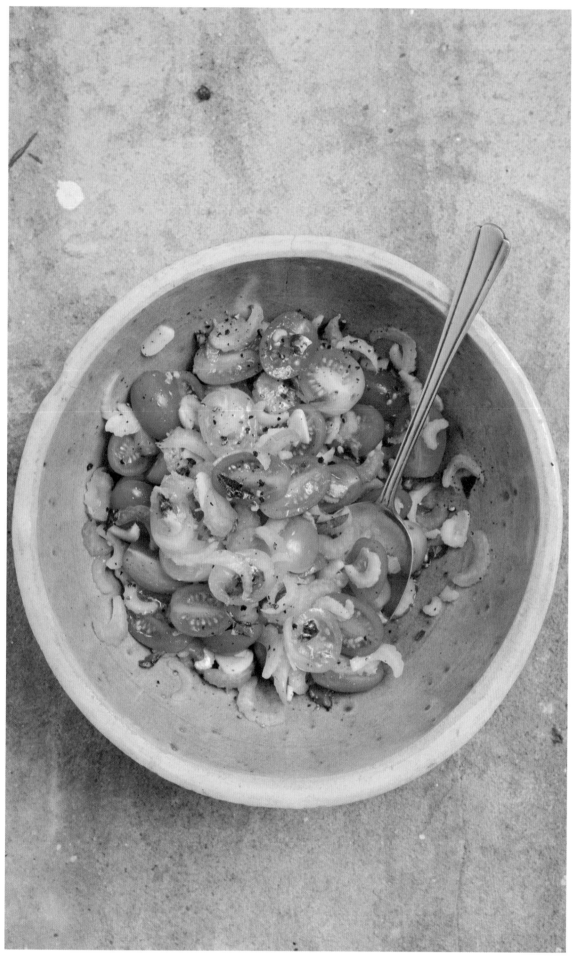

213

MARINATED CHERRY TOMATO SALAD

TOMATO AND BASIL RISOTTO

RISOTTO FILANTE AL POMODORO E BASILICO

Preparation time: *15 min*
Cooking time: *30 min*
Serves 4

— 5 cups vegetable stock
— 2 tablespoons olive oil
— 1 onion, finely chopped
— 1⅔ cups risotto rice
— 3 cups peeled, seeded, and
  diced ripe tomatoes
— 4–5 basil leaves, torn into
  pieces, plus extra to garnish
— 3 tablespoons butter
— 5 ounces mozzarella
  cheese, diced
— ½ cup grated Parmesan
  cheese
— salt and pepper

Pour the stock into a pan and bring to a boil. Meanwhile, heat the oil in a large pan. Add the onion and cook over low heat, stirring occasionally, for 5 minutes, until softened. Stir in the rice and cook, stirring continuously, for 2 minutes, until all the grains are coated in oil. Stir in the tomatoes. Add a ladleful of the hot stock and cook, stirring continuously, until absorbed. Continue to add the hot stock, a ladleful at a time, stirring continuously until each addition has been absorbed, for about 20 minutes. When the rice is nearly cooked, add the basil leaves and season with salt and pepper. Remove from the heat and stir in the butter and mozzarella. Transfer to a warm serving dish, garnish with a few basil leaves, and serve immediately.

BAKED TOMATOES WITH BALSAMIC VINEGAR

PHOTO PAGE 215

POMODORI ALL'ACETO BALSAMICO IN FORNO

Preparation time: *15 min*
Cooking time: *1¼ hours*
Serves 4

— 4 tablespoons olive oil,
  plus extra for brushing
— 1 teaspoon balsamic vinegar
— 8 tomatoes, halved
— 1 sprig thyme
— salt and pepper

Preheat the oven to 350°F. Brush an ovenproof dish with oil. Whisk together the oil and vinegar in a bowl and season with salt and pepper. Put the tomatoes into the prepared dish in a single layer, brush the oil and vinegar mixture over them, and sprinkle with the thyme. Bake for 15 minutes, then reduce the oven temperature to 225°F and bake for at least another 1 hour. Remove from the oven, transfer the tomatoes to a serving dish, and serve either hot or cold.

BAKED TOMATOES WITH BALSAMIC VINEGAR

TOMATO GRATIN

POMODORI GRATINATI

Preparation time: *45 min*
Cooking time: *30 min*
Serves 4

— 4 round tomatoes, halved
  and seeded
— ½ cup heavy cream
— 3 plum tomatoes,
  finely diced
— butter, for greasing
— 2 bread rolls, halved
— small bunch chives, finely
  chopped
— salt and pepper

Put the tomato halves, cut side down, on a layer of paper towels and let drain. Meanwhile, pour the cream into a small pan, add the diced plum tomatoes, and cook over medium-low heat, stirring occasionally, until reduced and thickened. Remove from the heat and let cool. Preheat the oven to 350°F. Grease an ovenproof dish with butter. Pull the crust away from the rolls in crumbs, put the crumb rolls into a bowl, and add 3–4 tablespoons water. Let soak for 5 minutes, then squeeze out the excess liquid, and put into a bowl. Stir in the chives and season with salt and pepper, then stir into the cooled cream and tomato sauce. Fill the tomato halves with this mixture and put them into the prepared dish. Bake for 30 minutes, then remove from the oven and serve.

PAN-FRIED TOMATOES

POMODORI IN TEGAME

Preparation time: *10 min*
Cooking time: *20 min*
Serves 4

— 3 tomatoes
— 2–3 tablespoons olive oil
— 1 large scallion, chopped
— 1 cup very fine
  fresh bread crumbs
— 1–2 tablespoons balsamic
  vinegar
— salt

Cut the tomatoes into wedges and remove the seeds, then let drain on a layer of paper towels. Heat the oil in a skillet. Add the scallion and cook over low heat, stirring occasionally, for 3 minutes. Roll the tomatoes in the bread crumbs and add to the skillet. Season with salt and cook, gently stirring occasionally, for 15 minutes. Remove the skillet from the heat, sprinkle the tomatoes with the balsamic vinegar, and mix well. Serve hot or warm.

FRIED GREEN TOMATOES

POMODORI VERDI FRITTI

Preparation time: 20 *min*,
plus 15 min resting
Cooking time: 25 *min*
Serves 4

For the batter:
— 1 egg yolk
— generous ¾ cup all-purpose
  flour

— 4 underripe tomatoes
  (more green than red), cut
  into ¼-inch slices
— 2 tablespoons finely
  chopped parsley
— 6 tablespoons olive oil
— salt

To make the batter, add scant 1 cup of ice water in a thin steady stream to the egg yolk, stirring continuously. Gradually stir in the flour until the mixture has a slightly granular texture (you may not need all of it). Cover the bowl with plastic wrap and let the batter stand for 15 minutes.

Remove the seeds from the tomato slices, then rinse the slices and pat dry with paper towels. Sprinkle with a little salt and chopped parsley. Heat the oil in a skillet. Dip the tomato slices into the batter, in batches, add to the hot oil, and cook, turning once, until golden brown. Remove with a slotted spoon and drain on paper towels. Transfer to a warm serving dish and serve immediately.

ORECCHIETTE WITH TOMATO
AND RICOTTA

ORECCHIETTE CON POMODORO E RICOTTA

Preparation time: 5 *min*
Cooking time: 40 *min*
Serves 4

— 4 tablespoons olive oil
— 4–5 ripe tomatoes
— 6 fresh basil leaves
— 12½ ounces orecchiette
— ½ cup grated firm ricotta
  cheese
— salt

Heat the oil in a small pan, add the tomatoes and a pinch of salt, and simmer for about 30 minutes. Mash the tomatoes with a fork, add the basil, turn off the heat, and cover. Cook the orecchiette in a large pan of salted, boiling water for 10 minutes, or according to the package directions, until al dente, drain well, and transfer to a warm serving dish. Pour the tomato sauce over the pasta and sprinkle with the ricotta.

RUSTIC TOMATO PIE

PHOTO PAGE 218

TORTINO RUSTICO DI POMODORI

Preparation time: *10 min*
Cooking time: *40 min*
Serves 6

— butter, for greasing
— 3 tablespoons olive oil
— 3 scallions, finely chopped
— 12 thin slices whole wheat
  bread, crusts removed
— 4 tomatoes, sliced
— pinch of dried oregano
— 1 egg
— ⅔ cup milk
— 2 ounces pecorino cheese,
  very thinly sliced
— salt and pepper

Preheat the oven to 350°F. Grease a rectangular pan with butter. Heat the oil in a pan, add the scallions, and cook over low heat, stirring occasionally, for 5 minutes. Lightly season with salt and remove from the heat. Cover the bottom of the prepared pan with half of the bread and spoon the scallions on top. Place the tomato slices on top, sprinkle with the oregano, and cover with the remaining the bread. Beat the egg with the milk in a bowl and season with salt and pepper. Pour the mixture over the bread, cover with the pecorino, and bake for 30 minutes or until the cheese has melted and turned golden brown. Let cool slightly, then turn out onto a serving dish.

TOMATOES WITH PROVOLONE CHEESE

POMODORI AL PROVOLONE

Preparation time: *15 min*
Cooking time: *20–25 min*
Serves 4

— ¼ cup dried
  bread crumbs
— 4 large tomatoes
— 1 large scallion, white
  part only, finely chopped
— 1 sprig parsley, finely
  chopped
— 3 tablespoons olive oil
— scant 1 cup grated provolone
  cheese
— salt and pepper

Light the barbecue or preheat the oven to 350°F. Put the bread crumbs into a bowl, add 4 tablespoons of water, and let soak. Slice the tops off the tomatoes and, using a teaspoon, scoop out the seeds and most of the flesh without piercing the "shells." Put the flesh into a bowl. Add the scallion, parsley, oil, and grated cheese. Drain the bread crumbs, squeeze out the excess moisture, and add to the bowl. Mix well and season with salt and pepper. Fill the tomatoes with the mixture, put into a flameproof dish, cover with a sheet of aluminum foil, and cook on the barbecue for 20–25 minutes. Alternatively, put into an ovenproof dish, cover with aluminum foil, and bake in the oven for 20–25 minutes. Serve immediately.

BELL PEPPER BUNDLES

Preparation time: *1 hour,*
plus 30 min draining
Cooking time: *30 min*
Serves *4*

— 6 red and yellow bell
 peppers, halved and seeded
— 1 large eggplant, diced
— 4 tablespoons olive oil,
 plus extra for brushing
 and drizzling
— ½ cup black olives, pitted
 and coarsely chopped
— 3 tablespoons capers, drained,
 rinsed, and coarsely chopped
— 1 clove garlic, chopped
 (optional)
— 1 tablespoon mixed finely
 chopped parsley and basil
— 2 tablespoons bread crumbs
— salt and pepper

Preheat the oven to 375°F. Line a baking sheet with aluminum foil. Put the bell peppers on the prepared baking sheet and bake for 20 minutes. Meanwhile, put the eggplants into a colander, sprinkle each layer with salt, and let drain for 30 minutes. Remove the bell peppers from the oven and let cool, then peel off the skins. Drain and rinse the eggplants, then pat dry with paper towels. Heat the oil in a large skillet. Add the eggplants and cook over medium-low heat, stirring frequently, for 8–10 minutes, until golden brown. Remove with a slotted spoon and drain on paper towels. Preheat the oven to 350°F. Brush an ovenproof dish with oil. Combine the eggplants, olives, capers, garlic, if using, herbs, and bread crumbs in a bowl and season with salt and pepper. Put the bell pepper halves on a counter, divide the stuffing among them, and roll up. Pack them into the prepared dish, drizzle with oil, and bake for 30 minutes. Remove from the oven and let cool before serving.

MACARONI WITH BELL PEPPERS

Preparation time: *20 min*
Cooking time: *30 min*
Serves *4*

— 2 tablespoons olive oil
— 1 clove garlic
— 4 canned anchovy fillets,
 drained
— 2 yellow bell peppers,
 seeded and cut into strips
— 11 ounces macaroni
— salt and pepper
— chopped oregano,
 to garnish (optional)

Heat the oil in a skillet. Add the garlic clove and cook over low heat, stirring frequently, for a few minutes, until browned. Remove the garlic with a slotted spoon and discard. Add the anchovies and cook, mashing with a wooden spoon until they have disintegrated. Add the bell pepper strips, season with salt and pepper, and cook, stirring occasionally, for 12–15 minutes, until the bell peppers are soft but not mushy. Cook the pasta in plenty of salted boiling water until al dente. Drain, turn into the skillet, toss well, and cook for another few minutes to let the flavors mingle. Serve sprinkled with a little oregano, if using.

SUMMER STUFFED BELL PEPPERS

PEPERONI RIPIENI D'ESTATE

Preparation time: *20 min,*
plus 30 min draining
Cooking time: *1 hour*
Serves 6

— 1 eggplant, diced
— 2 salted anchovies, with
    heads removed, cleaned, and
    filleted, then soaked in cold
    water for 10 min, and
    drained
— 2 tablespoons olive oil,
    plus extra for brushing
— 5 ounces Gruyère cheese,
    diced
— ½ cup olives, pitted
    and thinly sliced
— ¾ cup chopped parsley
— 6 basil leaves, chopped
— 3 tomatoes, peeled, seeded,
    and chopped
— 2 potatoes, diced
— 1 tablespoon capers,
    rinsed and drained
— pinch of dried oregano
— 6 green bell peppers
— salt and pepper

Put the eggplant cubes in a colander, sprinkle with salt, and let drain for 30 minutes. Meanwhile, chop the anchovy fillets. Preheat the oven to 180°/350°F. Brush an ovenproof dish with oil. Put the Gruyère, olives, parsley, basil, tomatoes, and potatoes into a large bowl. Rinse the eggplant, pat dry with a clean dish towel, and add to the bowl with the anchovies, capers, and oregano. Season with salt and pepper, and mix well. Remove the stalks from the bell peppers and cut off and reserve the tops. Remove the seeds and membranes using a small sharp knife and a teaspoon. Fill the bell peppers with the stuffing, drizzle a teaspoon of olive oil into each, and replace the tops, securing with a toothpick if necessary. Place the bell peppers in the prepared dish and bake for 1 hour. Serve hot or cold.

SWEET-AND-SOUR BELL PEPPERS

AGRODOLCE DI PEPERONI

Preparation time: *10 min*
Cooking time: *20 min*
Serves 4

— 2 red bell peppers
— 2 yellow bell peppers
— 3 tablespoons olive oil
— generous ¾ cup white wine
    vinegar
— 2 tablespoons sugar
— salt

Seed the bell peppers and cut into thick strips. Heat the oil in a pan and fry the bell peppers on low heat for about 15 minutes. Season with salt, remove the bell peppers from the pan, and set aside. Pour the vinegar and sugar into the pan juices, turn up the heat, and let simmer. When the vinegar has almost completely evaporated and the sugar has dissolved, return the bell peppers to the pan. Let cook for another two minutes, then place on a serving dish and serve at room temperature.

TUSCAN VEGETABLE SOUP

ACQUACOTTA

Preparation time: *35 min*
Cooking time: *30 min*
Serves 4

— 6 ripe tomatoes, peeled
— 2 tablespoons olive oil
— 1 large onion, finely chopped
— 4 red bell peppers, seeded
  and cut into thin strips
— 1 stalk celery, diced
— 6¼ cups vegetable stock
— 6 eggs
— ⅔ cup grated Parmesan
  cheese
— 4 thick slices coarse
  white bread
— salt and pepper

Press the tomatoes through a strainer into a bowl. Heat the oil in a deep, flameproof dish or large pan. Add the onion and cook over low heat, stirring occasionally, for 5 minutes, until softened. Stir in the bell peppers, add the celery, and cook, stirring occasionally, for 5 minutes. Add the tomatoes, season with salt and pepper, and cook, stirring occasionally, for 20 minutes, until reduced and thickened. Add the vegetable stock and bring to a boil, stirring. Lightly beat the eggs in a soup tureen. Pour in the soup, stirring vigorously, and sprinkle with the grated cheese. To serve, put a slice of bread into each of 4 individual soup bowls and ladle the soup over.

BAKED BELL PEPPERS WITH BASIL AND CHIVES

PHOTO PAGE 223

JULIENNE DI PEPERONI AL FORNO CON BASILICO ED ERBA CIPOLLINA

Preparation time: *15 min,*
plus 15 min cooling
Cooking time: *15 min*
Serves 4

— 4 red bell peppers, seeded
  and cut into quarters
— olive oil, for brushing
  and drizzling
— small bunch chives, chopped
— 1 sprig basil, chopped
— 1 dried chile, crumbled
— salt

Preheat the oven to 375°F. Cover a baking sheet with aluminum foil. Sprinkle the inner sides of the bell pepper quarters with salt and brush the outer sides with oil. Put them on the prepared baking sheet and bake for 15 minutes. Remove from the oven and let cool. Peel the bell peppers and cut the flesh into julienne strips. Put into a bowl, sprinkle with the chives and basil, and drizzle with olive oil. Season with salt and a pinch of crumbled chile.

BAKED BELL PEPPERS WITH BASIL AND CHIVES

STUFFED FRIED BELL PEPPERS

PEPERONI RIPIENI FRITTI

Preparation time: *30 min*
Cooking time: *20 min*
Serves *4*

— 4 red or yellow bell peppers,
  halved and seeded
— 12 ounces ground beef
— 1 onion, finely chopped
— 1 clove garlic, finely chopped
— 1 chile, seeded and
  finely chopped
— 3 tablespoons soy sauce
— ¼ cup all-purpose flour
— 2 eggs
— vegetable oil, for deep-frying
— salt

Bring a pan of lightly salted water to a boil. Add the bell peppers and blanch for 5 minutes, then drain and let cool. Meanwhile, combine the ground beef, onion, garlic, chile, and soy sauce in a bowl and season lightly with salt. Divide this mixture among the bell pepper halves. Spread out the flour in a shallow dish and beat the eggs with a pinch of salt in another shallow dish. Coat the bell peppers in flour and then in the beaten eggs. Heat the oil in a deep-fryer to 350–375°F or until a cube of day-old bread browns in 30 seconds. Add the bell peppers, in batches, and cook, carefully turning once, until golden brown. Remove with a slotted spoon, drain briefly on paper towels, transfer to a warm serving plate, and keep warm while you cook the remaining batches. Serve warm.

SAUTÉED PEPPERS WITH GARLIC

PEPERONI VERDI IN TEGAME

Preparation time: *15 min*
Cooking time: *30 min*
Serves *4*

— 4 medium green pointed,
  sweet peppers
— 3 tablespoons olive oil
— 1 clove garlic, peeled
— salt

Cut out the stalk, seeds, and membranes from the sweet peppers, otherwise leaving them whole. Bring a pan of water to a boil. Add the sweet peppers and cook for 5 minutes, then drain and turn upside down on paper towels. Heat the oil in a pan. Add the garlic and cook over low heat, stirring frequently, for a few minutes, until browned. Remove and discard. Add the sweet peppers to the pan and sprinkle with a little salt. Increase the heat to medium, cover, and cook for 30 minutes. Check that the sweet peppers are not drying out too much or sticking to the pan—there should be very little liquid left in the pan when they are cooked. Transfer them to a warm serving dish and serve immediately.

BELL PEPPER, EGGPLANT, OLIVE, ANCHOVY, AND CAPER MEDLEY

MISTO DI PEPERONI, MELANZANE, OLIVE, ACCIUGHE E CAPPERI

Preparation time: *1 hour, plus 15 min, for cooling*
Cooking time: *40 min*
Serves 4

— 4 bell peppers
— scant ½ cup olive oil, plus extra for brushing
— 2 eggplants, diced
— 1 clove garlic
— 2 tablespoons fresh bread crumbs
— ½ cup black olives, pitted
— 1 tablespoon capers, drained and rinsed
— 1 tomato, peeled and seeded
— 1 sprig oregano, finely chopped
— 1 sprig parsley
— 2 canned anchovy fillets, drained and chopped
— salt

Preheat the oven to 350°F. Put the bell peppers on a baking sheet and bake, turning once or twice, for 20 minutes. Remove from the oven, and, using tongs, transfer to a plastic bag and seal the top. When they are cold enough to handle, peel off the skins, cut out the stalks, and remove the seeds and the membranes, otherwise leaving them whole.

Heat 4 tablespoons of the oil in a large skillet. Add the eggplants and cook over medium-low heat, stirring frequently, for 5–8 minutes, until browned. Remove with a slotted spoon and drain on paper towels.

Preheat the oven to 325°F. Brush an ovenproof dish with oil. Heat the remaining oil with the garlic clove in another skillet and cook over low heat, stirring frequently, for a few minutes, until the garlic is lightly browned. Remove and discard. Sprinkle the bread crumbs into the garlic-flavored oil and add the olives, capers, tomato, oregano, and parsley. Season lightly with salt and cook over low heat, stirring occasionally, for 10 minutes. Stir in the anchovies and eggplants, and mix well. Remove the skillet from the heat and carefully fill the bell peppers with the mixture. Stand upright in the prepared dish and bake for 40 minutes. Serve immediately.

BAKED LAYERED BELL PEPPERS

PEPERONI IN TORTIERA

Preparation time: *1¼ hours, plus 15 min cooling*
Cooking time: *20 min*
Serves *6–8*

— 4½ pounds mixed red and yellow bell peppers
— 1 tablespoon olive oil, for brushing and drizzling
— 6 tablespoons fresh bread crumbs
— 1 tablespoon finely chopped parsley
— 1 tablespoon finely chopped capers
— 1 clove garlic (optional)
— salt and pepper

Preheat the oven to 350°F. Wrap the bell peppers in aluminum foil and bake for 1 hour. Remove from the oven and let cool in the aluminum foil, then unwrap and peel. Cut in half and remove the seeds and membranes. Cut the flesh into thin strips. Preheat the oven to 375°F. Brush an ovenproof dish with oil. Put the bread crumbs, parsley, capers, and oil in a bowl and mix well, then season with salt and pepper and stir in just enough water to make a soft mixture. Make alternate layers of the bell peppers and bread crumb mixture in the prepared dish. Bury the garlic clove, if using, in the center of the last layer. Drizzle with a little oil and bake for 20 minutes. Remove from the oven and let cool. Serve this delicious vegetable dish with a mixed broil.

BELL PEPPERS WITH BREAD CRUMBS AND CAPERS

PHOTO PAGE 227

PEPERONI AMMOLLICATI

Preparation time: *30 min*
Cooking time: *30 min*
Serves *4*

— 3 tablespoons olive oil
— 6 mixed yellow and green bell peppers, seeded and cut into chunks
— 2 tablespoons coarse fresh bread crumbs
— scant 1 cup grated pecorino cheese
— 2 tablespoons capers in oil, drained
— pinch of fresh oregano
— salt

Heat the oil in a pan. Add the bell peppers and cook over medium-low heat, stirring occasionally, for 15 minutes. (They should not be soft at this stage.) Season lightly with salt, stir well, and sprinkle with the bread crumbs, pecorino, capers, and oregano. Cook, stirring occasionally and sprinkling with a little hot water to moisten if necessary, for another 10 minutes. Remove from the heat, transfer to a warm serving dish, and serve immediately.

BELL PEPPERS WITH BREAD CRUMBS AND CAPERS

FENNEL AND PINK PEPPER RISOTTO

FENNEL AND PINK PEPPER RISOTTO

RISOTTO AI FINOCCHI E PEPE ROSA

Preparation time: *15 min*
Cooking time: *33 min*
Serves 4

— 4¼ cups vegetable stock
— 4 tablespoons butter
— 2 tablespoons olive oil
— 1 onion, finely chopped
— 3⅔ cups thinly sliced
  fennel bulbs
— pinch of freshly grated
  nutmeg
— 1½ cups risotto rice
— ⅓ cup grated Gruyère
  cheese
— ½ teaspoon pink
  peppercorns, lightly crushed
— salt

Pour the stock into a pan and bring to a boil. Meanwhile, melt half the butter with the oil in a large pan. Add the onion and cook over low heat, stirring occasionally, for 5 minutes, until softened and translucent. Add the fennel and nutmeg, stir well, and season with a pinch of salt. Cook, stirring occasionally, for 10 minutes, until the fennel is tender. Stir in the rice and cook for 1–2 minutes, until all the grains are coated in oil. Add a ladleful of the hot stock and cook, stirring continuously, until absorbed. Continue to add the hot stock, a ladleful at a time, stirring continuously until each addition has been absorbed, for about 20 minutes. When the rice is tender, remove the pan from the heat and stir in the Gruyère and remaining butter. Sprinkle the risotto with pink peppercorns, transfer to a warm serving dish, and serve immediately.

STUFFED FENNEL

FINOCCHI RIPIENI

Preparation time: *20 min*
Serves 4

— 7 ounces mild Gorgonzola
  cheese, crumbled
— 3½ ounces crescenza or
  Taleggio cheese
— 4 fennel bulbs
— ¼ cup finely chopped
  blanched almonds
— freshly ground white pepper

Mix the cheeses into a bowl and beat well until thoroughly combined, smooth, and creamy. Remove the tough outer layers of the fennel and cut out the cores. Halve the bulbs from top to bottom and separate the concave layers. Fill each of these vegetable "saucers" with some of the cheese mixture, season with white pepper, and sprinkle with the almonds. Put the stuffed fennel on a serving plate and keep cool until ready to serve, but do not chill in the refrigerator because this ruins the flavor of the cheese.

BUCATINI WITH WILD FENNEL

BUCATINI AL FINOCCHIETTO SELVATICO

Preparation time: *15 min*
Cooking time: *20 min*
Serves 4

— scant ½ cup raisins
— ½ wild fennel bulb,
   trimmed
— 2 tablespoons olive oil
— 1 onion, very thinly sliced
— ¼ cup pine nuts
— pinch of saffron threads
— 12 ounces bucatini
— salt

Put the raisins into a heatproof bowl, pour in warm water to cover, and let soak. Blanch the fennel in boiling water for 3–4 seconds, then drain and chop. Heat the oil in a pan. Add the onion and cook over low heat, stirring occasionally, for 5 minutes. Add the fennel and cook, stirring occasionally, for another 10 minutes. Drain the raisins and squeeze out the excess liquid, then add to the pan with the pine nuts and saffron. Cook the bucatini in plenty of salted boiling water until al dente. Drain, turn into a warm serving dish, and pour the sauce over. Serve immediately.

BRAISED FENNEL AND LEEKS

FINOCCHI E PORRI STUFATI

Preparation time: *20 min*
Cooking time: *50 min*
Serves 6

— 6 fennel bulbs
— 5 tablespoons butter
— 1 tablespoon olive oil
— 3 small leeks, sliced
— salt and pepper

Remove the tough outer layers of the fennel and cut out the cores. Thinly slice the bulbs. Melt the butter with the oil in a pan. Add the leeks and cook over low heat, stirring occasionally, for 5 minutes, until softened. Add the fennel and cook, stirring continuously, for 2 minutes. Pour in scant ½ cup of hot water, cover, and simmer over low heat, stirring occasionally and adding a little more hot water as necessary, for 45 minutes. Season with salt and pepper and remove the pan from the heat. Transfer the vegetables to a warm serving dish and spoon the cooking juices over. Serve hot with baked fillets of sole.

FENNEL WITH MOZZARELLA

Preparation time: *10 min*
Cooking time: *20 min*
Serves 4

— 8 fennel bulbs, trimmed
— 2 tablespoons butter
— 7 ounces mozzarella
   cheese, sliced
— 1 sprig parsley, chopped
— 4 eggs
— scant 1 cup heavy cream
— ½ cup grated Parmesan
   cheese
— salt and pepper

Cook the fennel in a pan of salted, boiling water for about 30 minutes, until tender. Drain, pat dry, and let cool slightly, then cut into thin wedges while still warm. Preheat the oven to 325°F. Melt the butter in a flameproof dish, add the fennel, and cook, stirring continuously, until lightly browned. Remove from the heat, cover with the mozzarella slices, and sprinkle with the parsley. Beat together the eggs, cream, and Parmesan in a bowl, season with salt and pepper, and pour the mixture over the fennel. Bake until the eggs are just set. Serve immediately.

FENNEL WITH SAUCE

Preparation time: *25 min*
Cooking time: *35 min*
Serves 4

— 4 fennel bulbs
— 2¼ cups vegetable stock
— 4 tablespoons mayonnaise
— 1 teaspoon ketchup
— 3 drops Tabasco sauce
— 4 tablespoons strained
   orange juice
— 2 tablespoons strained
   lemon juice

Discard the tough outer parts of the fennel, halve the bulbs, and put into a large pan. Pour in the stock and bring to a boil over high heat, then reduce the heat and simmer for about 30 minutes. Drain the fennel pieces in a fine-meshed strainer and let the liquid they will have absorbed during the cooking drain out. Combine the mayonnaise, ketchup, and Tabasco in a bowl, then gradually stir in the orange and lemon juices. Transfer the fennel to a serving plate and drizzle the citrus mayonnaise sauce over. Serve immediately.

FENNEL AND PINK GRAPEFRUIT

PHOTO PAGE 233

FINOCCHI E POMPELMI ROSA

Preparation time: *15 min*
Serves 4

— 4 tender fennel bulbs
— 2 pink grapefruit
— 5 stalks celery, blanched
   and julienned
— 5 tablespoons olive oil
— juice of ½ lemon, strained
— 1 sprig mint, finely chopped
— salt and pepper

Remove the tough outer layers of the fennel and cut out the cores. Thinly slice the bulbs. Peel the grapefruit, removing all traces of the bitter white pith. Cut out the segments between the membranes and put them into a large salad bowl. Add the celery and the fennel. Whisk the oil with the lemon juice in a bowl, add the mint, and season with salt and pepper. Drizzle this dressing over the salad, toss well, and serve.

FENNEL AND ARTICHOKE SALAD

INSALATA DI FINOCCHI E CARCIOFI

Preparation time: *30 min*
Serves 4

— ½ cup olive oil
— juice 1 orange, strained
— 3 fennel bulbs
— juice 1 lemon, strained
— 2 globe artichokes
— 1 tablespoon very small
   capers, drained and rinsed
— salt and pepper

Whisk together the oil and orange juice in a bowl and season with salt and pepper. Remove the tough outer layers of the fennel and cut out the cores, then slice very thinly, preferably using a mandoline. Fill a bowl halfway with water and stir in the lemon juice. Trim the artichoke stems, remove any coarse leaves and the chokes, and cut the artichokes into small pieces, then add the pieces immediately to the acidulated water to prevent discoloration. Drain the artichokes thoroughly and put into a salad bowl. Add the fennel and sprinkle with the capers. Finally, drizzle the oil and orange dressing over the salad.

FENNEL AND PINK GRAPEFRUIT

FENNEL AND POTATO BUNDLE

Preparation time: *35 min*
Cooking time: *20 min*
Serves *4*

— 2 fennel bulbs
— 2 potatoes, cut into
⅛-inch slices
— scant 1 cup black olives,
pitted
— olive oil, for drizzling
— salt

Preheat the oven to 350°F. Line an ovenproof dish with a large piece of aluminum foil, letting it overhang the sides. Remove the tougher outer layers of the fennel bulbs and cut out the cores. Slice the bulbs very thinly, preferably using a mandoline. Bring a pan of water to a boil. Add the potatoes and parboil for 3 minutes, then drain. Put the fennel in the bottom of the prepared dish, then cover with half of the potato slices. Sprinkle with the olives. Top with the remaining potato slices, drizzle with oil, and season with a pinch of salt. Loosely fold over the overhanging foil to enclose the vegetables, leaving space inside for air to circulate. Bake for 20 minutes. Remove the dish from the oven and open up the bundle carefully to avoid being scalded by hot steam. Let stand for 5 minutes before serving.

FENNEL PIE

Preparation time: *45 min*
Cooking time: *30 min*
Serves *6*

— 7 small fennel bulbs,
trimmed
— 3 eggs
— 4 tablespoons butter, plus
extra for greasing
— 5 slices whole wheat bread,
crusts removed
— 6 tablespoons milk
— 7 ounces Taleggio cheese,
sliced
— ⅔ cup grated Parmesan
cheese
— salt

Cook the fennel in salted, boiling water for 30 minutes. Meanwhile boil the eggs until hard-cooked, refresh under cold water, then shell, and slice thinly. Drain the fennel, pat dry with paper towels, and cut into crosswise slices. Preheat the oven to 350°F. Grease a deep ovenproof dish with butter. Sprinkle the slices of bread with milk and make a layer in the bottom of the prepared dish. Place a layer of fennel on top, followed by a layer of hard-cooked egg, and then a layer of taleggio. Continue making layers until all the ingredients are used, then sprinkle with the Parmesan. Bake until golden, remove from the oven, and serve warm.

ROASTED CORN ON THE COB

PANNOCCHIE ARROSTO

Preparation time: *15 min*
Cooking time: *20 min*
Serves 4

— 4 corncobs, leaves and
   silks removed
— 3 tablespoons butter, melted
— salt

Preheat the oven to 400°F or light the barbecue. Put the corncobs directly on an oven shelf or barbecue grill rack to roast. Turn frequently, for 20 minutes, until evenly browned. Remove from the oven or barbecue grill, brush with melted butter, and sprinkle with salt. Serve immediately.

CORN AND RADICCHIO SALAD

INSALATA DI MAIS E RADICCHIO

Preparation time: *15 min*
Serves 4

— generous 1 cup chopped
   baby spinach leaves
— 3 Treviso radicchio, chopped
— generous 1 cup diced
   smoked ham
— 1¼ cups fresh corn kernels
   or 7 ounces canned corn
   kernels, drained
— juice of 1 lemon, strained
— scant ½ cup olive oil
— salt

If using fresh corn, cook in a pan of salted boiling water for 5–10 minutes or until tender. Drain well. Put the spinach and radicchio in a salad bowl and add the ham and corn. Put a pinch of salt in a bowl, add the lemon juice, and stir to dissolve, then whisk in the olive oil. Pour the dressing over the salad and toss.

SHRIMP AND CORN SALAD

INSALATA DI GAMBERETTI E MAIS

Preparation time: *15 min*
Cooking time: *10–15 min*
Serves 4

— generous 1¾ cups fresh corn
  kernels or 9½ ounces canned
  corn kernels, drained
— 11 ounces uncooked shrimp,
  peeled and deveined
— olive oil
— juice of 1 lemon, strained
  (optional)
— salt

If using fresh corn, cook in a pan of salted boiling water for 5–10 minutes or until tender. Drain well and turn into a salad bowl. Cook the shrimp in another pan of salted boiling water for 5–6 minutes, then drain and add to the corn. Toss together, then drizzle with oil and lemon juice, if using, and season with salt. Let cool to room temperature before serving.

CORN AND BEAN SALAD

INSALATA DI MAIS E FAGIOLI

Preparation time: *10 min,
plus 1 hour chilling*
Serves 4

— 2½ cups fresh corn kernels
  or 14 ounces canned corn
  kernels, drained
— 1 yellow bell pepper, seeded
  and cut into thin strips
— 1 green bell pepper, seeded
  and cut into thin strips
— 1 hot chile, seeded and
  cut into thin strips
— 2 onions, thinly sliced
— 3½ ounces canned lima
  beans, drained
— 1 tablespoon chopped
  parsley

For the vinaigrette:
— 4 tablespoons olive oil
— 3 tablespoons red wine
  vinegar
— salt and pepper

If using fresh corn, cook in a pan of salted boiling water for 5–10 minutes or until tender. To make the vinaigrette, whisk together the oil and vinegar in a bowl and season with salt and pepper. Put the bell peppers, chile, and onions into a salad bowl, drizzle over the vinaigrette, and chill in the refrigerator for 1 hour. Add the corn, beans, and parsley, toss well, and serve.

CORN

MINI CORN FRITTERS

POLPETTINE DI MAIS

Preparation time: *40 min*
Cooking time: *10 min*
Serves 6

— 4 corncobs, leaves and
 silks removed
— 2 eggs, beaten
— 1 stalk celery, chopped
— 1 onion, chopped
— 1 clove garlic, chopped
— 2 tablespoons all-purpose
 flour
— ¾ teaspoon ground
 coriander
— ½ cup olive oil
— salt

Bring a large pan of water to a boil. Add the corncobs and
cook for 15 minutes, until the kernels are tender. Drain
and let cool slightly, then strip off the kernels and put into
a bowl. Stir in the eggs, celery, onion, and garlic, then stir
in the flour, coriander, and a pinch of salt until thoroughly
combined. Scoop up small portions of the mixture and
shape into balls. Heat the oil in a skillet. Add the fritters,
in batches, and cook, for 1–2 minutes on each side, until
golden. Remove with a slotted spoon, drain on paper towels,
and season with salt. Serve immediately.

PASTA WITH CORN, PANCETTA, AND BABY SPINACH

RUOTE AL MAIS, PANCETTA E SPINACI NOVELLI

PHOTO PAGE 239

Preparation time: *10 min*
Cooking time: *15 min*
Serves 4

— 1½ cups fresh corn kernels
 or 8 ounces canned corn
 kernels, drained
— 11 ounces ruote
 (pasta wheels)
— 2 tablespoons olive oil,
 plus extra for drizzling
— 5 ounces baby spinach
— 3 thin slices pancetta
 or bacon, diced
— salt and pepper

If using fresh corn, cook in a pan of salted boiling water
for 5–10 minutes or until tender. Bring a large pan of salted
water to a boil. Add the pasta, bring back to a boil, and
cook for 8–10 minutes, or according to pasta directions,
until tender but still al dente. Drain and refresh under cold
running water. Turn into a salad bowl, drizzle with a little
oil, and stir in the corn. Add the baby spinach leaves and
set aside in a cool place. Heat the oil in a small pan. Add
the pancetta or bacon and cook over high heat, stirring
frequently, for a few minutes, until tender. Remove the pan
from the heat, sprinkle the pancetta or bacon over the salad,
stir, and serve immediately.

PASTA WITH CORN, PANCETTA, AND BABY SPINACH

LETTUCE

CELERY

CHESTNUTS

MUSHROOMS

TRUFFLES

PUMPKIN

BEETS

CARROTS

POTATOES

SCORZONERA

TURNIPS

FALL

Fall's hearty vegetables may be less showy than the spring and summer crops, but they are equally prized. As the colors of the leaves change and the temperatures drop, Italians continue to cook with the freshest of the season's offerings, and many favourite vegetables mature during fall.

By September, the root vegetables have grown bigger, with the cooler temperatures sweetening the flavors. Carrots, potatoes, beets, and turnips dominate in the garden. Some root crops can be eaten raw in salads, such as Beets with Orange (see page 317) or Carrot, Apple, and Golden Raisin Salad (see page 325), but starchy sweet and savory root vegetables are more often enjoyed roasted or baked. Potato Gratin with Bacon and Thyme (see page 335), Roasted Turnips with Leeks and Pumpkin (see page 348), and Carrots with Taleggio Cheese (see page 320) can be served as a main course with a salad on the side, or as an accompaniment to roasted meat.

Mushrooms are immensely popular in the fall, when they are at their peak. Portobello and porcini are star varieties, but any type of mushroom can be used in many of the dishes in this section, whether for Tagliatelle with Mushrooms (see page 290), Mushroom Pilaf Timbale (see page 296), or Mushroom Flan (see page 292).

Fall offers a variety of interesting and unusual crops. Scorzonera, or black salsify, is a popular Italian root vegetable that can be served as a fricassee (see page 344) or with anchovies (see page 342). Chestnuts are not strictly vegetables, but they are included here since no Italian kitchen would be without them during the season. Cultivated by ancient villages in the Apennine woodlands, the chestnut features in many traditional recipes and is associated with *cucina povera*, or "poor cuisine," the cooking of locals who made the best of the limited produce available. The chewy texture and nutty taste of the chestnut is heightened when paired with Brussels sprouts. You may be surprised to find lettuce growing in the fall, but, like root vegetables, lettuce thrives in a cool climate.

Other long-haul vegetables also mature during fall. Winter squashes and pumpkins will thrive and take up more space than you imagined with their fast-growing vines. They are particularly valued in the Italian kitchen and appear in delicious savory dishes, such as Pumpkin Gnocchi with Orange Butter (see page 308) or Pumpkin with Wild Fennel (see page 312).

Harvest your root vegetables after the first cool weather for the best flavor, but do not hurry to harvest them all; root crops can be left in the garden for months, even in cold winter areas, and harvested as needed throughout fall and winter. However, if mice or other pests are enjoying your underground bounty, pull and store your root crops in a cool, dark basement or shed. Root vegetables are easier to pull up if you harvest them shortly after rainfall.

LETTUCE
LATTUGA

There are two main types of lettuce: round and romaine. Round lettuces such as butterheads have loosely packed leaves, a pale heart, and a mild flavor, while romaine lettuce, also known as cos, tends to be crisp with firm ribs and a fine flavor. It is the classic lettuce for Caesar salad and an Italian favorite.

Lettuce forms the basis of many salads, and leaves from different types may be combined. It can also be cooked to make a Lettuce and Mint Soup (see page 270) and served as a gratin or in an omelet.

Whatever the variety, look for undamaged, firm, crisp leaves with no signs of slime or insect damage. Store in the salad drawer of the refrigerator for a few days. Discard any coarse or wilted leaves and wash thoroughly in cold water. Dry in a salad spinner or with a dish towel.

IN THE GARDEN Sow lettuce seeds in spring or fall for a winter harvest in well-drained, raised beds to which compost has been added. Space them 1 inch apart in rows 18 inches apart. Once four leaves have formed, thin loose heads to 4 inches apart and other varieties to 10 inches. Use the thinned baby lettuce in salads. Harvest looseleaf and romaine varieties by picking individual leaves or cutting the whole lettuce to the ground. Heading lettuce are ready to harvest when the center feels firm; pick the entire plant.

LETTUCE RECIPES ON PAGES 270–277

CELERY

SEDANO

Italian cooks prefer to use green celery in soups and sauces and white celery for salads and braising. Celery has an affinity with cheese and nuts, and is used in salads, soups, gratins, and risotto. It may be filled with a cheese mixture to make little boats to serve as canapés or stuffed, rolled, and fried. It is a delicious accompaniment to chicken, pork, and fish when braised in stock and served sprinkled with grated Parmesan.

Look for straight, crisp stalks and fresh-looking leaves. Avoid bunches with missing, damaged, or floppy stalks. Buy unwashed celery if possible, because it will have a better flavor. It will keep for several days in the salad drawer of the refrigerator. Wash thoroughly and separate the stalks, cutting off the base with a sharp knife. Remove any coarse strings by pulling them up from the base. Slice or dice, according to the recipe.

IN THE GARDEN Celery takes all summer to produce edible stalks from a spring planting. Transplant purchased seedlings 12 inches apart in rows 18 inches apart in well-drained compost-enhanced soil. It grows best in cool, moist summer conditions. Feed monthly with a balanced fertilizer and mulch with straw to keep the soil moist and weed free. Insufficient water causes the stalks to crack. Harvest the plants when they're about 10 inches tall. For a milder flavor, blanch green stalks by covering them for the last two weeks before harvesting. Wrap each celery plant in a plastic cylinder or brown paper bag and the stalks with turn a paler color.

CELERY RECIPES ON PAGES 278–280

CHESTNUTS
CASTAGNE

This attractive, shiny nut is widely used in Italian cooking for both savory and sweet dishes. The nuts themselves feature in stuffings and side dishes that are perfect with poultry, game birds, rabbit, wild boar, and pork. The flour ground from chestnuts is often used to make gnocchi, bread, and rustic desserts, such as Chestnut Cake (see page 286).

Look for rich brown, hard nuts with no blemishes or mold. Chestnuts bought in their shells are fresh and cannot be kept for longer than a week. Dried skinned chestnuts are also available, but must be soaked overnight before use. To peel and skin fresh chestnuts, make a slit in the shells and either roast in a preheated oven, 350°F, for 5–8 minutes or boil for 5 minutes, then drain. Peel off the shells and rub off the skins with a dish towel. They are then ready to be braised, broiled, cooked in butter or milk, or combined with other vegetables, most notably Brussels sprouts.

IN THE GARDEN Chestnut trees grow to 40 feet tall, so are not common in yards. However, the nuts can be collected in the wild in fall in temperate regions. Do not confuse the sweet chestnut with the horse chestnut, the nuts of which are inedible although not poisonous. The sweet chestnut has long, narrow, toothed leaves, while the horse chestnut has large leaves with five to seven leaflets. The casings of sweet chestnuts are covered in small, prickly spines—wear gloves when foraging—while those of the horse chestnut have fewer, very sharp spikes.

CHESTNUT RECIPES ON PAGES 282–288

MUSHROOMS
FUNGHI

Italians are passionate about mushrooms and about harvesting them in the wild, where they will pick rich-flavored porcini, also known as ceps, delicate yellow chanterelles, large parasols, and clusters of honey fungus. Never pick wild mushrooms unless you are certain that you can identify edible species. Cooks in many other countries rely on cultivated mushrooms, which still have a concentrated earthy flavor, although not quite so intense as wild mushrooms.

Mushrooms are hugely versatile. They add texture to warm salads and deep flavor to dishes such as Tagliatelle with Mushrooms (see page 290) or a traditional Mushroom Risotto (see page 295). They work just as well in sauces, gratins, pies, fricassees, omelets, timbales, and flans. However, one of the easiest and most delicious ways to serve any kind of mushrooms is *trifolati*, cooked with oil, parsley, and lemon juice.

Mushrooms should be firm to the touch and without slime. They should have a pleasant earthy smell. Do not wash cultivated mushrooms; simply wipe clean with damp paper towels. Gently brush grit and dirt from wild mushrooms, rinse very briefly, and dry immediately.

IN THE GARDEN Mushrooms, such as portobello, oyster, and white, can be grown in box kits or outdoor beds. Mushrooms should appear in a few weeks and you can get two to three harvests from a box. To grow outdoors, fill a bed in a shady area with straw, bark mulch, or wood chips. Wet the organic material thoroughly, then spread the spore. Cover until mushrooms begin to emerge, then uncover and begin to harvest.

MUSHROOM RECIPES ON PAGES 289–300

TRUFFLES
TARTUFI

Not a vegetable but an underground fungus, and certainly not a garden plant, the truffle is prized for its out-of-this-world fragrance, flavor, and price. There are many kinds of truffle but the most valued are simply called black and white. Black truffles have a milder flavor and less intense aroma than white and are usually cooked, while white truffles are used uncooked. Both are found in Italy, and the white truffles of Alba are generally acknowledged as the best in the world.

Both kinds have an affinity with eggs—black features in an upmarket frittata, while white shaved over fried eggs creates the most gourmet breakfast imaginable. Black truffles also go well with fish and chicken. White truffles can be shaved over all kinds of dishes, especially risotto and carpaccio, to turn a simple meal into a feast. Truffles also seem to go with all types of ingredients without surrendering their unique qualities.

Fresh truffles should be well rounded, not broken up, and completely ripe. Store wrapped in two layers of damp paper towels, then three layers of dry paper towels in the refrigerator for up to 1 week. Clean by brushing hard and wiping with a damp cloth.

IN THE GARDEN Attempts to cultivate truffles have never been successful because they are neither sown nor planted, but spring up spontaneously. Black truffles are found near oak and hazel trees, while white truffles grow among poplars, willows, oaks, and lime trees. Professional foragers use trained dogs or pigs to sniff out a crop after warm rain, because they grow about 6 inches below the ground.

TRUFFLE RECIPES ON PAGES 301–302

PUMPKIN
ZUCCA

As one of the best known winter squashes, pumpkin has a sweet flesh with a hint of honey that works as well in sweet dishes as it does in savory. A favorite Italian treat is baked pumpkin sprinkled with sugar. Pumpkin can be added to soup and gnocchi; used in a pie, flan, or roulade; and made into a filling for pasta.

Look for firm specimens with unblemished skin. Some pumpkins are huge so may be sold by the piece. In that case, look for firm flesh that is not fibrous. Pumpkins can be stored in a cool, dark place for a long time. To prepare the pumpkin, peel the skin, cut into pieces, and scoop out the seeds, then slice or dice, according to the recipe. The flesh may be steamed or boiled for 20–30 minutes, sautéed in butter, or roasted in a preheated oven at 400°F for 15 minutes, and then for another 5 minutes at 425°F.

IN THE GARDEN Plant pumpkin and other winter squash in spring after all danger of frost has passed in fertile, compost-enhanced soil. Sow two seeds per hole, spaced 2 feet apart in rows spaced 5 feet apart. After germination, thin to the strongest seedlings. Vining varieties will spread across the yard or up a trellis and produce the most fruit. Harvest in fall before the first frost, when pumpkins are in full color and the skin is hard when pressed with your thumb. Cure (the process that encourages a plant to naturally heal its own wounds, making it less susceptible to damage and disease) in a humid place at 80°F for 2 weeks, then store for winter in a dark place at 50°F for 3–6 months.

PUMPKIN RECIPES ON PAGES 304–314

BEETS
BARBABIETOLE

Italians really appreciate the sweet root and green tops of this vegetable, which is often underrated elsewhere. An easy north Italian dish combines roasted beet and onions in a salad, served simply drizzled with olive oil and sprinkled with salt. The young beet greens may be used in salads or boiled for just a few minutes, drained, and dressed with olive oil or melted butter.

While beets are often sold already cooked, the raw roots are usually available, too. Look for undamaged whiskery roots, intact skin, and at least 2 inches of stalk. Beets will keep for several weeks in a cool place. To prepare, rinse well under cold running water. Trim the leaves to 2 inches above the root, but do not peel. Simmer or steam for about 1½ hours, or wrap in aluminum foil and bake in a preheated oven, 400°F, for 2 hours. The beet is ready when the skin begins to wrinkle and can be easily rubbed off with your finger, or it is tender when pierced with a knife.

IN THE GARDEN Sow in spring before the last frost and again in late summer for a fall harvest. Sow seeds 1 inch apart in rows 1 foot apart on raised beds of sandy loam soil to which compost has been added. Keep the seed bed well watered. Thin to 4 inches apart when the seedlings are 3 inches tall, otherwise plants will become overcrowded and few roots will develop. Harvest young beets when they are 1–2 inches in diameter. The roots of most varieties will become woody if they get larger than this. Store in a dark, airy place at 40°F for up to 3 months.

BEET RECIPES ON PAGES 315–318

CARROTS
CAROTE

Although ranging in color from white to purple, traditional orange carrots remain the favorites in Italy. They feature in dishes with cheese, herbs, Belgian endive, cream, and various glazes, and are made into soups, salads, fritters, molds, and croquettes.

Look for well-shaped, smooth-skinned carrots with no blemishes and preferably with their green tops intact. They can be stored in the salad drawer of the refrigerator for a few days. Young carrots need no more than washing under cold running water. Medium carrots should be washed and scraped, while larger, older carrots need to be washed, then thinly peeled. Raw carrots may be grated or cut into julienne strips and served drizzled with olive oil and lemon juice. Carrots can be braised in stock or wine, boiled in lightly salted water, cooked in butter, or roasted to enhance their sweetness.

IN THE GARDEN Sow seeds in spring for an early summer harvest and in late summer for a fall harvest. Sprinkle the seeds on raised beds and cover with a ¼-inch-thick layer of potting mix. Once germinated, thin to 1–2 inches apart and again 3 weeks later to 3–4 inches apart. Overcrowded carrots will form small roots. Begin harvesting when carrots have developed their full color. The sweet flavor will be enhanced by colder weather.

CARROT RECIPES ON PAGES 319–326

POTATOES
PATATE

Although a staple accompaniment in most European countries, potatoes have never played the same role in Italian cooking and are treated as a dish in their own right. They can be made into gnocchi, baked in sauce, made into cakes, patties, fritters, and gratins, and chilled in salads.

Look for potatoes with smooth, undamaged tight skins without any sign of green or sprouts. The skins of new potatoes should rub off easily. New potatoes should be used as soon as possible after purchase, but regular potatoes will keep for months if stored in a cool, dry, dark place. Always remove them from plastic bags before storing.

Simply wash new potatoes, then cook and serve in their skins. Scrub potatoes under running water. Cook them in their skins and peel afterward—except for French fries—to preserve vitamins and minerals.

IN THE GARDEN Plant certified seed potatoes (ones that are government-certified as disease free) in 4–6 inch-deep trenches spaced 1 foot apart in spring. As the leaves begin to emerge, bury them with soil until the trench is filled. Mound soil around the plants when they reach 8 inches tall and again 2 weeks later. Keep the soil moist. Begin to harvest new potatoes 8–12 weeks after planting. Gently dig under the plant to remove a few egg-size potatoes per hill, then replace the soil. Harvest mature potatoes when the tops start to yellow and die back. Cure potatoes in a warm, well-ventilated room for 2 weeks before storing them in a dark, dry place at 40°F for up to 8 months.

POTATO RECIPES ON PAGES 327–341

SCORZONERA
SCORZONERA

Popular in continental Europe but not so well known elsewhere, scorzonera is an unattractive looking root with a deliciously delicate flavor. Sometimes called black salsify, which it closely resembles, it has blackish brown skin and butter-colored flesh.

Scorzonera is delicious in soup, sautéed in butter, frittered, and in fricassee. It goes wonderfully well with seafood, pork, chicken, and game. Salsify can be substituted for scorzonera in all recipes. Look for firm, smooth roots, preferably with fresh-looking tops intact. They will keep for several days in a cool, dark place. Scorzonera is difficult to peel. Either scrub the root under cold running water and peel after cooking or peel with a stainless steel knife and cut into pieces, then immediately drop them into acidulated water to prevent discoloration. Simmer in acidulated, lightly salted water for about 30 minutes, until tender, then drain. Serve with a cream, lemon, or anchovy sauce, cold with a garlic vinaigrette, or cook with other ingredients.

IN THE GARDEN Sow seeds ½ inch apart in a raised bed on well-drained, loose sandy soil in spring. The grasslike seedlings are slow to germinate and easily confused with weeds. Thin them to 3 inches apart. The plants grow slowly all summer, are pest free, and drought tolerant. Harvest 12-inch-long roots after a few frosts but before the soil freezes. Carefully dig out the brittle roots, remove the tops, and clean off the soil. Scorzonera is a perennial crop. If left in the soil in fall, the young greens and yellow flowers that appear in spring make an excellent addition to salads or may be cooked like asparagus.

SCORZONERA RECIPES ON PAGES 342–344

TURNIPS

RAPE

The tennis ball-size turnip root is not so popular today in Italy as it was in earlier centuries, but turnip greens remain a favorite vegetable. Roots are used for soups and may also be stuffed or roasted with other vegetables. The greens are used for soups and salads and served with bread crumbs, garlic and oil, or Parmesan, garlic, and tomatoes or chile. A simple way to serve them is cooked with pasta, then drained and dressed with olive oil and chopped garlic.

For a sweet, nutty flavor, choose small roots—large turnips tend to have a coarser flavor and texture. Look for a firm texture, smooth, undamaged skins, and fresh greens. Store in a cool, dry place. Simply trim tender, young turnips but peel and slice or dice older ones. Cook in salted, boiling water until tender, then drain.

IN THE GARDEN Plant in spring or early fall. Fall-sown seeds can be harvested into winter. Sow seeds 2 inches apart in rows spaced 1 foot apart in well-drained, fertile soil. Thin seedlings to 4 inches apart and use the baby greens in salads. Keep the soil well watered and mulch with straw once the plants are established. Harvest young roots when they are 2 inches in diameter for salads. Harvest for cooking when they are 4 inches in diameter. Turnips develop a sweeter taste after a light frost. Store roots in the ground in mild winter areas or in a dark place at 40°F for a few months.

TURNIP RECIPES ON PAGES 345–351

STUFFED LETTUCE

LATTUGA RIPIENA

Preparation time: *20 min*
Cooking time: *30 min*
Serves 4

— 1- or ¾-inch-thick slice
   bread, crust removed
— scant ½ cup milk
— 3 ½ ounces ground meat
— 3 ½ ounces bulk sausage
— 1 tablespoon grated
   Parmesan cheese
— 1 egg, lightly beaten
— 4 round lettuce
— 2 ounces lardons
— 3 tablespoons olive oil
— 3 tablespoons butter
— salt and pepper

Tear the bread into pieces, place in a bowl, add the milk, and let soak for 10 minutes, then squeeze out. Combine the bread, meat, sausage, and Parmesan in a bowl and season with salt and pepper. Add the egg and mix until combined. Remove and discard the outer leaves and part of the centers of the lettuce, and wash the lettuce. Bring a pan of salted water to a boil and blanch for 3 minutes. Drain, gently open out the leaves, and stuff with the meat mixture. Reshape and tie the tops with kitchen string. Spread out the lardons in a flameproof casserole and place the lettuce on top. Pour the olive oil into the casserole and dot the lettuce with the butter. Add scant ½ cup of water, cover, and cook over medium heat for about 30 minutes.

LETTUCE AND MINT SOUP

CREMA DI LATTUGA E MENTA

PHOTO PAGE 271

Preparation time: *10 min*
Cooking time: *20 min*
Serves 4

— 2 tablespoons butter
— 1 onion, thinly sliced
   into rings
— 1 lettuce, shredded
— 4¼ cups vegetable stock
— 15 mint leaves
— 2 tablespoons heavy cream
— salt and pepper
— croutons, to serve

Melt the butter in a pan. Add the onion and cook over low heat, stirring occasionally, for 5 minutes, until softened and translucent. Add the lettuce and cook for a few minutes, then pour in the stock and season with salt and pepper. Increase the heat to medium and bring to a boil, then reduce the heat and simmer for 5 minutes. Stir in the mint leaves and remove the pan from the heat. Pour the soup into a foodprocessor or blender and process until smooth. Return the soup to the pan, stir in the cream, and reheat gently but do not let boil. Ladle into warm soup bowls and serve with croutons.

LETTUCE AND MINT SOUP

BROTH WITH EGGS AND LETTUCE

STRACCIATELLA ALLA LATTUGA

Preparation time: *18 min*
Cooking time: *20 min*
Serves 4

— 3 cups beef stock
— 2 romaine lettuce, shredded
— 3 eggs
— generous 1 cup grated
Parmesan cheese
— salt
— 4 thick slices oven-toasted
bread, to serve

Pour the stock into a pan and bring to a boil, then reduce the heat to a simmer. Add the lettuce and simmer for 10 minutes. Beat the eggs in a bowl, add the cheese, and season with salt, then gradually pour the mixture into the simmering stock, stirring continuously with a fork. Simmer, stirring continuously, for 10 minutes, until the egg mixture has formed fine threads. Place a slice of toasted bread into each of 4 soup bowls, ladle the soup over them, and serve immediately.

LETTUCE SOUFFLÉ OMELET

FRITTATA SOUFFLE DI LATTUGA

Preparation time: *15 min*
Cooking time: *20 min*
Serves 4

— 1½ tablespoons olive oil
— 1 shallot, very finely chopped
— 1 butterhead lettuce,
shredded
— 5 eggs, separated
— 2 drops lemon juice
— salt and pepper

Preheat the broiler. Meanwhile, heat ½ tablespoon of the oil with ½ tablespoon of water in a pan. Add the shallot and cook over low heat, stirring occasionally, for 5 minutes, until softened. Season lightly with salt and pepper, stir in the lettuce, and cook for 1 minute, then remove from the heat. Set aside and keep warm. Beat the egg yolks with 1 tablespoon of water in a bowl, season lightly with salt, and beat. Using a grease-free bowl, whisk the egg whites with the lemon juice to stiff peaks, then gently fold into the egg yolks. Add the lettuce mixture. Heat the remaining oil in a skillet. Pour in the egg and lettuce mixture and cook for 1 minute, then turn the omelet over and cook the second side for 1 minute, until soft and golden brown. Slide the omelet onto a flameproof serving plate and cook under the broiler for another 30 seconds. Remove and serve immediately.

LETTUCE GNOCCHI

GNOCCHI ALLA LATTUGA

Preparation time: *1 hour,
plus 1 hour resting*
Cooking time: *15 min*
Serves 4

— 2¼ pounds potatoes
— 1¾ cup all-purpose flour,
  plus extra for dusting
— 1 egg, lightly beaten
— salt

For the sauce:
— 2 tablespoons olive oil
— 1 shallot, finely chopped
— 3½ ounces sliced ham,
  julienned
— 1 romaine lettuce, shredded
— 1 cup heavy cream
— ¼ cup grated Parmesan
  cheese
— salt and pepper

To make the gnocchi, peel the potatoes, cut into 1-inch cubes, and put them into a steamer basket. Bring 2 inches of water to a boil in a pan. Insert the steamer, cover, and steam for 20 minutes, until tender. Remove the potatoes from the steamer, put into a bowl, and mash. Stir in the flour, egg, and a pinch of salt. Shape the dough into long sausages about ¾ inch in diameter and cut into 1-inch lengths. Press them gently against a grater and spread out on a dish towel lightly dusted with flour. Let rest for 1 hour.

To make the sauce, heat the oil in a skillet. Add the shallot and cook over low heat, stirring occasionally, for 10 minutes, until softened. Stir in the ham and cook for 2 minutes, then add the lettuce and cream. Season with salt and pepper and simmer for 10 minutes. Meanwhile, bring a large pan of salted water to a boil. Add the gnocchi in batches, cooking for about 5 minutes, or until they rise to the surface. Cook for another minute, then remove with a slotted spoon. Add the cooked gnocchi to the sauce and simmer for a few seconds. Transfer to a warm serving dish, sprinkle with grated cheese, and serve immediately.

LETTUCE AND PASTA GRATIN

PASTA GRATINATA ALLA LATTUGA

Preparation time: *30 min*
Cooking time: *20 min*
Serves 4

— 14 cups shredded lettuce
  leaves
— olive oil, for drizzling
— 11 ounces short pasta,
  such as sedani (celery stalks)
— 4 tablespoons butter
— scant 1 cup grated Gruyère
  cheese
— salt and pepper

Preheat the oven to 350°F. Put the lettuce into a bowl, drizzle with a little oil, stir, and set aside. Bring a large pan of salted water to a boil. Add the pasta, bring back to a boil, and cook for about 10 minutes, until tender but still al dente. Drain, add 2 tablespoons of the butter, and toss well, then turn into an ovenproof dish and spread out. Cover with the shredded lettuce, sprinkle with the Gruyère cheese, season lightly with pepper, and dot with the remaining butter. Bake for 20 minutes, until golden brown. Serve immediately straight from the dish.

SEA SCALLOPS WITH ORANGE JUICE AND LETTUCE HEARTS

PHOTO PAGE 274

CAPESANTE ALL'ARANCIA E CUORI DI LATTUGA

Preparation time: *30 min*
Cooking time: *6 min*
Serves 4

— ½ cup olive oil
— 8 sea scallops, shucked
— juice 1 orange, strained
— 3½ cups shredded lettuce hearts
— 3 tomatoes, peeled, seeded, and finely diced
— 1 tablespoon white wine vinegar
— salt and pepper

Heat 2 tablespoons of the oil in a skillet. Add the sea scallops and cook over high heat for 2 minutes on each side. Season lightly with salt and drizzle with 2 tablespoons of the orange juice. Cook until the juice has evaporated, gently turn the sea scallops, and remove them from the heat. Put the lettuce hearts and tomatoes into a salad bowl. Stir a pinch of salt into the vinegar in a bowl, then whisk in the remaining oil, a pinch of pepper, and the remaining orange juice. Drizzle the dressing over the salad, toss lightly, and place the sea scallops on top. Season with pepper and serve immediately.

CAESAR SALAD

CAESAR SALAD

Preparation time: *30 min*
Cooking time: *10 min*
Serves 6–8

— ½ cup olive oil
— 2 cloves garlic, peeled
— 9 cups small bread cubes
— 1 romaine lettuce, torn into pieces
— ½ teaspoon dry mustard
— ⅓ cup grated Parmesan cheese
— juice of ½ lemon, strained
— 3 bacon slices, cooked until crisp and finely chopped
— salt and pepper

Heat half of the oil with 1 garlic clove. Cook, stirring frequently, for a few minutes, until the garlic is lightly browned. Remove and discard. Add the bread cubes to the pan and cook over medium-low heat, stirring and turning frequently, for 5–10 minutes, until pale golden brown. Remove and drain on paper towels. Lightly crush the remaining garlic clove. Rub the bruised garlic clove over the inside of a salad bowl, put the lettuce into it, and sprinkle with the dry mustard and grated cheese. Whisk together the remaining oil and the lemon juice in a small bowl. Pour the dressing over the lettuce, season with salt and pepper, and toss well. Sprinkle the chopped bacon and croutons over the salad and serve.

LETTUCE, AVOCADO AND PEPPER SALAD

PHOTO PAGE 277

INSALATA DI LATTUGA, AVOCADO E PEPERONI

Preparation time: *15 min*
Serves 4

— 1 large lettuce heart
— 1 ripe avocado
— juice of ½ lemon, strained
— 5 tablespoons olive oil
— 2 teaspoons strong mustard
— 1 small red bell pepper,
   seeded and julienned
— salt

Separate the lettuce leaves. Peel and halve the avocado, remove and discard the pit, and thinly slice the flesh. Sprinkle the slices with lemon juice to prevent discoloration. Whisk together the olive oil, mustard, and a pinch of salt in a bowl. Put the lettuce leaves, bell pepper, and avocado slices on a serving dish, pour over the dressing, and serve.

SALAD WITH GORGONZOLA VINAIGRETTE

INSALATA DI LATTUGA CON VINAIGRETTE AL GORGONZOLA

Preparation time: *20 min*
Serves 6

— 3–4 lettuce hearts, quartered
   lengthwise
— 1 small bunch chives, finely
   chopped

For the vinaigrette:
— 4 ounces sharp Gorgonzola
   cheese, crumbled
— 2–3 tablespoons light cream
— 6 tablespoons olive oil
— 4 tablespoons white wine
   vinegar
— salt

To the make the vinaigrette, whisk together the Gorgonzola, cream, oil, and vinegar until smooth, and season with salt. Put the lettuce hearts on a serving dish, spoon the dressing over, and garnish with the chopped chives.

LETTUCE, AVOCADO, AND BELL PEPPER SALAD

STUFFED CELERY

SEDANI RIPIENI

Preparation time: *25 min*
Cooking time: *30 min*
Serves 6

— 1 large head celery
— 2 ounces chopped ham
— 2 ounces chopped mortadella
— 3½ ounces ground veal
— 3½ ounces ground pork
— ⅔ cup grated Parmesan
  cheese
— 2 egg yolks
— ½ cup all-purpose flour
— 2 eggs
— olive oil, for frying
— salt

Select the most tender celery stalks and discard the leaves. Bring a pan of salted water to a boil. Add the celery and cook for 3–4 minutes. Drain and place on a dish towel to dry. Combine the ham, mortadella, veal, and pork in a bowl. Add the cheese and egg yolks and season with salt. Mix well until thoroughly combined. Fill the celery stalks with the meat mixture and roll them up lengthwise. Spread out the flour in a shallow dish. Beat the eggs with a pinch of salt in another shallow dish. Roll the celery in the flour and secure with toothpicks, then dip in the beaten egg. Pour oil to a depth of about 1½ inches into a large skillet and heat. Add the stuffed celery rolls and cook until golden. Remove from the skillet with a slotted spoon and drain on paper towels. Serve immediately.

CELERY SOUP

ZUPPA DI SEDANO

Preparation time: *30 min*
Cooking time: *1 hour 10 min*
Serves 6

— 2 large heads celery, trimmed
  and thinly sliced
— 1 tablespoon lard
— scant 1 cup olive oil
— 4¼ cups vegetable stock
  or water
— 3½ ounces caciocavallo
  or Provolone cheese, sliced
— 2¾ ounces sopressata
  salami, diced
— 2¾ ounces salami,
  skinned and diced
— 2–3 hard-cooked eggs, shelled
— salt and pepper
— small slices crusty whole wheat
  bread, toasted, to serve
— grated pecorino cheese,
  to serve

Select the most tender celery stalks and cut into thin slices. Melt the lard with the oil in a large pan. Add the celery and cook over low heat, stirring occasionally, for 5 minutes. Pour in the vegetable stock or water, season with salt and pepper, and simmer for 1 hour. Put the cheese slices in the bottom of a soup tureen, then add the sopressata and salami. Quarter the hard-cooked eggs and add. Pour the soup over them. Serve immediately, handing around the toasted bread and grated pecorino separately.

CELERY RISOTTO

RISOTTO AL SEDANO

Preparation time: *10 min*
Cooking time: *28 min*
Serves 4

— 4¼ cups vegetable stock
— 2 tablespoons olive oil
— 1 onion, chopped
— 2¾ cups chopped white celery
— 2¼ cups risotto rice
— scant 1 cup dry white wine
— ½ cup grated Parmesan
cheese
— salt and pepper

Pour the stock into a pan and bring to a boil. Meanwhile, heat the oil in another pan. Add the onion and cook over low heat, stirring occasionally, for 5 minutes, until softened. Add the celery and cook, stirring occasionally, for 2–3 minutes. Stir in the rice and cook, stirring continuously, for 1–2 minutes, until all the grains are translucent and coated with oil. Add the wine and cook until the alcohol has evaporated, then season with salt. Add a ladleful of the hot stock and cook, stirring continuously, until it has been absorbed. Continue to add the hot stock, a ladleful at a time, stirring continuously until each addition has been absorbed before adding the next, for about 20 minutes. Remove from the heat, sprinkle with the grated cheese, stir, and season. Transfer to warm plates and serve immediately.

CELERY AND FONTINA SALAD

INSALATA DI SEDANO E FONTINA

Preparation time: *10 min*
Serves 4

— 4 stalks celery, cut into
strips
— 7 ounces mild fontina
cheese, cut into strips
— 2 ounces sharp fontina,
cut into strips
— olive oil, for drizzling
— salt and pepper

Put the celery and both kinds of cheese into a salad bowl. Drizzle with olive oil, season with salt and pepper, toss well, and serve.

MOLISE CELERY

PHOTO PAGE 281

SEDANO ALLA MOLISANA

Preparation time: *15 min*
Cooking time: *15 min*
Serves *4*

— 2 tablespoons olive oil, plus
  extra for brushing
— 1 head celery,
  trimmed and sliced
— 8 scallions, thinly sliced
— 1 scant cup pitted black
  olives
— 3 tablespoons bread crumbs
— salt and pepper

Preheat the oven to 400°F. Brush an ovenproof dish with oil. Bring a pan of salted water to a boil. Add the celery and cook for 10 minutes, then drain, turn into a bowl, and let cool slightly. Meanwhile, heat the oil and 1 tablespoon of water in a pan, add the scallions, and cook over low heat for 5 minutes, until softened, then season with salt and pepper. Put the celery into the prepared dish, top with the scallions and olives, sprinkle with the bread crumbs, and bake for 15 minutes.

CELERY AND WALNUT SALAD

SEDANO ALLE NOCI

Preparation time: *15 min*
Serves *4*

— 4 ounces white celery,
  trimmed
— 1 green apple, peeled, cored,
  and diced
— juice of 1 lemon, strained
— 4 ounces low-fat tomino or
  other semihard cheese, diced
— 1 tablespoon chopped parsley
— ½ cup chopped walnuts
— 5 tablespoons olive oil
— salt and pepper

Halve the celery stalks lengthwise and cut into thin strips. Place the celery and apple in a salad bowl and stir in half of the lemon juice. Add the cheese, parsley, and half of the walnuts. Whisk together the olive oil and remaining lemon juice in a pitcher and season with salt and pepper. Stir in the remaining walnuts and pour the dressing over the salad.

MOLISE CELERY

CHESTNUT FLOUR GNOCCHI

GNOCCHI DI FARINA DI CASTAGNE

Preparation time: *20 min, plus 30 min resting*
Cooking time: *10 min*
Serves 4

— 4½ cups chestnut flour
— 2¼ cups all-purpose flour
— 1 quantity Pesto
  (see page 159)
— salt

Sift together the chestnut and all-purpose flours into a mound on a counter and make a well in the center. Add a pinch of salt to the well and just enough water to obtain a smooth, firm dough as you mix with your fingers. Shape the dough into a ball, cover, and let rest for 30 minutes. Break off small pieces of the dough and shape into balls, then cut each ball into ¼-inch pieces. Bring a pan of salted water to a boil. Add the gnocchi and cook for about 10 minutes, until they rise to the surface. Drain well, turn into a serving dish, and stir in the pesto. Serve immediately.

BOILED CHESTNUTS

CASTAGNE LESSE

Preparation time: *30 min*
Cooking time: *45 min*
Serves 4

— 1½ tablespoons butter
— 1 pound 5 ounces chestnuts, peeled
— 5 cups beef stock
— 1 bay leaf
— 1 sprig thyme
— 1 stalk celery
— salt and pepper

Preheat the oven to 425°F. Melt the butter in an ovenproof casserole. Add the chestnuts and cook for 1 minute, then pour in the stock. Add the bay leaf, thyme, and celery, and bring to a boil. Cover the casserole, transfer to the oven, and cook, gently shaking the casserole occasionally, for 45 minutes. Remove from the oven and season with salt and pepper.

CHESTNUT SOUFFLÉ

SOUFFLÉ DI CASTAGNE

Preparation time: *45 min*
Cooking time: *15 min*
Serves 4

— 4 tablespoons butter, plus
  extra for greasing
— 1 pounds 5 ounces chestnuts,
  peeled
— ⅔ cup beef stock
— 2 egg whites
— salt

Preheat the oven to 400°F. Grease a soufflé dish with butter. Blanch the chestnuts in boiling water for 5 minutes, then drain and peel. Bring a pan of lightly salted water to a boil, add the chestnuts, and simmer for 30 minutes. Mash the chestnuts in a pan. Pour in the stock, add the butter, and season with salt. Place on low heat and stir until the puree is fairly dry, then remove from the heat and let cool. Whisk the egg whites until stiff and fold into the mixture. Spoon into four ramekins, place on a baking sheet and bake for about 12–15 minutes, until the soufflé only has a slight wobble in the center. Serve in the ramekins on individual plates.

CHESTNUT FRITTERS

FRITTELLE DI CASTAGNE

Preparation time: *10 min*
Cooking time: *10 min*
Serves 4

— 4½ cups sweet chestnut flour
— scant 1 cup pine nuts
— 1 pinch baking powder
— olive oil, for frying
— confectioners' sugar,
  for dusting

Sift the flour into a large bowl and stir in enough water, a spoonful at a time, until a fairly soft batter is formed. Stir in the pine nuts and baking powder. Heat plenty of olive oil in a skillet, then add spoonfuls of the batter and fry, turning once, for a few minutes, until golden brown. Remove with a spatula and drain on paper towels. Dust with confectioners' sugar and serve hot.

MASHED CHESTNUTS

PURÉ DI CASTAGNE

Preparation time: *20 min*
Cooking time: *1¼ hours*
Serves 4

— 1¾ pounds chestnuts
— 1 bay leaf
— 1 cup hot milk
— 2 tablespoons butter

Make a horizontal slit in the concave part of each chestnut shell. Put the nuts into a pan, add the bay leaf, pour in boiling water to cover, and cook for 1 hour. Drain and discard the bay leaf. When the chestnuts are cool enough to handle, peel off the shells and skins and mash in a bowl. Warm a serving dish. Heat gently, gradually stirring in the hot milk, stir in the butter, transfer to the serving dish, and serve immediately.

ROASTED CHESTNUTS WITH BRUSSELS SPROUTS

PHOTO PAGE 285

CASTAGNE ARROSTO CON CAVOLINI DI BRUXELLES

Preparation time: *1 hour*
Cooking time: *30 min*
Serves 4

— 1 pound 2 ounces chestnuts,
— 4 tablespoons butter, plus extra for greasing
— 1 shallot, chopped
— 1 pound 2 ounces Brussels sprouts, trimmed and coarse leaves removed
— juice of 1 lemon, strained
— pinch of freshly grated nutmeg
— scant 1 cup grated fontina cheese
— salt and pepper

Make a slit in each chestnut with a small knife. Put them into a pan, pour in water to cover, bring to a boil, and simmer for 20 minutes. Melt half the butter in another pan. Add the shallot and cook over low heat, stirring occasionally, for 5 minutes, until softened. Add the Brussels sprouts and lemon juice and pour in ½ cup of water. Season with salt and pepper and stir in the nutmeg. Cover and cook for about 10 minutes. Meanwhile, preheat the oven to 400°F. Grease an ovenproof dish with butter. Drain the chestnuts and rinse under cold running water. Remove and discard the shells and inner skins and put the chestnuts into the prepared dish. Add the Brussels sprouts, together with some of the cooking liquid. Sprinkle with the cheese, dot with the remaining butter, and bake for 30 minutes. Serve immediately straight from the dish.

ROASTED CHESTNUTS WITH BRUSSELS SPROUTS

CHESTNUT CAKE

PHOTO PAGE 287

CASTAGNACCIO

Preparation time: *15 min*
Cooking time: *40 min*
Serves 8

— 3 tablespoons olive oil,
  plus extra for brushing
  and drizzling
— 3½ cups chestnut flour
— 1 cup milk
— ¼ cup superfine sugar
— 2 tablespoons pine nuts
— 1 sprig rosemary
— salt

Preheat the oven to 350°F. Brush a round ¾-inch-deep cake pan with oil. Sift the chestnut flour into a bowl and gradually whisk in the milk and 1½ cups of water. (The mixture should be runny and creamy, so add a little more water if necessary.) Stir in the sugar, a pinch of salt, and the oil. Spoon the batter into the prepared pan, sprinkle with the pine nuts and rosemary needles, and drizzle with a little oil. Bake for 40 minutes. Remove the pan from the oven, put it on a wire rack, and let cool before turning out and serving.

LUCCHESE SOUFFLÉ

SOUFFLÉ LUCCHESE

Preparation time: *20 min*
Cooking time: *30 min*
Serves 4

— 7 tablespoons butter, melted,
  plus extra for greasing
— all-purpose flour, for greasing
— 2 eggs, separated
— scant ½ cup superfine sugar
— generous ¾ cup chestnut
  flour, sifted
— sifted confectioners' sugar,
  for dusting
— 1 cup heavy cream, whipped

Preheat the oven to 350°F. Grease and flour a 8-inch soufflé dish. Whisk together the egg yolks and superfine sugar in a bowl until pale and fluffy. Stir in the melted butter and chestnut flour. In a grease-free bowl, whisk the egg whites to stiff peaks and fold into the mixture. Pour the soufflé mixture into the prepared dish and bake for about 30 minutes. Remove the soufflé from the oven and let cool slightly before turning it out onto a serving plate. Dust with the confectioners' sugar and serve lukewarm, handing around the whipped cream separately.

CHESTNUT CAKE

CHESTNUT PUDDING

BUDINO DI CASTAGNE

Preparation time: *45 min, plus 3 hours chilling*
Cooking time: *45 min*
Serves 6

— 1 pound 2 ounces chestnuts, shelled
— 2¼ cups milk
— ½ teaspoon vanilla extract
— scant 1 cup blanched almonds, plus extra to garnish
— ¼ cup superfine sugar
— ⅔ cup light cream
— salt

Blanch the chestnuts in boiling water for 20 minutes, then drain and peel. Put the chestnuts into a pan. Combine the milk, vanilla, and a pinch of salt in a pitcher and pour over. Cover and cook over medium heat for 45 minutes, until the chestnuts are soft. Meanwhile, preheat the oven to 350°F. Spread out the almonds on a baking sheet and toast in the oven, stirring occasionally, for about 5 minutes, until golden brown and aromatic. Remove from the oven, let cool, then chop. Mash the chestnuts, together with the cooking liquid, into a clean pan. Heat the chestnut puree and stir in the sugar and chopped almonds until evenly mixed. Remove the pan from the heat and stir in the cream. Pour the mixture into a mold and let cool, then chill in the refrigerator for 3 hours. Just before serving, turn out the pudding onto a dish and garnish with almonds.

CHESTNUT CREAM

CREMA DI CASTAGNE

Preparation time: *15 min*
Cooking time: *1 hour*
Serves 6–8

— 2¼ pounds chestnuts, shelled, or 1¼ pounds canned chestnuts
— 1 cup superfine sugar
— 1 teaspoon vanilla extract
— scant 1 cup heavy cream
— salt

Blanch the chestnuts in boiling water for 5 minutes, then drain and peel. Bring a pan of lightly salted water to a boil, add the chestnuts, and simmer for 30 minutes. Meanwhile, put the superfine sugar and vanilla extract into a small pan, pour in 1 cup of water, and heat gently, stirring until the sugar has dissolved, then simmer, without stirring, for about 10 minutes, until syrupy. Remove the pan from the heat. Drain the chestnuts, stir into the syrup, return the pan to the heat, and boil for 15 minutes. Remove the pan from the heat, remove the chestnuts with a slotted spoon, reserving the syrup, and mash in a bowl. Stir in the syrup and let cool. Whip the cream until thick, then fold it into the chestnut mixture. Divide the mixture among 6 serving dishes and store in a cool place until required.

MUSHROOM SAUCE

SALSA DI FUNGHI

Preparation time: *10 min,*
plus 1 hour soaking
Cooking time: *40 min*
Serves *4*

— 20 g/¾ oz dried mushrooms
— 65 g/2½ oz butter
— ½ shallot, chopped
— 100 ml/3½ fl oz dry
   white wine
— dash Marsala
— 200 ml/7 fl oz vegetable stock
— salt

Put the mushrooms into a heatproof bowl, pour in hot water to cover and leave to soak for 1 hour, then drain, reserving the soaking liquid. Squeeze out the excess moisture and chop the mushrooms. Strain the soaking liquid into a bowl. Melt the butter in a frying pan. Add the shallot and cook over low heat, stirring occasionally, for 5 minutes, until softened. Stir in the mushrooms and cook, occasionally stirring in 1 tablespoon of the reserved liquid, for 15 minutes. Mix together the wine and Marsala in a jug, pour the mixture over the mushrooms and cook until the alcohol has evaporated. Pour in the stock and cook for a further 15 minutes, then season to taste with salt.

MELTING BAKED PORCINI

FUNGHI CROGIOLATI AL FORNO

Preparation time: *25 min*
Cooking time: *10 min*
Serves *4*

— 100 ml/3½ fl oz olive oil,
   plus extra for brushing
— 800 g/1¾ lb porcini
   mushrooms
— 1 sprig parsley, chopped
— 1 clove garlic, chopped
— soft part of 2 bread rolls,
   crumbled
— salt and pepper

Preheat the oven to 180°C/350°F/Gas Mark 4. Brush an ovenproof dish with oil. Separate the mushroom caps and stems and clean, wash and dry both. Pour 5 tablespoons of the olive oil into a bowl and season with salt and pepper. Add the mushroom caps and leave to marinate. Mix together the parsley, garlic, breadcrumbs and remaining oil in another bowl. Take the mushroom caps out of the marinade, put them on a rack and put in the oven briefly to dry. Chop the mushroom stems and place in the prepared dish. Put them into the caps, gill side up, on top of the chopped stems and sprinkle with the breadcrumb mixture. Drizzle with a little of the marinade. Bake for 10 minutes.

PORCINI MUSHROOM DUMPLINGS

CANEDERLI AI FUNGHI PORCINI

Preparation time: *45 min*
Cooking time: *20 min*
Serves 6

— 300 g/11 oz day-old bread,
   crusts removed and torn into
   very small pieces
— 100 ml/3½ fl oz single
   cream
— 3 tablespoons warmed milk
— 100 g/3½ oz butter
— 3 eggs, lightly beaten
— 1 clove garlic
— 200 g/7 oz porcini
   mushrooms, thinly sliced
— 1 sprig parsley,
   finely chopped
— 1 sprig marjoram,
   finely chopped
— salt and pepper

To serve:
— 50 g/2 oz butter, melted
— 50 g/2 oz Parmesan
   cheese, grated

Put the pieces of bread into a large heatproof bowl. Stir in the cream and warmed milk, and leave to soak until the bread has absorbed all the liquid. Melt 50 g/2 oz of the butter and add to the bread. Stir in the eggs and season with salt and pepper. Heat the remaining butter with the garlic clove in a pan. Add the mushrooms and cook over low heat, stirring occasionally, for 15 minutes. Remove and discard the garlic, and stir in the parsley, marjoram and a pinch of salt. Remove from the heat and leave to cool slightly, then stir the mushrooms into the bread mixture. Shape the mixture into balls 5–6 cm/2–2½ inches in diameter. Bring a large pan of salted water to the boil, then reduce the heat to a simmer. Add the dumplings and simmer for 15 minutes. Remove with a slotted spoon and transfer to a warmed serving dish. Drizzle with the melted butter and serve immediately with the grated cheese.

TAGLIATELLE WITH MUSHROOMS

TAGLIATELLE AI FUNGHI

Preparation time: *30 min*
Cooking time: *45 min*
Serves 4

— 25 g/1 oz dried porcini
   mushrooms
— 1 small onion
— 2 tablespoons olive oil
— 5 tablespoons dry white wine
— 3 tablespoons concentrated
   tomato purée
— 275 g/10 oz fresh tagliatelle
— 40 g/1½ oz Parmesan
   cheese, grated
— salt

Put the mushrooms into a bowl, add warm water to cover and leave to soak for 20 minutes. Drain, squeeze out the liquid and chop finely with the onion. Heat the oil in a pan, add the mushrooms and onion and cook over low heat, stirring occasionally, for 5 minutes. Stir in 120 ml/ 4 fl oz water and season lightly with salt. Add the white wine and cook until the alcohol has evaporated, then stir in the tomato purée. Simmer over medium heat for 30 minutes. Bring a large pan of salted water to the boil. Add the tagliatelle and cook for 2–3 minutes until al dente. Drain, sprinkle with the cheese and toss with the mushroom sauce.

BARLEY AND PORCINI SOUP

ZUPPA D'ORZO E PORCINI

Preparation time: *30 min*
Cooking time: *35 min*
Serves 4–6

— 40 g/1½ oz dried porcini
  mushrooms
— 150 g/15 oz pearl barley
— 2 tablespoons olive oil
— 1 onion, chopped
— 200 g/7 oz courgettes,
  thinly sliced
— 1.5 litres/2½ pints
  beef stock
— salt

Put the mushrooms into a bowl, add warm water to cover and leave to soak for 20 minutes. Meanwhile, bring a large pan of salted water to the boil. Add the barley and cook for 10 minutes, then drain. Heat the oil in a small pan. Add the onion and cook over low heat, stirring occasionally, for 5 minutes. Meanwhile, drain the mushrooms and squeeze out the excess moisture. Tear them into small pieces and add to the pan. Cook for a few minutes, then add the courgettes and cook for a few more minutes. Stir in the pearl barley and the stock, season with salt and cook, stirring occasionally, for 20 minutes, until the barley, mushrooms and vegetables are tender. Ladle into warmed soup bowls and serve immediately.

MUSHROOM OMELETTE

OMELETTE AGLI CHAMPIGNON

Preparation time: *10 min*
Cooking time: *10 min*
Serves 4

— 50 g/2 oz butter
— 2 shallots, finely chopped
— 100 g/3½ oz button
  mushrooms, finely chopped
— 1 sprig parsley, finely chopped
— 6 eggs
— salt and pepper

Melt half the butter in a pan. Add the shallots and cook over low heat, stirring occasionally, for 2 minutes. Add the mushrooms and parsley, and cook for a further 2 minutes, then remove the pan from the heat. Lightly beat the eggs with 1 tablespoon water and season lightly with salt and pepper. Melt the remaining butter in a frying pan over medium-high heat. Pour in the egg mixture and tilt and rotate the pan to spread evenly. Cook for 10 seconds, then lift the cooked base with a palette knife to allow the uncooked egg to run underneath. Continue cooking in this way until the omelette is just set underneath but the top is still soft and creamy. Spoon the mushroom and shallot mixture on top of one half of the omelette and fold the other half over it. Slide onto a plate and serve immediately.

MUSHROOM AND PINE NUT SALAD

PHOTO PAGE 293

INSALATA DI FUNGHI E PINOLI

Preparation time: *50 min,
plus 2 hours chilling*
Cooking time: *15–20 min*
Serves *8–10*

— 300 g/11 oz mixed salad
  leaves, such as Cos lettuce,
  frisée, radicchio and chicory
— 120 ml/4 fl oz olive oil
— 1 clove garlic, lightly crushed
— 450 g/1 lb porcini
  mushrooms, thinly sliced
— 50 g/2 oz pine nuts
— 2 tablespoons raspberry
  vinegar
— 200 g/7 oz Brie cheese, diced
— salt and pepper
— basil leaves, to garnish

Separate all the salad leaves, put them into a bowl, cover with clingfilm and chill in the refrigerator for 2 hours. Shortly before serving, take the salad leaves out of the refrigerator and transfer to a salad bowl. Heat half the oil in a frying pan with the garlic clove and cook until the garlic is lightly browned, then remove with a slotted spoon and discard. Add the mushrooms and cook over low heat, stirring occasionally, for 10–15 minutes. Stir in the pine nuts and cook for a further 5 minutes, then remove from the heat and tip the contents of the frying pan over the salad. Pour the remaining oil into the same frying pan, add the raspberry vinegar and season with salt and pepper. Heat quickly, taste and add a little more raspberry vinegar if necessary, then drizzle over the salad. Sprinkle with the diced cheese, garnish with basil leaves and serve immediately.

MUSHROOM FLAN

SFOGLIATA AI FUNGHI

Preparation time: *40 min*
Cooking time: *25 min*
Serves *4*

— 3 tablespoons olive oil
— 1 clove garlic, crushed
— 500 g/1 lb 2 oz mixed
  mushrooms, such as field,
  parasols and porcini
— ¼ quantity béchamel
  sauce (see page 51)
— 5 tablespoons grated
  Parmesan cheese
— 2 tablespoons finely chopped
  chervil
— 225 g/8 oz puff pastry dough,
  thawed if frozen
— plain flour, for dusting
— salt and pepper

Heat the oil in a pan, add the garlic clove and cook over low heat, stirring frequently, for a few minutes, until the garlic is lightly browned. Remove the garlic and discard. Increase the heat to medium. Add the mushrooms and cook, stirring occasionally, for 15 minutes. Meanwhile, gently heat the béchamel sauce, stirring occasionally, then remove from the heat, stir in the Parmesan and season lightly with salt and pepper. Season the mushrooms with salt and pepper and remove from the heat, sprinkle with the chopped chervil, stir and set aside. Preheat the oven to 220°C/425°F/Gas Mark 7. Line a 24-cm/9½-inch flan tin with baking parchment. Roll out the dough on a lightly floured surface and use to line the prepared tin, trimming off the excess. Chill the pastry case for 20 minutes or until firm, then prick it all over with a fork. Spoon the mushroom mixture into the pastry case and spread out evenly, then pour the cheese sauce evenly over the top. Bake for 20 minutes, until set. Remove from the oven, transfer the flan to a serving dish and serve immediately.

MUSHROOM AND PINE NUT SALAD

MUSHROOM RISOTTO

PHOTO PAGE 294

RISOTTO AI FUNGHI

Preparation time: *10 min*
Cooking time: *30 min*
Serves 4

— 1 litre/1¾ pints hot
  vegetable stock
— 80 g/3 oz butter
— 3 tablespoons olive oil
— 400 g/14 oz mixed
  mushrooms, thinly sliced
— 1 onion, finely chopped
— 320 g/11½ oz risotto rice
— salt and pepper

Pour the stock into a pan and bring to the boil. Meanwhile, melt 25 g/1 oz of the butter with 1 tablespoon of the oil in a pan. Add the mushrooms, season with salt and pepper, cover and cook over low heat. Melt half the remaining butter with the remaining oil in a large pan. Add the onion and cook over low heat, stirring occasionally, for 5 minutes, until softened. Stir in the rice and cook, stirring constantly, for 1–2 minutes, until all the grains are coated with oil. Add a ladleful of the hot stock and cook, stirring constantly, until it has been absorbed. Continue to add the hot stock, a ladleful at a time, stirring constantly until each addition has been absorbed before adding the next, about 20 minutes. Gently stir about one-third of the mushrooms into the risotto. Remove from the heat, gently stir in the remaining butter and transfer to a warmed serving dish. Spoon the remaining mushrooms into the centre and serve immediately.

PORCINI WITH TARRAGON

FUNGHI PORCINI AL DRAGONCELLO

Preparation time: *35 min*
Cooking time: *25 min*
Serves 4

— 8 porcini mushrooms
— 50 g/2 oz butter
— 1 sprig tarragon, chopped
— juice 1 lemon, strained
— salt and pepper

Preheat the oven to 160°C/325°F/Gas Mark 3. Line a roasting tin with foil. Separate the porcini caps and stems and set the stems aside for another dish. Put the caps in the roasting tin and place in the oven for 25 minutes, or until they have dried out. If the caps are very big, make a cut in their tops with a knife. Melt the butter in a pan, add the mushrooms and tarragon, season with salt and pepper and cook over low heat for 20 minutes. Sprinkle with the lemon juice and cook until it has evaporated, then serve.

MUSHROOM PILAF TIMBALE

PHOTO PAGE 297

TORTINO DI PILAF AI FUNGHI

Preparation time: 20 *min,*
plus 6 hours soaking
Cooking time: 35 *min*
Serves 4

— 50 g/2 oz dried mixed
  mushrooms
— 2 tablespoons olive oil
— 1 sprig parsley, finely chopped
— 100 ml/3½ fl oz dry
  white wine
— 475 ml/17 fl oz hot
  vegetable stock
— 200 g/7 oz risotto rice
— pinch saffron threads

Put the mushrooms in a heatproof bowl, add warm water to cover and leave to soak for at least 6 hours. Drain well, squeeze out the excess moisture and chop finely. Heat the oil in a large pan. Add the mushrooms and half the parsley and cook over low heat, stirring constantly, for 1 minute. Pour in the wine and a very little hot stock and simmer gently for 15 minutes. Add the rice and cook, stirring constantly, for 1 minute, then pour in the remaining hot stock and simmer for 5 minutes. Cover with a tight-fitting lid, turn off the heat and leave to stand for 12 minutes until the rice has absorbed all the stock and is tender. Do not lift the lid during this time. Stir in the remaining parsley. Rinse out a dariole or other small mould with water and spoon a quarter of the rice mixture into it, pressing it down gently and levelling the surface. Turn out on to an individual serving plate. Repeat this process for each serving. Sprinkle with saffron threads.

MUSHROOM FRICASSÉE

FUNGHI IN FRICASSEA

Preparation time: 20 *min*
Cooking time: 25 *min*
Serves 4

— 2 tablespoons olive oil
— 1 clove garlic, crushed
— 1 tablespoon finely chopped
  wild mint leaves or 3 sprigs
  parsley, finely chopped
— 600 g/1 lb 5 oz porcini
  mushrooms, thinly sliced
— 2 egg yolks
— juice 1 lemon, strained
— salt

Heat the oil in a pan. Add the garlic clove and wild mint or parsley and cook over low heat, stirring frequently, for a few minutes, until the garlic is lightly brown. Remove with a slotted spoon and discard. Add the mushrooms, season lightly with salt and cook over very low heat, stirring occasionally, for 20 minutes, sprinkling occasionally with a little hot water if becoming too dry. Beat the egg yolks with the lemon juice and a pinch of salt in a bowl. Remove the pan from the heat and add the egg and lemon mixture, constantly stirring quickly. (The egg mixture should not become hot enough to cook and solidify but should remain creamy.) Transfer to a warmed serving dish and serve immediately.

MUSHROOM PILAF TIMBALES

POLENTA PASTICCIATA WITH MUSHROOMS

FLORENTINE MUSHROOMS

CHAMPIGNON ALLA FIORENTINA

Preparation time: *20 min*
Cooking time: *40 min*
Serves 4

— 500 g/1 lb 2 oz spinach,
  coarse stalks removed
— 80 g/3 oz butter, plus extra
  for greasing
— 1 tablespoon olive oil
— 1 onion, finely chopped
— 500 g/1 lb 2 oz button
  mushrooms, thinly sliced
— 2–3 tablespoons grated
  Parmesan cheese
— salt and pepper

Wash spinach but do not dry and and cook in a pan over low heat, turning once or twice for 5 minutes, until wilted. Drain and squeeze out the excess moisture, then chop. Melt 25 g/1 oz of the butter with the oil in a small pan. Add the onion and 1 tablespoon water and cook, stirring occasionally, for 5 minutes, until softened. Melt half the remaining butter in another pan, add the spinach and heat gently. Melt the remaining butter in a third pan. Add the mushrooms, season lightly with salt and cook over low heat, stirring occasionally, for 20 minutes. Meanwhile, preheat the oven to 180°C/350°F/Gas Mark 4. Grease an ovenproof dish with butter. Spread the spinach evenly over the prepared dish and top with half the onion. Sprinkle with half the cheese and season with pepper. Cover with the mushrooms, the remaining onion and the remaining cheese and season lightly with pepper. Bake for 20 minutes and serve immediately.

POLENTA PASTICCIATA WITH MUSHROOMS

PHOTO PAGE 298

POLENTA PASTICCIATA AI FUNGHI

Preparation time: *1½ hours, plus cooling*
Cooking time: *1 hour*
Serves 4

— 100 g/3½ oz dried
  mushrooms
— 350 g/12 oz coarse
  polenta
— 50 g/2 oz butter, plus extra
  for greasing
— 1 clove garlic
— 1 quantity béchamel sauce
  (see page 51)
— 50 g/2 oz Parmesan cheese,
  grated
— salt and pepper

Soak the mushrooms in warm water for 20 minutes. To make a stiff polenta, bring 500 ml / 2½ pints of salted water to a boil. Sprinkle the flour into the pan while stirring it frequently, about 45–60 minutes. Pour into a tray and leave to cool and set. Meanwhile, melt 25 g/1 oz of the butter in a pan, add the garlic and cook until it turns golden brown, then discard it. Drain the mushrooms, squeezing out as much liquid as possible, and add to the pan. Season with salt and pepper and cook for 10 minutes. Stir the mushrooms and their cooking juices into the béchamel sauce with half the Parmesan. Preheat the oven to 180°C/350°F/Gas Mark 4 and grease an ovenproof dish with butter. Cut the cold polenta into slices and arrange in alternating layers with the mushroom mixture in the prepared dish, ending with a layer of polenta. Dot with the remaining butter, sprinkle with the remaining Parmesan and bake for about 1 hour.

MUSHROOM AND CHEESE TIMBALES

SFORMATINI DI FUNGHI ALLA FONTINA

Preparation time: *25 min*
Cooking time: *15–20 min*
Serves 6

— 25 g/1 oz butter, plus extra
  for greasing
— 3 tablespoons olive oil
— 1 clove garlic, crushed
— 750 g/1 lb 10 oz mixed
  mushrooms
— 150 g/5 oz fontina cheese,
  diced
— 500 ml/18 fl oz lukewarm
  béchamel sauce (see page 51)
— 3 egg yolks
— 1 sprig parsley, finely chopped
— 1 egg white
— 3 tablespoons fine fresh
  breadcrumbs
— salt and pepper

Heat the butter, oil and garlic clove in a frying pan, stirring frequently, for a few minutes, until the garlic is lightly browned. Remove the garlic and discard. Add the mushrooms to the pan, cover and cook, stirring occasionally, for 15–20 minutes. Preheat the oven to 200°C/400°F/Gas Mark 6. Grease 6 ramekins with butter and chill in the refrigerator. Stir the fontina into the béchamel sauce, then add the egg yolks, 1 at a time, and stir in the parsley. Using a grease-free bowl, whisk the egg white to stiff peaks and fold into the sauce, then season with salt and pepper. Remove the ramekins from the refrigerator and sprinkle with the breadcrumbs. Put 3 tablespoons of the béchamel mixture into each ramekin. Divide the mushrooms and their cooking juices among the ramekins and cover with the remaining béchamel sauce. Put the ramekins into a roasting tin, pour in hot water to come about halfway up the sides and bake for 15–20 minutes. Remove from the oven and leave to stand for a few minutes, then turn out onto a serving dish. Serve hot or warm.

WARM MUSHROOM SALAD WITH ORANGE DRESSING

INSALATA TIEPIDA DI PORCINI IN SALSETTA
AL SUCCO D'ARANCIA

Preparation time: *20 min*
Cooking time: *25 min*
Serves 4

— thinly pared rind and juice of
  ½ orange
— 800 g/1¾ lb porcini
  mushrooms, thinly sliced
— 4–5 tablespoons olive oil
— 1 clove garlic, lightly crushed
— 2 tablespoons sherry vinegar
— 1 red onion, very thinly sliced
— salt and pepper

Cut the orange rind into strips, add to a small pan of boiling water and blanch for 2 minutes, then drain and set aside. Heat 2 tablespoons of the oil in a frying pan with the garlic clove. Cook over low heat until the garlic is golden brown. Remove and discard. Add the mushrooms and cook over low heat, stirring occasionally, for 5–10 minutes, but do not allow them to brown. Transfer the mushrooms to a salad bowl. Strain the orange juice into a bowl, whisk in the remaining oil, the vinegar and strips of orange rind and season with salt and pepper. Pour the dressing over the mushrooms, add the onion slices, toss well and leave to stand for 15 minutes. Toss once more and serve.

BLACK TRUFFLE SAUCE

SALSA AL TARTUFO NERO

Preparation time: *25 min*
Serves 4

— 2 fresh black truffles
— 3 salted anchovies, heads
    removed, cleaned and filleted,
    soaked in cold water for
    10 minutes, drained and
    finely chopped
— 150 ml/¼ pint light olive oil
— dash lemon juice

Clean the truffles with a small damp brush. Grate into a bowl and add the anchovies. Stir in the olive oil to make a fairly runny sauce. (Use a light, delicately flavoured oil so that the truffle flavour dominates.) Just before serving, sprinkle with a dash of lemon juice. This sauce can be served with tagliolini.

RISOTTO WITH WHITE TRUFFLE AND PARMESAN

RISOTTO AL PARMIGIANO E TARTUFO BIANCO D'ALBA

Preparation time: *10 min*
Cooking time: *25 min*
Serves 4

— 1.5 litres/2½ pints
    vegetable stock
— 65 g/2½ oz butter
— 1 shallot, finely chopped
— 320 g/11½ oz risotto rice
— 50 g/2 oz Parmesan
    cheese, grated
— 25 g/1 oz white truffle,
    very thinly sliced
— salt

Pour the stock into a pan and bring to the boil. Meanwhile, melt half the butter in a deep pan. Add the shallot and cook over low heat, stirring occasionally, for 5 minutes, until softened. Stir in the rice and cook, stirring, for 2 minutes, until all the grains are coated with butter. Add a ladleful of the hot stock and cook, stirring constantly, until absorbed. Continue to add the hot stock, a ladleful at a time, stirring constantly after each addition, about 20 minutes. Remove from the heat, season generously with salt, add the remaining butter and the Parmesan and stir. Transfer to a warmed serving dish and sprinkle with the truffle slices. Serve immediately.

TAGLIERINI WITH TRUFFLES

TAGLIERINI TARTUFATI

Preparation time: *15 min*
Cooking time: *8 min*
Serves 4

— 50 g/2 oz butter
— 1 tablespoon double cream
— 25 g/1 oz tube truffle paste
— 275 g/10 oz fresh taglierini
— 40 g/1½ oz Parmesan
  cheese, grated
— salt and freshly ground
  white pepper

Melt the butter in a heatproof bowl set over a pan of simmering water. Add the cream and mix well. Add about 10 cm/4 inches of the truffle paste and mix well again. Taste and, if necessary, add more truffle paste. Cook the taglierini in plenty of salted boiling water for 2–3 minutes until al dente. Drain, transfer to a warmed serving dish and toss with the truffle butter. Season with white pepper, sprinkle with Parmesan and serve immediately.

FRIED EGGS WITH POLENTA AND TRUFFLE

PHOTO PAGE 303

UOVA FRITTE CON POLENTA E TARTUFO

Preparation time: *5 min*
Cooking time: *10 min*
Serves 4

— 80 g/3 oz butter
— 8 slices cooked polenta
— 8 eggs
— 1 small white truffle
— salt and pepper

Melt half the butter in a frying pan. Add the polenta slices and cook, turning once, until golden brown. Remove with a fish slice, drain on kitchen paper and keep warm. Melt half the remaining butter in another frying pan. Break the eggs on to a plate, 1 at a time, and slide into the pan. (Don't try to cook more than 4 at the same time.) Gather the whites around the yolks with a slotted spoon to keep them neat and separated. Cook until the whites are set and very lightly browned and the yolks are still soft. Remove with a fish slice and drain on kitchen paper. Season with salt and pepper and place on top of the polenta slices. Cook the remaining eggs in the same way, adding more butter. Shave the truffle over the eggs and serve immediately.

FRIED EGGS WITH POLENTA AND TRUFFLE

PUMPKIN GRATIN SOUP

MINESTRA DI ZUCCA GRATINATA

Preparation time: *25 min*
Cooking time: *50 min*
Serves 4

— 1 litre/1¾ pints milk
— 3 potatoes, cut into wedges
— 500 g/1 lb 2 oz pumpkin,
  peeled, de-seeded and
  chopped
— 1 sage leaf
— 100 ml/3½ fl oz double cream
— 4 slices rustic bread
— 50 g/2 oz Parmesan cheese,
  grated
— salt and pepper

Pour the milk and 350 ml/12 fl oz water into a large pan and bring to the boil. Add the potatoes, pumpkin and sage, season with salt and pepper and bring back to the boil. Reduce the heat to medium and simmer for 40 minutes. Remove the sage leaf, transfer the mixture to a food processor or blender and process to a purée. Pour the purée into a pan, stir in the cream, taste and adjust the seasoning, if necessary, and cook for a few minutes more. Meanwhile, preheat the grill. Ladle the soup into individual flameproof soup plates, top with a slice of bread, sprinkle with the Parmesan and place under the grill. Serve as soon as the cheese has melted.

FUSILLI IN PUMPKIN CREAM

FUSILLI CON CREMA ALLA ZUCCA

Preparation time: *10 min*
Cooking time: *1¼ hours*
Serves 4

— 500 g/1 lb 2 oz pumpkin
— 500 g/1 lb 2 oz turnip tops,
  coarse leaves removed
— 350 g/12 oz fusilli
— 3 tablespoons olive oil
— 1 clove garlic, finely chopped
— 1 onion, chopped
— 150 ml/¼ pint double
  cream
— 50 g/2 oz Parmesan cheese,
  grated
— salt and pepper

Preheat the oven to 180°C/350°F/Gas Mark 4. Slice the top off the pumpkin, scoop out and discard the seeds and membranes, then scoop out the pulp and slice. Reserve the pumpkin shell. Put the pumpkin slices into a large ovenproof dish and bake for 40 minutes. Meanwhile, bring a large pan of salted water to the boil. Add the turnip tops and cook for 10–15 minutes, then drain well and leave to cool. Remove the pumpkin from the oven and mash well until smooth. Bring a large pan of salted water to the boil. Add the pasta, bring back to the boil and cook for 8–10 minutes, until tender but still al dente. Meanwhile, heat the oil in a large pan. Add the garlic and onion, and cook over low heat, stirring occasionally, for 5 minutes, until softened. Drain the pasta and add to the pan with the turnip tops, pumpkin purée, cream and grated cheese, and season with salt and pepper. Mix gently and cook for a few minutes to heat through, then spoon the mixture into the reserved pumpkin shell and serve.

PUMPKIN, RICE, AND BEAN SOUP

MINESTRA DI ZUCCA, RISO E FAGIOLI

Preparation time: *25 min*
Cooking time: *1¼ hours*
Serves 4

— 2¼ cups milk
— 1 x 2¼-pounds pumpkin,
  peeled, seeded, and diced
— ¾ cup fresh borlotti beans
— 4–5 mint leaves, chopped
— ½ cup risotto rice
— 2 tablespoons butter
— ⅔ cup grated Parmesan
  cheese
— salt and pepper

Pour the milk into a large pan and add 8½ cups of water, the diced pumpkin, beans, and mint. Bring to a boil, reduce the heat, cover, and simmer, stirring occasionally, for 1 hour. Season with salt and pepper and mash the pumpkin. Add the rice and simmer for another 15–20 minutes, until tender. Add the butter and sprinkle with the cheese, remove from the heat, and serve.

SAVORY PUMPKIN TART

TORTA DI ZUCCA

Preparation time: *30 min*
Cooking time: *55 min*
Serves 4

— ¾ cup dried mushrooms
— 4 tablespoons olive oil
— 1 onion, chopped
— 1 x 2¼-pounds pumpkin,
  peeled, seeded, and diced
— all-purpose flour, for dusting
— 1 clove garlic
— butter, for greasing
— 2 eggs, lightly beaten
— generous 1 cup grated
  Parmesan cheese
— pinch freshly grated nutmeg
— 14 ounces basic pie dough,
  thawed if frozen
— 3½ ounces fontina cheese,
  sliced
— salt and pepper

Put the mushrooms into a heatproof bowl, pour in lukewarm water to cover, and let soak. Heat half of the oil in a pan. Add the onion and cook over low heat, stirring occasionally, for 5 minutes, until softened and translucent. Add the pumpkin, 3–4 tablespoons of water, and a pinch of salt and cook, stirring continuously, until the pumpkin has broken down into a puree. Remove the pan from the heat. Drain the mushrooms and squeeze out the excess liquid. Heat the remaining oil in a skillet. Add the garlic clove and cook over low heat, stirring frequently, for a few minutes, until golden, then remove and discard. Add the mushrooms and cook over low heat, stirring frequently, for 15 minutes, then remove from the heat. Meanwhile, preheat the oven to 400°F. Grease and flour a cake pan. Combine the pumpkin puree, eggs, Parmesan, mushrooms, and nutmeg in a bowl and season with pepper. Roll out the dough on a lightly floured counter and use to line the pan, making sure that it comes up the sides. Spoon in the pumpkin mixture, place the slices of fontina on top, and bake for 40 minutes.

PUMPKIN FLAN

PUMPKIN FLAN

PHOTO PAGE 306

FLAN DI ZUCCA

Preparation time: *45 min, plus cooling*
Cooking time: *1 hour 10 min*
Serves 4

— 2 tablespoons butter, plus extra for greasing
— 1 quantity béchamel sauce (see page 51)
— 1 onion, sliced
— 1 x 2¼-pounds pumpkin, peeled, seeded, and diced
— ⅔ cup grated Parmesan cheese
— 2 egg yolks
— ⅓ cup pine nuts
— salt and pepper

Preheat the oven to 325°F. Grease a tart pan with butter. Make the béchamel sauce. Melt the butter in a large pan. Add the onion and cook over low heat, stirring occasionally, for 5 minutes, until softened. Add the pumpkin and ⅔ cup of water and cook, stirring and mashing occasionally, until the pumpkin turns to a soft puree. Stir in the béchamel sauce, Parmesan, egg yolks, and pine nuts, and season with salt and pepper. Pour the mixture into the prepared pan and bake for 1 hour, then increase the oven temperature to 350°F and bake for another 10 minutes. Remove the pan from the oven and let cool completely before turning out. This flan is excellent served with spinach in butter.

PUMPKIN SOUP

VELLUTATA DI ZUCCA

Preparation time: *20 min*
Cooking time: *35 min*
Serves 4

— 4¼ cups vegetable stock
— 1 x 1¾-pounds pumpkin, peeled, seeded, and cut into chunks
— 1 onion, chopped
— 1 clove garlic, chopped
— pinch freshly grated nutmeg
— 4 tablespoons heavy cream
— salt and pepper

Pour the stock into a large pan and bring to a boil. Add the pumpkin, onion, and garlic, reduce the heat, cover, and simmer for 30 minutes. Drain the pumpkin mixture, reserving the stock. Put the pumpkin mixture into a food processor or blender and process until smooth—if necessary, add some of the reserved stock, and process again. Pour the soup into a clean pan and reheat. Season to taste with salt and stir in the nutmeg. Ladle the soup into individual bowls, swirl in the cream, and add a pinch of pepper. Serve immediately.

PUMPKIN GNOCCHI WITH ORANGE BUTTER

GNOCCHETTI DI ZUCCA AL BURRO E SUCCO D'ARANCIA

Preparation time: *1 hour,*
plus 1 hour resting
Cooking time: *15–20 min*
Serves 6

— 1 x 2-pound pumpkin,
   peeled, seeded, and chopped
— 3½ potatoes, peeled
   and cut into wedges
— 1 egg, lightly beaten
— 1 tablespoon olive oil
— 2¾ cups all-purpose flour
— ⅔ cups Parmesan cheese,
   grated
— salt

For the sauce:
— 2 oranges
— 6 tablespoons butter
— freshly ground white pepper

Steam the pumpkin flesh for 25 minutes, until tender. Steam the potatoes for 25 minutes, until tender. Remove from the heat and mash the pumpkin and potatoes in a bowl. Stir in the egg, oil, and flour, then cover with plastic wrap and let rest for 1 hour. Shape the dough into long rolls about ¾ inch in diameter and cut into 1-inch lengths. Press the little rolls of dough against the prongs of a fork to make them curved and ribbed on one side to make the gnocchi. For the sauce, thinly pare a strip of rind from half of an orange and cut into very thin strips. Squeeze both the oranges and strain the juice. Melt the butter in a heatproof bowl set over a pan of barely simmering water, then pour into a pan and heat gently until it turns very pale golden brown. Stir in the orange juice and simmer over low heat.

Bring a large pan of salted water to a boil. Add the gnocchi and cook for about 5 minutes, until they rise to the surface. Remove with a slotted spoon and transfer to a warm serving dish, spoon the orange butter sauce over them, sprinkle with the Parmesan, and season lightly with pepper. Garnish with orange rind and serve immediately.

BAKED PUMPKIN WITH POTATOES

ZUCCA AL FORNO CON PATATE

Preparation time: *25 min*
Cooking time: *1 hour*
Serves 4

— olive oil, for brushing
   and drizzling
— 1 x 1¼-pounds pumpkin,
   peeled and seeded
— 4 potatoes, cut into ¼-inch
   slices
— 1 onion, sliced into rings
— 4 ripe tomatoes, peeled
   and diced
— salt and pepper

Preheat the oven to 350°F. Brush a roasting pan with olive oil. Cut the pumpkin flesh into ½-inch slices. Make alternate layers of potato, onion, and pumpkin in the prepared pan. Sprinkle with the diced tomatoes, drizzle with oil, and season with salt and pepper. Bake for 1 hour, until all the vegetables are tender. Let stand for 5 minutes, then serve.

PUMPKIN GNOCCHI WITH ORANGE BUTTER

PUMPKIN WITH ROSEMARY

PUMPKIN WITH ROSEMARY

PHOTO PAGE 310

ZUCCA AL ROSMARINO

Preparation time: *15 min*
Cooking time: *25 min*
Serves 4

— 2 tablespoons olive oil
— 2 cloves garlic
— 1 x 1½-pounds pumpkin,
  peeled, seeded, and thinly
  sliced
— ¾ cup dry white wine
— 1½ teaspoons fresh rosemary,
  finely chopped
— salt and pepper

Heat the oil in a pan, add the garlic and pumpkin, and cook over medium heat, stirring occasionally, until the garlic cloves start to turn brown, then remove and discard. Pour in the wine and cook until the alcohol has evaporated, then lower the heat and simmer until tender. Season with salt and pepper to taste and sprinkle with the rosemary. Cook for another few minutes, then serve.

PUMPKIN AND SHRIMP RISOTTO

RISOTTO CON ZUCCA E GAMBERONI

Preparation time: *45 min*
Cooking time: *25 min*
Serves 4

— 8 large shrimp
— 6 tablespoons butter
— 1 shallot, finely chopped
— 1½ cups diced pumpkin flesh
— 4¼ cups hot vegetable
  or fish stock
— 1 tablespoon olive oil
— 1⅔ cups risotto rice
— scant ½ cup dry white wine
— salt and pepper

Peel the shrimp and reserve the heads and shells. Devein and coarsely chop the shrimp. Melt 2 tablespoons of the butter in a pan. Add the shallot and shrimp heads and shells and cook over low heat, occasionally stirring and crushing the heads and shells with the prongs of a fork, for 10 minutes. Remove and discard the heads and shells, add the diced pumpkin, season with salt and pepper, and cook for another 5 minutes. Pour the stock into a large pan and bring to a boil. Meanwhile, melt half of the remaining butter with the oil in another large pan. Add the pumpkin and shrimp, then stir in the rice and cook, stirring continuously, for 1–2 minutes, until all the grains are coated with oil. Pour in the wine and cook until the alcohol has evaporated. Add a ladleful of the hot stock and cook, stirring continuously, until it has been absorbed. Continue to add the hot stock, a ladleful at a time, stirring continuously until each addition has been absorbed, for about 20 minutes. Remove the risotto from the heat, stir in the remaining butter, transfer to a warm serving dish, and serve immediately.

SPICED PUMPKIN WITH PARSLEY

ZUCCA PICCANTE AL PREZZEMOLO

Preparation time: *15 min*
Cooking time: *15 min*
Serves 4

— 1 x 1¾-pounds pumpkin,
  peeled, halved, and seeded
— 2–3 tablespoons olive oil
— 1 hot chile
— 1 onion, finely chopped
— pinch of freshly grated
  nutmeg
— 2 tablespoons chopped
  curly parsley
— salt

Cut the pumpkin into wedges and then into slices about ¼-inch thick. Heat the oil in a large skillet. Add the chile and onion and cook over low heat, stirring occasionally, for 5 minutes, until the onion is softened and translucent. Add the pumpkin slices and nutmeg and season with salt. Stir well and cook for 5–7 minutes, until the pumpkin is tender, then remove the pan from the heat. Remove and discard the chile, transfer the mixture to a serving dish, sprinkle with the parsley, and serve. This is an excellent accompaniment to a selection of seasonal cheeses.

PUMPKIN WITH WILD FENNEL

ZUCCA GIALLA AL FINOCCHIO SELVATICO

Preparation time: *25 min*
Cooking time: *20 min*
Serves 4–6

— 1 x 2¼-pounds pumpkin,
  peeled, seeded, and diced
— 3 tablespoons olive oil
— 1 clove garlic, crushed
— 1 bunch wild fennel,
  chopped, or 1 teaspoon
  fennel seeds, crushed
— salt and pepper

Put the pumpkin, oil, garlic, and fennel into a large skillet, pour in scant 1 tablespoon water, and season with salt and pepper. Cover and cook over low heat, stirring occasionally, for 20 minutes, until all the liquid has been absorbed. Transfer to a warm serving dish and serve lukewarm.

PUMPKIN ROULADE WITH CHEESE AND SPINACH

ROTOLO DI ZUCCA CACIOTTA E SPINACI

Preparation time: *2 ½ hours,*
plus 7 hours chilling
Cooking time: *30 min*
Serves 8

For the pasta dough:
— 2¾ cups all-purpose flour,
   plus extra for dusting
— 2 eggs
— 2 egg yolks

For the filling:
— 1 x 1¾-pounds pumpkin,
   peeled, seeded, and diced
— scant ½ cup olive oil
— 4 shallots, chopped
— 1 clove garlic, peeled
— 4 leaves sage, chopped
— 1 pound 5 ounces spinach,
   coarse stalks removed
— 3 cups grated caciotta or
   provolone cheese,
— 1 egg, lightly beaten
— butter, for greasing
— salt and pepper

To make the pasta dough, sift the flour into a mound on a counter and make a well in the center. Add the eggs and egg yolks to the well and, using your fingers, gradually incorporate the dry ingredients. Knead well for about 10 minutes, then shape into a ball, wrap in plastic wrap, and let rest in the refrigerator for at least 1 hour. Remove the dough from the refrigerator, unwrap, and divide in half. Roll out each piece into a very thin rectangular sheet on a lightly floured counter. Bring a large pan of salted water to a boil. Add 1 pasta sheet and boil for 2–3 minutes, then remove with tongs, and spread out to dry on a dish towel. Repeat with the second sheet.

Let the sheets cool to a leathery consistency while preparing the filling. For the filling, bring a pan of water to a boil. Add the pumpkin and cook for 10 minutes, then drain and set aside. Heat 4 tablespoons of the oil in a skillet. Add the shallots, garlic, and sage leaves and cook over low heat, stirring frequently, for 10 minutes. Remove and discard the garlic clove. Season with salt and pepper and heat through. Remove from the heat, transfer to a bowl, mash, and let cool. Heat the remaining oil in the same skillet. Add the spinach, cover, and cook over low heat, stirring and turning once or twice, for 10 minutes. Season with salt, remove from the heat, drain well, chop, and let cool.

Spread out the pumpkin mixture, spinach, and cheese on 1 pasta sheet, leaving a ¾-inch margin all around. Brush the edges with the beaten egg, cover with the second pasta sheet, pressing the edges to seal. Using the dish towel to help you and, starting at a short side, roll up lengthwise like a jelly roll. Twist the ends of the roulade together like candy wrappers and chill in the refrigerator for 6 hours.

Preheat the oven to 350°F. Grease an ovenproof dish with butter. Cut the roulade into ¾-inch slices and put them, overlapping slightly, into the prepared dish. Bake until golden.

SWEET PUMPKIN TART

CROSTATA DI ZUCCA

Preparation time: *1 hour plus 1 hour draining*
Cooking time: *40 min*
Serves 8

— 1 x 1 pound 10 ounce-pumpkin, peeled, seeded, and chopped
— butter, for greasing
— 9 ounces basic pie dough, thawed if frozen
— all-purpose flour, for dusting
— 2 eggs
— ¾ cup cane sugar
— ½ cup heavy cream
— 1 tablespoon sherry
— pinch of ground cinnamon
— pinch of freshly grated nutmeg
— pinch of ground ginger
— salt
— ice cream, to serve

Put the pumpkin into a pan, pour in 1 cup of water, add a pinch of salt, and bring to a boil. Reduce the heat, cover, and simmer gently for 25 minutes, until tender. Drain well and mash. Put into a strainer, then top with a bowl weighed down with a couple of cans. Let drain for an hour, then put in a food processor or blender, and process until smooth.

Preheat the oven to 350°F. Grease an 8-inch cake pan with butter. Roll out the dough on a lightly floured counter and use to line the prepared pan. Trim the edges and reserve the offcuts. Line the pie shell with aluminum foil and fill it halfway with pie weights. Put the pan on a baking sheet and bake for 10 minutes, then remove from the oven and remove the pie weights and foil. Return the pan to the oven and bake for another 5–10 minutes, until dry and just beginning to color.

Meanwhile, roll out the reserved dough trimmings and cut out leaves for decoration. Beat together the eggs and sugar in a bowl until pale and fluffy. Stir in the pumpkin, then add the cream, sherry, cinnamon, nutmeg, and ginger, and mix well. Remove the pan from the oven and pour the mixture into the pie shell. Arrange the pastry leaves on top and cover with a sheet of aluminum foil with holes punched in it. Bake for 10 minutes, then remove the aluminum foil and bake for another 20 minutes. Remove from the oven and serve the tart warm or at room temperature, accompanied by ice cream.

BEET RISOTTO

RISOTTO AL SUCO DI BARBABIETOLE

Preparation time: *15 min*
Cooking time: *30 min*
Serves 4

— 1 pound 5 ounces beets, peeled
— 4¼ cups vegetable stock
— 4 tablespoons butter
— 1 shallot, chopped
— 1⅔ cups risotto rice
— scant 1 cup dry white wine
— ½ cup grated Parmesan cheese
— 4 tablespoons heavy cream
— salt

Juice the beet in a juicer and set the juice aside. Pour the stock into a pan and bring to a boil, then reduce the heat and simmer. Meanwhile, melt half of the butter in another pan. Add the shallot and cook over low heat, stirring occasionally, for 5 minutes, until softened. Add the rice and cook, stirring continuously, for 2 minutes, until all the grains are coated in butter and are translucent. Sprinkle in the wine and cook until the alcohol has evaporated. Add a ladleful of the hot stock and cook, stirring continuously, until absorbed. Continue to add the hot stock, a ladleful at a time, stirring continuously until each addition has been absorbed, about 20 minutes. Remove the pan from the heat. Stir in the remaining butter, grated cheese, and cream. Season with salt, stir well, then pour the beet juice over the risotto. Mix gently until the color is even. Let rest for 1 minute, then serve.

BEET SOUP

ZUPPA DI BARBABIETOLE

Preparation time: *30 min*
Cooking time: *1 hour*
Serves 4

— 2 tablespoons butter
— 2 tablespoons all-purpose flour
— 1 tablespoon red wine vinegar
— 1 onion, diced
— 2 carrots, diced
— 11 ounces beet, peeled and diced
— scant 1 cup plain yogurt
— 1 tablespoon chopped parsley
— salt
— croutons, to serve

Melt the butter in a large pan. Stir in the flour and cook, stirring continuously, for 2 minutes. Add the vinegar and 6¼ cups warm water, stirring until smooth. Season with salt, add the onion, carrots, and beets and bring to a boil. Reduce the heat, cover, and simmer for 1 hour. Remove the pan from the heat, let cool slightly, then ladle the mixture into a food processor or blender. Process to a smooth puree. Ladle into a warm soup tureen and stir in the yogurt and parsley. Serve with croutons.

BEET GREENS AND POTATO PIE

PASTICCIO DI BIETOLE E PATATE

Preparation time: *1 hour*
Cooking time: *20 min*
Serves 6

— 2¼ pounds wild sea beet
    greens or Swiss chard, coarse
    stalks removed
— 2 tablespoons olive oil,
    plus extra for brushing
— 10 ounces Italian sausage,
    skinned
— 1 chile, seeded and
    finely chopped
— 1 clove garlic, peeled
— 4 potatoes, peeled and cut
    into wedges
— 3 hard-cooked eggs, shelled
    and cut into small pieces
— 3 ounces smoked mozzarella
    or Provolone cheese,
    coarsely grated
— 2–3 tablespoons fresh
    bread crumbs
— salt and pepper

Bring a pan of salted water to a boil. Add the beet greens and blanch for a few minutes, then drain, reserving the cooking liquid. Chop the greens coarsely and set aside.

Heat the oil in a large pan. Crumble in the sausage meat and add the chile and garlic clove. Cook over low heat, stirring occasionally, for a few minutes, until the garlic is lightly browned. Remove the garlic with a slotted spoon and discard. Add the beet greens and potatoes, pour in the reserved cooking liquid, season with salt and pepper, and cook for about 40 minutes, adding more liquid, if necessary.

Meanwhile, preheat the oven to 375°F. Brush a 9-inch ovenproof dish with oil. Drain the mixture in a colander, then place in a bowl. Stir in the hard-cooked eggs, cheese, and bread crumbs. Transfer the mixture to the prepared dish and bake for 15–20 minutes. Remove from the oven and let stand for 5 minutes before serving.

BEET AND CAVIAR SALAD

INSALATA DI BARBABIETOLE AL CAVIALE

Preparation time: *20 min*
Serves 4

— 2 cooked beets
— 1 chive, finely chopped
— olive oil, for drizzling
— red wine vinegar, for
    drizzling
— scant 1 cup heavy cream
— few drops lemon juice
— 4 teaspoons caviar
— salt and pepper

Peel the beets, cut into slices, then into strips. Put into a bowl, add the chive, and drizzle with oil and vinegar. Season with salt and pepper. Lightly whip the cream and add the lemon juice. Divide the beet strips among 4 individual plates and add a spoonful of the cream, topped with a teaspoonful of caviar, on the side.

MIXED BEET SALAD

INSALATA MISTA DI BARBABIETOLE

Preparation time: *25 min*
Cooking time: *15–20 min*
Serves 4

— 3 potatoes
— scant 1 cup green beans
— 2 cooked beets, sliced
— 1 tomato, cut into wedges
— 3 hard-cooked eggs, shelled
— 3½ ounces Gruyere cheese, diced
— 3½ tablespoons capers, rinsed and drained
— 3 pickled gherkins, drained and coarsely chopped
— 1 tablespoon chopped parsley
— 1 tablespoon white wine vinegar
— ⅔-1 cup olive oil
— salt and pepper

Cook the potatoes in a pan of salted boiling water for 15–20 minutes, until tender. Cook the green beans in another pan of salted boiling water for 5–10 minutes, or until tender but still al dente, then drain and refresh under cold running water. Drain the potatoes and cut into slices. Put the potatoes, beets, and tomato into a salad bowl. Cut 2 of the eggs into wedges and add to the bowl with the cheese. Surround these ingredients with the green beans. Coarsely chop the remaining egg. Put the chopped egg, capers, gherkins, parsley, vinegar, and ⅔ cup of the oil in a blender, season with salt and pepper, and process to a thick sauce, adding more oil if necessary. Serve the salad handing around the dressing separately.

BEETS WITH ORANGE

BARBABIETOLE ALL'ARANCIA

Preparation time: *20 min*
Serves 4

— 3 cooked beets
— 2 oranges
— small bunch chives, chopped
— olive oil, for drizzling
— apple vinegar, for drizzling

Peel the beets and cut them into ⅛-inch thick slices. Peel the oranges, removing all traces of bitter white pith, and slice thinly. Put alternate slices of beet and orange on a serving plate in concentric circles. Sprinkle the chives over them and drizzle with a little oil and apple vinegar. Set aside in a cool place for a few minutes for the flavors to mingle, then serve.

BEET AND CELERY ROOT WITH MUSTARD MAYONNAISE

BARBABIETOLE E SEDANO RAPA CON MAIONESE ALLA SENAPE

Preparation time: *40 min, plus 1 hour draining*
Serves 4–6

— 1 pound 10 ounces celery root
— 1 tablespoon white wine vinegar
— 1 tablespoon medium-hot mustard
— 1 teaspoon honey
— 4 tablespoons light olive oil
— 1 pound 2 ounces cooked beets, peeled
— olive oil, for drizzling
— strained lemon juice, for drizzling
— salt

For the mayonnaise:
— 1 egg yolk
— 2 tablespoons whole-grain mustard
— scant 1 cup sunflower oil
— 1–2 teaspoons white wine vinegar
— salt

Grate the celery root into thin strips, put them into a fine strainer, sprinkling each layer with salt, and let drain for 1 hour.

Meanwhile, whisk together the vinegar, medium mustard, and honey in a bowl, then gradually whisk in the light olive oil until thoroughly combined.

Pat the beet dry with paper towels, cut into strips, and put into a bowl. Drizzle with olive oil and lemon juice to taste and set aside.

To make the mayonnaise, beat the egg yolk with the mustard in a bowl. Gradually beat in the oil, a drop at a time, until the mixture begins to thicken, then in a steady stream until it has been completely incorporated. Stir in a small pinch of salt and the vinegar, and let rest in a cool place.

Rinse the celery root and pat dry with paper towels, then add to the vinaigrette. Set aside and keep cool until ready to serve. Put the celery root mixture and beet mixture separately on a serving plate and serve immediately, handing around the mustard mayonnaise separately.

CARROTS WITH BELGIAN ENDIVE

CAROTE CON CICORIA

Preparation time: *10 min*
Serves 4

— 1¾ pounds carrots,
  thinly sliced
— olive oil, for drizzling
— juice 1 lemon, strained
— 2 slices fresh pineapple,
  cored and diced
— 1 head Belgian endive
— salt and pepper

Put the carrot slices into a bowl, drizzle with olive oil and lemon juice, and season with salt and pepper. Stir in the pineapple. Separate the Belgian endive leaves and put them on a serving plate in concentric circles. Spoon the carrot mixture into the Belgian endive leaves and serve.

CARROT AND PAPRIKA SOUP

CAROTE ALLA PAPRIKA IN BRODO

Preparation time: *25 min*
Cooking time: *30 min*
Serves 4

— 4¼ cups vegetable stock
— 4¼ cups grated carrots
— ¾ cup diced potatoes
— pinch of sweet paprika
— 2 tablespoons butter
— juice of 1 lemon, strained
— salt

To serve:
— 4 slices rye bread
— grated Parmesan cheese

Bring the stock to a boil in a large pan. Add the carrots and potatoes, stir in the paprika, and season with salt. Reduce the heat and simmer for 30 minutes, then remove from the heat. Transfer the soup to a food processor or blender and process until smooth. Pour the soup into a bowl and stir in the butter and lemon juice. Put the slices of bread into 4 individual soup bowls and sprinkle with grated cheese. Ladle the carrot soup over them and serve immediately.

CREAM OF CARROT AND FENNEL SOUP

CREMA DI CAROTE E FINOCCHI

Preparation time: *25 min*
Cooking time: *25 min*
Serves 4

— 6 carrots, trimmed
— 3 fennel bulbs, trimmed
— olive oil, for drizzling
— ½ grated Parmesan cheese
— salt and pepper
— small slices bread, fried in
   a little oil or butter, to serve

Put the carrots and fennel into a pan, pour in 4¼ cups of water, add a pinch of salt, and bring to a boil. Reduce the heat and simmer for 15–20 minutes, until tender. Transfer to a food processor or blender and process until smooth. Pour the mixture into a clean pan and cook briefly to thicken. Season to taste with salt. Ladle into 4 soup plates, drizzle with a little oil, season with a pinch of pepper, and sprinkle with the grated cheese. Serve immediately, handing around the fried bread separately.

CARROTS WITH TALEGGIO CHEESE

PHOTO PAGE 321

CAROTE AL TALEGGIO

Preparation time: *50 min*
Cooking time: *20 min*
Serves 4

— 2 tablespoons olive oil
— 1 shallot, finely chopped
— 1¾ pounds carrots, cut into
   ½-inch slices
— butter, for greasing
— 6 ounces Taleggio cheese
— 2 eggs, lightly beaten
— ½ cup grated Parmesan
   cheese
— scant ½ cup milk
— 1 tablespoon chopped
   parsley
— salt and pepper

Heat the oil in a skillet. Add the shallot and cook over low heat, stirring occasionally, for 5 minutes, until softened and translucent. Stir in the carrots and cook, stirring occasionally, for 10 minutes. Season with salt and pepper and cook for another 5 minutes, then remove from the heat. Preheat the oven to 425°F. Grease an ovenproof dish with butter. Mash the Taleggio in a bowl until creamy, then beat in the eggs, Parmesan, and milk. Season with salt and pepper. Put the carrots into the prepared dish, spreading them out evenly. Cover with the taleggio cream and bake for 20 minutes. Remove from the oven, sprinkle with the chopped parsley, and serve.

CARROTS WITH TALEGGIO CHEESE

BABY CARROTS IN HERB SAUCE

BABY CARROTS IN HERB SAUCE

PHOTO PAGE 322

CAROTE NOVELLE IN SALSA D'ERBE

Preparation time: *10 min*
Cooking time: *25 min*
Serves *4*

— 1¾ pounds baby carrots,
  trimmed
— 3 tablespoons butter
— 1 tablespoon olive oil
— 1 clove garlic, peeled
— 2 tablespoons mixed herbs,
  such as parsley, basil,
  and marjoram, chopped
— 4 tablespoons heavy cream
— salt and pepper

Bring a pan of lightly salted water to a boil. Add the carrots and cook for 10 minutes, until tender. Melt the butter with the oil in a skillet. Add the garlic clove and cook over low heat, stirring frequently, for a few minutes, until golden brown. Remove the garlic and discard. Add the carrots to the pan and cook for a few minutes, then add the chopped herbs, season with salt and pepper, and stir in the cream. Simmer gently for 10–15 minutes, until the sauce has reduced. If the sauce seems a little too thick, stir in a little lukewarm water or milk. Remove from the heat and serve warm.

CARROT FRITTERS

SCHIACCIATE DI CAROTE

Preparation time: *45 min*
Cooking time: *20 min*
Serves *4*

— 1 pound 2 ounces carrots,
  trimmed
— ⅔ cup all-purpose flour
— 1 egg, separated
— 2 tablespoons butter
— 1 tablespoon brandy
— pinch of freshly grated
  nutmeg
— ½ cup olive oil
— salt

Put the carrots into a pan, pour in water to cover, add a pinch of salt, and bring to a boil. Reduce the heat and simmer for 20 minutes. Drain and slice, then put into a clean pan and mash to a puree. Heat gently, stirring frequently, for a few minutes to eliminate any excess moisture and to thicken. Remove from the heat, stir in 2 tablespoons of the flour, the egg yolk, butter, brandy, and nutmeg, and season with salt. Spread out the remaining flour in a shallow dish. Using a grease-free bowl, whisk the egg white until soft peaks form. Shape the carrot mixture into balls and flatten gently. Coat with flour, then dip into the beaten egg white. Heat the oil in a large skillet. Add the carrot fritters, in batches if necessary, and cook until lightly browned. Remove with a slotted spoon and drain on paper towels. Transfer to a warm serving dish and serve immediately.

BRAISED CARROTS WITH CELERY

CAROTE BRASATE AL SEDANO

Preparation time: 30 *min*
Cooking time: 55 *min*
Serves 6

— 2 tablespoons butter
— 2 tablespoons olive oil
— 5 ounces pearl onions, peeled
— 1¾ pounds carrots, thinly sliced
— 1 celery heart, cut into small pieces
— 1 sprig rosemary, very finely chopped
— pinch of ground cinnamon (optional)
— salt and pepper

Melt the butter with the oil in a pan. Add the onions and cook over low heat, stirring occasionally, for 10–15 minutes, until golden brown. Add the carrots and celery, season with salt and pepper, and stir in the rosemary leaves and 2 tablespoons of hot water. Cover and simmer gently, shaking the pan occasionally, for 40 minutes. Sprinkle with the cinnamon, if using, stir well, and transfer to a warm serving dish. Serve immediately.

GNOCCHETTI SALAD WITH CARROTS AND MINT

GNOCCHETTI SARDI CON CAROTE ALLA MENTA

Preparation time: 30 *min*
Cooking time: 35 *min*
Serves 4

— 11 ounces gnocchetti sardi pasta
— 2 tablespoons olive oil, plus extra for drizzling
— 1 clove garlic
— 1 onion, chopped
— 11 ounces baby carrots, cut into thin sticks
— 10 small mint leaves, chopped
— salt and pepper

Bring a pan of salted water to a boil. Add the pasta, bring back to a boil, and cook for about 10 minutes, or according to the package directions, until tender but still al dente. Drain and refresh under cold running water, then transfer to a salad bowl and drizzle over a little oil. Heat the oil in a skillet. Add the garlic clove and onion and cook over low heat, stirring occasionally, for 10 minutes, until golden. Remove and discard the garlic. Add the carrots and cook, stirring occasionally, for 15 minutes. Add the mint and cook for another 5 minutes. Season with salt and pepper and mix well. Add the carrot mixture to the gnocchetti, stir well, and let cool before serving.

CARROT, APPLE, AND RAISIN SALAD

INSALATA DI CAROTE E MELE ALL'UVETTA

Preparation time: *25 min*
Serves 4

— ⅓ cup golden raisins
— 2 tablespoons sugar
— grated rind and strained juice of 1 lemon
— juice of 1 lime, strained
— 6 carrots, thinly sliced
— 2 tart apples, such as Granny Smith
— olive oil, for drizzling
— salt and pepper

Put the golden raisins into a heatproof bowl, pour in warm water to cover, and let soak for 15 minutes. Meanwhile, dissolve the sugar in 2 tablespoons of warm water in a small bowl. Put the lemon rind and juice and lime juice into a salad bowl and stir in the sugar mixture. Add the carrots. Peel and coarsely grate the apples, and stir into the salad. Drain the golden raisins, squeeze out the excess liquid, and add to the salad. Drizzle with the olive oil, season with salt and pepper, and serve immediately.

CARROTS WITH ACACIA HONEY

CAROTE AL MIELE D'ACACIA

Preparation time: *15 min*
Cooking time: *25–35 min*
Serves 4

— 7 tablespoons butter
— 1¾ pounds carrots, thickly sliced
— 1 tablespoon acacia honey
— scant ½ cup brandy
— 2 tablespoons chopped parsley
— salt

Melt the butter in a skillet. Add the carrots and cook over medium heat, stirring occasionally, for a few minutes. Season with salt and stir again, then stir in the honey. Cover and cook, stirring occasionally, for 20–30 minutes. If necessary, add a little hot water from time to time. Towards the end of the cooking time, sprinkle the brandy over the carrots and cook until the alcohol has evaporated. Remove from the heat and sprinkle over the parsley.

SESAME-GLAZED CARROTS

CAROTE GLASSATE AL SESAMO

Preparation time: *25 min*
Cooking time: *25 min*
Serves 4

— 1 pound 5 ounces carrots,
  thickly sliced
— 3 tablespoons butter
— 2 small onions, chopped
— grated rind and strained juice
  of ½ lemon
— 1 tablespoon toasted
  sesame seeds
— 2 tablespoons chopped
  parsley
— olive oil, for drizzling
— salt and pepper

Put the carrots into a large bowl, pour in water to cover, and stir in 2 teaspoons of salt. Let soak for 15 minutes. Meanwhile, melt the butter in a skillet. Add the onion and cook over low heat, stirring occasionally, for 5 minutes, until softened. Stir in the lemon rind and juice and cook for 2 minutes. Drain the carrots well and add to the skillet. Season with salt and a little pepper and cook for 10–15 minutes. Remove from the heat, transfer to a serving dish, and sprinkle over the toasted sesame seeds and chopped parsley. Drizzle with a little oil and serve.

CARROT, MÂCHE, AND BLACK OLIVE SALAD

INSALATA DI CAROTE, SONCINO E OLIVE NERE

Preparation time: *20 min*
Serves 4

— 3 carrots, julienned
— 7 ounces mâche,
  separated into leaves
— 1 cup pitted black olives
— olive oil, for drizzling
— white wine vinegar,
  for drizzling
— salt and pepper

Put the carrot strips into a salad bowl and add the mâche and olives. Drizzle with the oil and vinegar to taste, season with salt and pepper, and toss to mix. Let stand for 5 minutes to let the flavors mingle, then serve.

NEW POTATOES WITH ROSEMARY

PATATINE NOVELLE AL ROSMARINO

Preparation time: *15 min*
Cooking time: *15 min*
Serves 4

— 2 tablespoons butter
— scant ½ cup olive oil
— 1 sprig rosemary
— 1 clove garlic
— 1½ pounds new potatoes
— salt

Heat the butter and oil in a large pan, add the rosemary, garlic, and potatoes, stir, and cover. Cook over low heat until golden brown. Remove and discard the garlic and rosemary, sprinkle with salt, and serve.

POTATO, BEET GREENS, RICOTTA, AND PARMESAN ROLL

ROTOLO DI PATATE, ERBETTE, RICOTTA E PARMIGIANO

Preparation time: *1½ hours*
Cooking time: *40 min*
Serves 6

— 2¼ pounds potatoes
— scant 1 cup all-purpose flour, plus extra for dusting
— 1¾ pounds beet tops, coarse stalks removed
— 4 tablespoons butter, plus extra for greasing
— 2¼ cups ricotta cheese
— 1 egg, lightly beaten
— ⅔ grated Parmesan cheese
— pinch of freshly grated nutmeg
— salt and pepper

Put the unpeeled potatoes into a large pan, pour in water to cover, add a pinch of salt, and bring to a boil. Cook for 40 minutes, until tender. Drain, peel, and press them through a potato masher into a bowl. Sift in the flour and mix to a smooth and even dough. Roll out to ½-inch thick on a lightly floured counter. Bring a pan of salted water to a boil. Add the beet greens and cook for 10 minutes, then drain and chop finely. Melt 2 tablespoons of the butter in a pan. Add the beet greens and cook over low heat, stirring occasionally, for 10 minutes. Season with salt and pepper, and remove from the heat. Put the ricotta into a bowl and stir until light and creamy, then stir in the beet greens, egg, Parmesan, and nutmeg. Spread the mixture over the potato dough, roll up, wrap in a clean dish towel, tying the ends securely. Bring a large pan of water to a boil, then reduce the heat so that it is just simmering. Add the roll and simmer for 40 minutes. Lift out the roll and drain well, then unwrap and cut into thick slices. Preheat the broiler and grease a flameproof dish with butter. Put the slices into the prepared dish, dot with the remaining butter, and brown under the broiler. Serve immediately.

POTATO PUFFS

SGONFIOTTI DI PATATE

Preparation time: *35 min*
Cooking time: *40 min*
Serves *4*

— 4 potatoes, peeled
— 4¼ cups all-purpose flour,
  plus extra for dusting
— 4 tablespoons olive oil
— salt and pepper

Put the potatoes into a pan, pour in water to cover, add a pinch of salt, and bring to a boil. Cook for 25 minutes, then drain and mash in a bowl. Let cool, then stir in just enough flour to form a smooth dough that does not stick to your hands. Season with salt and pepper. Roll out on a lightly floured counter into a sheet and stamp out 1¾–2-inch rounds with a cookie cutter or small glass. Heat the oil in a skillet. Add the potato rounds, in batches, and cook for 5–10 minutes on each side, until puffed up and golden brown. Remove and keep warm while cooking the rest of the batches. Serve immediately.

POTATO GNOCCHI WITH TOMATOES AND BASIL

PHOTO PAGE 329

GNOCCHI DI PATATE AL POMODORO E BASILICO

Preparation time: *1 hour,
plus 1 hour resting*
Cooking time: *30 min*
Serves *4*

— 2¼ pounds potatoes
— 1¾ cups all-purpose flour,
  plus extra for dusting
— 1 egg, lightly beaten
— salt

For the sauce:
— 2¼ pounds plum tomatoes,
  peeled, seeded, and
  coarsely chopped
— 3 tablespoons olive oil
— 2 cloves garlic, finely
  chopped
— pinch of sugar
— 10 basil leaves
— ¼ cup grated Parmesan
  cheese
— salt and pepper

To make the gnocchi, peel the potatoes and steam for 25 minutes, until tender. Remove the potatoes from the steamer, then mash in a bowl. Stir in the flour, egg, and a pinch of salt. Shape the dough into long rolls about ¾ inch in diameter and cut into 1-inch lengths. Press them gently against a grater and spread out on a dish towel lightly dusted with flour. Let rest for 1 hour.

Meanwhile, make the sauce. Put the tomatoes, olive oil, garlic, and sugar into a pan and season with salt and pepper. Cover and cook over low heat, stirring occasionally, for 30 minutes, until pulpy. Bring a large pan of lightly salted water to a boil. Add the gnocchi, in batches, and cook until they rise to the surface. Remove with a slotted spoon and transfer to a warm serving dish. While the gnocchi are cooking, add the basil to the sauce. When all the gnocchi are cooked, pour the tomato sauce over them, sprinkle with the grated cheese, and serve immediately.

POTATO GNOCCHI WITH TOMATOES AND BASIL

PAN-FRIED POTATO PATTIES

PANCAKES DI PATATE

Preparation time: *40 min*
Cooking time: *25 min*
Serves *4*

— 4 potatoes
— 1–2 eggs
— 1 tablespoon all-purpose flour
— pinch of baking powder
— ½ teaspoon grated lemon rind
— 1 tablespoon finely chopped parsley
— 4 tablespoons olive oil
— salt and pepper

Preheat the oven to 300°F. Peel the potatoes and dry thoroughly with paper towels, then grate. Lightly beat the eggs in a bowl, then sift in the flour, baking powder, and a pinch each of salt and pepper. Add the lemon rind, parsley, and, last of all, the potatoes and mix well. Divide the mixture into 8 portions. Heat the oil in a large skillet. Add half of the patties and cook for 8–10 minutes on each side, until well browned. Remove with a spatula and keep warm in the oven while you cook the remaining patties. Serve immediately.

POTATO SALAD WITH DANDELIONS AND BLACK TRUFFLES

INSALATA DI PATATE DENTI DI LEONE E TARTUFO NERO

Preparation time: *25 min*
Cooking time: *40 min*
Serves *6*

— 5 potatoes
— 2 shallots, finely chopped
— olive oil, for drizzling
— 5½ cups dandelion leaves, torn into small pieces
— 2 tablespoons butter
— 20 walnut halves
— 2 small black truffles
— salt and pepper

Put the unpeeled potatoes into a pan, pour in water to cover, add a pinch of salt, and bring to a boil. Cook for 30–40 minutes, until tender. Drain, peel, and slice. Put the slices into a salad bowl and add the shallots. Drizzle with oil, season with salt and pepper, and stir gently. Let stand for a few minutes, then add the dandelion leaves. Melt the butter in a small pan, add the walnut halves, and cook, stirring frequently, for a few minutes, until very lightly browned. Remove with a slotted spoon and sprinkle over the lukewarm potato salad. Shave wafer-thin slices of truffle on top of the salad and serve immediately.

POTATO BUNDLES WITH PAPRIKA

CARTOCCIO DI PATATE ALL PAPRICA DOLCE

Preparation time: *10 min*
Cooking time: *1 hour*
Serves 4

— 2 tablespoons sweet paprika
— 4 large potatoes
— 7 tablespoons butter
— 2 sprigs tender rosemary
— salt

Preheat the oven to 400°F. Combine the paprika and salt in a bowl and roll the potatoes in the mixture. Cut out 4 sheets of aluminum foil, each large enough to enclose a potato. Put a pat of butter in the center of each. Put a potato on top, put another pat of butter on the potato, and sprinkle with 2–3 chopped rosemary needles. Fold up the aluminum foil to enclose the potatoes completely. Put the bundles on a baking sheet and bake for 1 hour. Remove from the oven and serve the potatoes in their bundles.

POTATO FRITTERS WITH GOAT CHEESE AND TOMATO

CROSTATINE DI PATATE AL POMODORO E FORMAGGIO CAPRINO

Preparation time: *30 min*
Cooking time: *30 min*
Serves 6

— 10 potatoes
— 3 small, semisharp goat cheeses, thinly sliced into rounds
— 3 plum tomatoes, thinly sliced into rounds
— 1 sprig rosemary, finely chopped
— 3 tablespoons olive oil, plus extra for drizzling
— salt and pepper

Peel and grate the potatoes into a colander. Sprinkle with salt and let drain for 10 minutes. Put the cheese and tomato slices on a plate, sprinkle with the rosemary, and season with pepper. Preheat the oven to 425°F. Heat the oil in a skillet. Add a few tablespoons of the grated potatoes and press each of them flat with the back of the spoon. Cook, turning occasionally, until a thin crust has formed on both sides. Remove from the skillet with a spatula and drain on paper towels. Repeat with the remaining potatoes. Put a slice of tomato and a slice of goat cheese on top of each potato fritter, drizzle with a couple of drops of oil, and season with salt. Put the fritters on 1–2 baking sheets and bake for 15 minutes. Remove from the oven and serve immediately.

BAKED POTATOES WITH GORGONZOLA CREAM

PATATE AL CARTOCCIO CON CREMA DI GORGONZOLA

Preparation time: *20 min*
Cooking time: *1 hour*
Serves 4

— 4 large potatoes, scrubbed
— 4 ounces Gorgonzola cheese
— 6 shelled walnuts, chopped
— 4 bay leaves
— salt

Preheat the oven to 400°F. Make 3 shallow cuts across the width of the potatoes, sprinkle them with salt, and wrap each potato in a square of aluminum foil. Bake in the oven for 50–60 minutes. Meanwhile, mash the Gorgonzola in a bowl until smooth and creamy, then mix in the chopped walnuts. When the potatoes are cooked, remove from the oven, open up the aluminum foil wrappings, and use a teaspoon to scoop out some of the flesh from the cuts. Fill each hollow with 1 tablespoon of the Gorgonzola mixture. Preheat the broiler and line the broil pan with aluminum foil. Place the potatoes in the broiler pan, filled side uppermost, put a bay leaf in each one, and broil until the cheese starts to melt. Discard the bay leaves. Serve immediately.

NEW POTATO AND BLACK OLIVE SALAD WITH LEMON MAYONNAISE

PHOTO PAGE 333

INSALATA DI PATATE NOVELLE E OLIVE NERE CON SALSA AL LIMONE

Preparation time: *20 min*
Cooking time: *35 min*
Serves 6

— 1¾ pounds new potatoes
— scant 1 cup dried black olives, pitted and halved
— 2 hard-cooked eggs, shelled and sliced
— salt

For the mayonnaise:
— 1 egg yolk
— 1 tablespoon Dijon mustard
— juice of 3 lemons, strained
— ¾ cup sunflower oil
— thinly pared rind of 1 lemon, julienned
— salt and pepper

Bring a pan of lightly salted water to a boil. Add the unpeeled potatoes and cook for 18 minutes, then drain and let cool. When they are cold, slice them and put into a salad bowl. Add the olives and hard-cooked eggs.

To make the dressing, whisk the egg yolk with the mustard and lemon juice in a bowl. Gradually whisk in the oil, 1 drop at a time to begin with. When the mixture begins to thicken, add the oil in a continuous thin stream. Stir in the lemon rind and season with salt and pepper. Stir the mayonnaise into the potato mixture and serve.

NEW POTATO AND BLACK OLIVE SALAD WITH MAYONNAISE

POTATO GRATIN WITH BACON AND THYME

POTATO CAKES WITH CHEESE AND SAGE

SCHIACCIATINE ALLA SALVIA

Preparation time: *15 min*
Cooking time: *40 min*
Serves 4

— 2¼ pounds potatoes
— 1 egg, lightly beaten
— ⅔ cup grated Parmesan
  cheese
— 2 tablespoons milk
— 3–4 sage leaves, finely
  chopped
— 1 teaspoon grated lemon rind
— all-purpose flour, for dusting
— 2 tablespoons butter
— 3 tablespoons olive oil
— salt and pepper

Put the unpeeled potatoes into a pan, pour in water to cover, add a pinch of salt, and bring to a boil. Cook for 25 minutes, until tender. Drain well, peel, and mash in a bowl. Stir in the egg, Parmesan, milk, sage, and grated lemon rind, and season with salt and pepper. Shape the mixture into about 12 balls, then slightly flatten each and dust with flour. Melt the butter with the oil in a skillet. Add the potato cakes, in batches, and cook for 5–8 minutes on each side, until golden brown. Remove and drain on paper towels. Keep warm while you cook the remaining batches, then serve.

POTATO GRATIN WITH BACON AND THYME

PHOTO PAGE 334

PURÈ GRATINATO CON BACON E TIMO

Preparation time: *30 min*
Cooking time: *1¼ hours*
Serves 4

— 2¼ pounds potatoes
— 4 tablespoons butter, plus
  extra for greasing
— 1 tablespoon olive oil
— 3½ ounces thick bacon, cut
  crosswise into thin strips
— 1 egg, lightly beaten
— 3 ounces provolone
  cheese, coarsely grated
— 3 sprigs thyme, finely
  chopped
— 4 tablespoons fresh
  bread crumbs
— salt and pepper

Peel the potatoes, cut into large pieces, and put into a steaming basket. Bring 2 inches of water to a boil in a pan. Insert the steamer, cover, and cook for 20–30 minutes, until tender. Transfer the potatoes to a bowl and crush with a fork, then let cool slightly.

Meanwhile, preheat the oven to 400°F. Grease an ovenproof dish with butter. Heat the oil in a skillet. Add the bacon strips and cook, turning occasionally, for 6–8 minutes, until slightly crisp. Combine the crushed potatoes, egg, and cheese and season with salt and pepper. Add the bacon and thyme. Spoon the potato mixture into the prepared dish, sprinkle with the bread crumbs, and dot with the butter. Bake for 30 minutes, until golden brown and crunchy on top. Serve immediately.

POTATOES BAKED IN SALT

PHOTO PAGE 337

PATATE AL SALE

Preparation time: *20 min*
Cooking time: *40 min*
Serves 6–8

— 3¼ pounds potatoes
— 2 tablespoons all-purpose flour
— 3 pounds coarse sea salt
— 2 egg whites
— 1 sprig sage, finely chopped
— 1 sprig rosemary, finely chopped
— pepper

Preheat the oven to 375°F. Peel and slice the potatoes, put them into a bowl of cold water, and set aside. In another bowl, Combine the flour, salt, egg whites, and just enough cold water to moisten the mixture without making it runny. Drain the potatoes and pat dry with a dish towel. Spread out half of the salt mixture in an ovenproof dish and put the potato slices on top, being careful not to leave any empty spaces. Sprinkle with the sage and rosemary, and cover with the remaining salt mixture. Bake for 40 minutes. Remove the dish from the oven, discard the salt "shell", making sure that no salt remains on the potatoes, and serve.

POTATO, CHEESE, AND LEEK GRATIN

TORTINO DI PATATE, FORMAGGIO E PORRI

Preparation time: *20 min*
Cooking time: *1 hour*
Serves 8

— 4½ pounds potatoes
— 5 tablespoons butter, plus extra for greasing
— 2 tablespoons olive oil
— 2 leeks, finely chopped
— 2 onions, thinly sliced
— ¼ cup fresh bread crumbs
— 1¾ cups mascarpone cheese
— 1 egg, lightly beaten
— salt and pepper

Put the unpeeled potatoes into a large pan, pour in water to cover, add a pinch of salt, and bring to a boil. Cook for 25 minutes, until tender. Drain, peel, and mash in a bowl. Melt 2 tablespoons of the butter with the oil in a pan. Add the leeks and onions and cook over low heat, stirring occasionally, for 5 minutes, until softened and translucent. Season lightly with salt and remove the pan from the heat. Preheat the oven to 350°F. Grease an ovenproof dish with butter and sprinkle with the bread crumbs. Melt the remaining butter in a heatproof bowl set over a pan of barely simmering water. Combine the potatoes, leek and onion mixture, mascarpone, and melted butter, and season with salt and pepper. Spoon the mixture into the prepared dish and gently smooth the surface with a spatula. Brush the surface with the beaten egg and bake for 20 minutes, until the top is golden brown. Serve immediately.

POTATOES BAKED IN SALT

POTATO TORTE WITH JUNIPER BERRIES

TORTIERA DI PATA AL GINEPRO

Preparation time: *25 min*
Cooking time: *50 min*
Serves *6*

— 1 tablespoon olive oil, plus
  extra for brushing
— 3 pounds potatoes
— 1 shallot, chopped
— 3–4 juniper berries, crushed
— 3 ounces bacon slices,
  chopped
—4 tablespoons butter
— salt and pepper

Preheat the oven to 425°F. Brush a 10½-inch cake pan with oil. Peel and thinly slice the potatoes, then pat dry with paper towels. Heat the oil in a skillet. Add the shallot and cook over low heat, stirring occasionally, for 5 minutes, until softened and translucent. Add the juniper berries and bacon, and cook, stirring occasionally, for another 5 minutes, then remove the skillet from the heat. Put a layer of potato slices, slightly overlapping, on the bottom of the prepared pan. Season with salt and pepper, top with some of the juniper-flavored bacon, and dot with 1 tablespoon of the butter. Continue making layers in this way until all the ingredients have been used, ending with a layer of potato slices dotted with butter. Cover with aluminum foil and bake for 20 minutes. Remove the foil, return the pan to the oven, and bake for another 30 minutes. Remove from the oven, cut into wedges, and serve.

CRISPY POTATOES WITH HORSERADISH SAUCE

PATATE CROCCANTI CON CREMA DI RAFANO

Preparation time: *20 min*
Cooking time: *40 min*
Serves *4*

— 1 tablespoon creamed
  horseradish
— ½ cup heavy cream
— small bunch chives, coarsely
  chopped
— 2 ½ pounds potatoes
— 3–4 tablespoons olive oil
— salt

Preheat the oven to 325°F. Line a roasting pan with aluminum foil. To make the horseradish sauce, combine the creamed horseradish, cream, chives, and a small pinch of salt in a bowl. Cover with plastic wrap and set aside in the refrigerator until required. Peel the potatoes, cut in half lengthwise, and then cut each half lengthwise into 2–3 pieces. Put into a bowl and toss with enough oil to coat well. Transfer to the prepared roasting pan and roast, turning occasionally, for 40 minutes, until golden brown and crisp. Transfer to a warm serving dish and sprinkle with a little salt. Serve immediately, handing around the horseradish sauce separately.

BAKED POTATOES WITH OREGANO

PATATE IN FORNO AL PROFUMO DI ORIGANO

Preparation time: *15 min*
Cooking time: *50 min*
Serves 8

— 8 potatoes
— ½ cup olive oil
— juice 3 lemons, strained
— 1 teaspoon dried oregano
— salt and pepper

Preheat the oven to 475°F. Cut the potatoes into quarters and place in a casserole. Pour in 1 cup of water, add the oil, lemon juice, and oregano, and season with salt and pepper. Stir well. Bake for 25 minutes, then turn the potatoes and add a very little water if necessary. Return to the oven and bake for another 25 minutes. Remove from the oven and serve immediately straight from the casserole.

POTATO, CHEESE, AND HAM CAKES

PICCOLI GATTÒ DI PATATE

Preparation time: *40 min*
Cooking time: *30 min*
Serves 6–8

— 2½ pounds potatoes
— 4 tablespoons butter, plus extra for greasing
— scant 1 cup milk
— 1½ cups fresh bread crumbs
— 1 cup grated Parmesan cheese
— scant 1 cup ricotta cheese, strained
— 2 eggs, lightly beaten
— 4½ ounces mozzarella cheese, diced
— 3 ounces ham, finely chopped
— 3 slices processed cheese, finely chopped
— salt and pepper

Put the unpeeled potatoes into a steaming basket. Bring 2 inches of water to a boil in a pan. Insert the steamer, cover, and steam for 20 minutes. Remove the potatoes from the steamer and peel. Mash in a bowl and set aside. Melt the butter, add the potatoes, and set over low heat. In a separate pan, warm the milk, then stir into the potatoes. Remove from the heat and let cool until lukewarm.

Meanwhile, preheat the oven to 350°F. Grease 6–8 ramekins and sprinkle with the bread crumbs, tipping out any excess. Reserve the remainder. Stir the Parmesan, ricotta, eggs, and a pinch each of salt and pepper into the potato mixture. Spoon the mixture into the prepared ramekins, filling them halfway. Combine the mozzarella, ham, and processed cheese, and sprinkle over the potato mixture. Cover with the remaining potato mixture and sprinkle with the remaining bread crumbs. Bake for about 30 minutes. Remove from the oven and turn out onto a warm serving dish. Serve immediately.

POTATO AND BELL PEPPER FRITTERS

POLENTA AND POTATO CAKE

POLENTA E PATATE ROSTIDE

Preparation time: *45 min*
Cooking time: *30 min*
Serves 4

— 6 potatoes
— ¼ cup olive oil
— 1 onion, very thinly sliced
— 2 slices cold, cooked polenta
  (see page 299), chopped
— salt and pepper

Put the unpeeled potatoes into a pan, pour in water to cover, add a pinch of salt, and bring to a boil. Cook for 20–25 minutes, until tender, then drain, peel, and chop. Heat 2 tablespoons of the oil in a skillet. Add the onion and cook over low heat, stirring occasionally, for 15 minutes, until softened and translucent. Add the polenta and potatoes and use a potato masher to crush the contents of the pan into a rough cake. After a few minutes, when the cake has browned on the underside, turn it with a spatula. Continue cooking, turning the cake once or twice more, until a crunchy crust has formed on both sides. Slide out of the skillet and serve immediately.

POTATO AND BELL PEPPER FRITTERS

PHOTO PAGE 340

FRITTELLE DI PATATE AL PEPERONE VERDE

Preparation time: *40 min*
Cooking time: *20 min*
Serves 4

— 4–5 potatoes
— 2 eggs, lightly beaten
— 1 small onion, finely
  chopped
— 1 small green bell pepper,
  seeded and julienned
— 6 tablespoons olive oil
— salt

Put the unpeeled potatoes into a large pan, pour in water to cover, add a pinch of salt, and bring to a boil. Cook for 20–25 minutes, until tender. Drain, peel, and mash into a bowl. Stir in the eggs, onion, bell pepper strips, and a pinch of salt, and mix well. Shape the mixture into thick, round patties. Chill for 30 minutes. Heat the oil in a large skillet. Add the patties, in batches, and cook for 5 minutes on each side, until lightly browned. Remove and drain on paper towels. Season with salt. Serve immediately.

SCORZONERA WITH ANCHOVIES

SCORZONERA ALLE ACCIUGHE

Preparation time: *20 min*
Cooking time: *30 min*
Serves 4

— juice of 1 lemon, strained
— 1½ pounds scorzonera,
   trimmed and peeled
— 4 ounces salted anchovies,
   heads removed, cleaned, and
   filleted, soaked in cold water
   for 10 minutes, and drained
— 2 tablespoons olive oil
— 1 tablespoon capers, drained,
   rinsed, and chopped
— 1 tablespoon white wine
   vinegar
— 1 sprig parsley, chopped
— salt

Fill a large pan with water, add the lemon juice, a pinch of salt, and the scorzonera, and bring to a boil. Lower the heat and simmer for 30 minutes. Meanwhile, chop the anchovy fillets. Heat the oil in a skillet, add the anchovies, and cook over low heat, mashing with a wooden spoon until almost disintegrated. Add the capers and vinegar and cook until the vinegar has evaporated, then remove the skillet from the heat. Drain and chop the scorzonera, and place on a warm serving dish. Spoon the anchovy sauce over, sprinkle with the parsley, and serve.

SCORZONERA WITH HORSERADISH

SCORZONERA AL CREN

Preparation time: *15 min*
Cooking time: *40 min*
Serves 4

— juice of 1 lemon, strained
— 1 pound 5 ounces scorzonera,
   peeled and chopped
— 1 tablespoon all-purpose flour
— scant 1 cup heavy cream
— 2 tablespoons white wine
   vinegar
— 2 tablespoons finely grated
   horseradish
— salt and pepper

Fill a bowl halfway with water and add half of the lemon juice, then immerse the scorzonera, in the acidulated water. Fill a large pan with water, add the flour, a pinch of salt, the scorzonera, and the remaining lemon juice, and bring to a boil. Lower the heat and simmer for about 30 minutes. Drain and let cool. Meanwhile, stiffly whip the cream, season with salt and pepper, and gently stir in the vinegar and horseradish. Place the scorzonera on a serving dish and spoon over the horseradish cream.

SCORZONERA FRITTERS

FRITTELLE DI SCORZONERA

Preparation time: *1 hour 10 min,
plus 2 hours resting*
Cooking time: *15–20 min*
Serves *4*

— juice of 1 lemon, strained
— 2¼ pounds scorzonera
— ⅔ cup grated Parmesan
 cheese
— 5 ounces thick ham slice,
 coarsely chopped
— 4–6 tablespoons olive oil
— salt

For the batter:
— ½ cup lukewarm milk
— 1¼ teaspoons dry active yeast
— 2¼ cups all-purpose flour
— 2 egg yolks
— salt

To make the batter, pour the milk into a small bowl and sprinkle the yeast over the surface. Let stand for 10–15 minutes, until frothy, then stir well. Sift the flour and a pinch of salt into a bowl and stir in the egg yolks. Stir in the yeast mixture and ½ cup of water and beat well to a thick, but fluid batter. Cover and let rest for 2 hours.

Fill a bowl halfway with water and stir in half the lemon juice. Trim off the ends of the scorzonera and scrape off the skin. Dice the flesh, adding it immediately to the acidulated water to prevent discoloration. Drain the scorzonera, transfer to a large pan, add the remaining lemon juice and a pinch of salt, and bring to a boil. Cook for 30 minutes, then drain and set aside. Add the scorzonera to the batter, stir in the cheese and ham, and mix. Heat 4 tablespoons of the oil in a large skillet. Add tablespoons of the scorzonera mixture, spaced well apart, and cook until golden. Remove and drain on paper towels. Cook the remaining mixture in the same way, adding more oil as required. Put the fritters on a warm serving plate, season with salt, and serve immediately.

SCORZONERA FRICASSEE

SCORZONERA IN FRICASSEA

Preparation time: *40 min*
Cooking time: *10 min*
Serves *4*

— juice of 2 lemons, strained
— 1½ pounds scorzonera,
 trimmed and peeled
— 2 tablespoons butter
— 2 egg yolks
— 1 sprig parsley, chopped
— salt

Fill a large pan with water, add half of the lemon juice, a pinch of salt, and the scorzonera, and bring to a boil. Lower the heat and simmer for 30 minutes, then drain and slice. Melt the butter in a pan, add the scorzonera, and cook over low heat, stirring occasionally, for 5 minutes. Meanwhile, beat the egg yolks with the remaining lemon juice and a pinch of salt in a bowl. Remove the pan from the heat, stir in the egg, return to the heat, and cook, stirring continuously, until the eggs are lightly cooked. Remove from the heat, sprinkle with the parsley, and serve.

GLAZED TURNIPS

RAPE STUFATE

Preparation time: *30 min*
Cooking time: *15 min*
Serves 6

— 2¼ pounds baby turnips,
  trimmed and cut into
  even chunks
— 3 tablespoons butter
— 1 tablespoon sugar
— 2–3 tablespoons vegetable
  stock (optional)
— salt and pepper

Bring a pan of salted water to a boil. Add the turnips and cook for 10 minutes, then drain. Melt the butter in a skillet. Add the turnips and sugar, and cook over medium-low heat, stirring frequently, for 5 minutes, until beginning to caramelize. Reduce the heat, cover, and cook for another 10 minutes. Remove the lid, season with salt and pepper, and, if necessary, moisten the mixture by sprinkling over a little stock and stirring well. Transfer to a warm serving dish and serve immediately.

TURNIP GREENS WITH HAM

CIME DI RAPA AL PROSCIUTTO

Preparation time: *15 min*
Cooking time: *15 min*
Serves 4

— 2¼ pounds turnip greens
— 2 tablespoons olive oil
— 2 cloves garlic
— ½ chile, seeded and chopped
— 3½ ounces cooked ham, cut
  into strips
— ½ cup fresh bread crumbs
— salt

Cook the turnip greens in salted, boiling water for 10 minutes, then drain well, place on a serving dish, and keep warm. Heat the olive oil in a pan, add the garlic, and cook until lightly browned, then remove and discard. Add the chile, ham, and bread crumbs to the pan and cook, stirring occasionally, for a few minutes. Spoon the ham mixture over the turnip greens and serve.

ORECCHIETTE WITH TURNIP GREENS

ORECCHIETTE WITH TURNIP GREENS

PHOTO PAGE 346

ORECCHIETTE CON CIME DI RAPA

Preparation time: *5 min*
Cooking time: *15 min*
Serves 4

— 12 ½ ounces orecchiette
— 14 ounces turnip greens
— olive oil, for drizzling
— salt and pepper

Cook the orecchiette in a large pan of salted, boiling water for 10 minutes, or according to packet directions, until al dente, then add the turnip greens and cook for another 5 minutes, until tender. Drain, transfer to a warm serving dish, drizzle with plenty of olive oil, and season with pepper.

Alternatively, heat 4 tablespoons of olive oil with 2 garlic cloves, add the drained orecchiette mixture, cook for a few minutes, then discard the garlic and serve immediately.

TURNIP AND BARLEY SOUP

ZUPPA DI RAPE E ORZO

Preparation time: *15 min*
Cooking time: *1 hour*
Serves 4

— 1 tablespoon olive oil
— 2 leeks, thinly sliced
— 4 turnips, peeled and diced
— scant ½ dry white wine
— 2 tablespoons whole wheat flour
— 2 ¼ cups vegetable stock
— 1 bay leaf
— 1 carrot, diced
— ¼ cup pearl barley
— pinch saffron threads, lightly crushed
— 1 tablespoon finely chopped parsley
— salt
— grated Parmesan cheese, to serve

Heat the oil with 2 tablespoons of water in a pan. Add the leeks, cover tightly, and cook over low heat for 5 minutes, until translucent. Stir in the turnips, sprinkle in the wine, increase the heat to medium, and cook until the alcohol has evaporated. Stir in the flour, then add the stock and the bay leaf, and bring to a boil. Add the carrot and the pearl barley, cover, and simmer over low heat, stirring occasionally, for 40 minutes, until the barley is very tender. Remove and discard the bay leaf. Put a ladleful of the stock into a small bowl and stir in the saffron, then add to the soup. Season lightly with salt. Ladle the soup into a warm tureen and sprinkle with the parsley. Serve immediately, handing around the Parmesan separately.

TURNIP GREENS WITH GARLIC AND OIL

BROCCOLETTI DI RAPE ALL'AGLIO E OLIO

Preparation time: *20 min*
Cooking time: *30 min*
Serves 4

— 2 ½ pounds turnip greens,
  coarse leaves removed
— 3 tablespoons olive oil
— 2 cloves garlic
— ½ chile, seeded and
  chopped
— salt

Slice the stalks of the turnip greens, and split the leaves in half lengthwise. Bring a pan of lightly salted water to a boil, add the turnip greens, and cook for 15 minutes, then drain. Heat the oil in a large skillet. Add the garlic cloves and chile and cook, stirring frequently, for a few minutes, until the garlic is golden brown. Remove and discard. Add the turnip greens, separating them out with 2 forks. Cook, stirring occasionally, for 15 minutes. Season to taste with salt and remove from the heat. Transfer to a warm serving dish and serve immediately.

ROASTED TURNIPS WITH LEEKS AND PUMPKIN

RAPE IN TEGLIA CON PORRI E ZUCCA

PHOTO PAGE 349

Preparation time: *15 min*
Cooking time: *45 min*
Serves 4

— 7 ounces pumpkin, peeled,
  seeded, and sliced
— 1 teaspoon thyme leaves
— 3 tablespoons olive oil,
  plus extra for drizzling
— 7 ounces leeks, white parts
  only, sliced
— 11 ounces turnips, trimmed
  and sliced
— 2 tablespoons sesame seeds
— salt

Preheat the oven to 400°F. Put the pumpkin slices on a sheet of aluminum foil, season with salt, and sprinkle with the thyme leaves. Fold over the aluminum foil to enclose the pumpkin completely, place on a baking sheet, and bake for 30 minutes. Heat the oil in a large pan, add the leeks and turnips, and cook over medium heat, stirring occasionally, until tender. Add the pumpkin and cook for another few minutes. Sprinkle with the sesame seeds and drizzle with olive oil, then serve.

ROASTED TURNIPS WITH LEEKS AND PUMPKIN

TURNIP GREENS WITH BREAD CRUMBS

TURNIPS WITH BACON

RAPE AL BACON

Preparation time: *15 min*
Cooking time: *30 min*
Serves 4

— 8 small turnips, trimmed
— scant ¾ cup (1⅜ sticks) butter
— 3 ounces bacon, cut into
   strips
— ⅓ cup all-purpose flour
— 1¾ cups milk
— salt and pepper

Scoop out a hole in the middle of each turnip with a small sharp knife. Push 1 tablespoon of the butter into each hole, season with salt and pepper, and put into a deep pan. Pour 5 tablespoons of water into the pan, cover, and bring to a boil, then lower the heat and cook until the turnips are tender, adding more boiling water if necessary. Put the bacon in a skillet and cook over low heat until the fat runs, then remove and drain on paper towels. Make a béchamel sauce (see page 51) with the remaining butter, the flour, and milk, and season with salt and pepper. Stir in the bacon. Remove the turnips from the pan, cut into slices, place on a warm serving dish, and cover with the sauce.

TURNIP GREENS WITH BREAD CRUMBS

PHOTO PAGE 350

CIME DI RAPA AL PANGRATTATO

Preparation time: *50 min*
Cooking time: *15 min*
Serves 4

— 3¼ pounds turnip greens,
   coarse stalks removed
— scant ½ cup olive oil
— 1 chile
— 1 large onion, finely chopped
— 2 tablespoons fresh
   bread crumbs
— salt

Bring a pan of salted water to a boil. Add the turnip greens and cook for 10 minutes, then drain onto paper towels. Heat 4 tablespoons of the oil in a pan. Add the chile and cook over low heat, stirring frequently, for a few minutes, until lightly browned. Remove and discard. Add the onion to the pan and cook over low heat, stirring occasionally, for 5 minutes, until softened and translucent. Add the turnip greens, stir well, and cook for 5 minutes, then transfer to a warm serving dish. Heat the remaining oil in a small pan. Add the bread crumbs and cook, stirring frequently, for a few minutes, until golden brown. Remove from the heat and sprinkle over the turnip greens.

RADICCHIO

CARDOONS

BRUSSELS SPROUTS

CABBAGE

BROCCOLI

CAULIFLOWER

LEEKS

CELERY ROOT

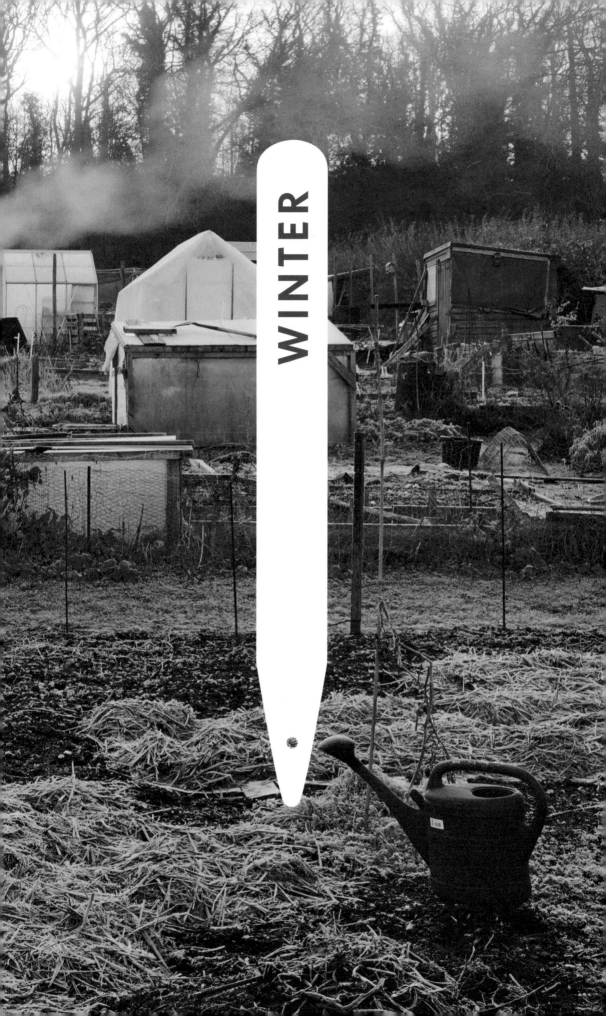

WINTER

Winter is a quiet time in the Italian garden. The cold weather slows plant growth, and vegetables are waiting for the longer and warmer days of spring. However, that does not mean the garden is empty; there are hardy vegetables that can be harvested all season long in mild areas. Even in colder areas buried under snow, there is scope to harvest fresh vegetables.

Winter cooking provides the opportunity to exploit a narrower range of root crops and robust greens. Broccoli, cauliflower, cabbage, and Brussels sprouts can be harvested into early winter, with some overwintering varieties growing on into early spring. The season is perfect for hearty soups, slow-simmered stews, and roasted vegetables that fill the house with mouthwatering aromas. From Pappardelle with Cauliflower and Gorgonzola (see page 412) and Red Cabbage, Pancetta, and Roquefort Salad (see page 401) to Spicy Broccoli with Yogurt (see page 408) and Parmesan Brussels Sprouts (see page 394), these comforting dishes taste great on their own or as accompaniments to broiled meat dishes. Winter brings out the sweetness of these crops, making them less pungent than summer-grown varieties.

Other vegetables thrive in the winter garden. With a soft texture and celery taste, celery root is versatile enough for roasting, braising, frying, and boiling. Radicchio, meanwhile, adds color and can spice up a winter salad or add a strong flavor to soup and risotto dishes. As part of the onion and garlic family, leeks grow well in winter and have a mild and sweet flavor, ideal for roasting, sauces, or simply sautéed in butter.

Brassicas, or vegetables of the cabbage family, survive the winter in mild areas if grown in free-draining raised beds. Plants need to have grown large enough by fall to survive the winter. Watch for slugs and snails attacking the plants and control them using organic methods. Root crops, such as celery root, can survive in cold and mild winter areas, if protected. In cold winter areas, protect root crops by mulching with a 6–8-inch-thick layer of straw in late fall. This will insulate the ground and prevent it from freezing in most areas. Simply remove the straw in winter to harvest and then replace it.

In mild winter areas, a lighter protection of floating row covers may be all you need. The cold soil temperatures help to sweeten root vegetables, making them excellent additions to soups and stews. Watch out for mice and other pests eating your roots and harvest them quickly if you notice damage.

By late winter, it is time to remove the last of the root crops and brassicas, encourage new growth on remaining winter hardy greens with additions of fertilizer, and prepare the ground for spring planting.

RADICCHIO

RADICCHIO

Radicchio is the Italian name for several varieties of red chicory, some with pointed red leaves and broad, white ribs and others more variegated and cabbage-shaped. Their spectacular appearance, slightly bitter flavor, and crisp texture makes them a welcome addition to winter salads. Radicchio is often cooked in Italy and, when tossed in olive oil and broiled or cooked on the barbecue for 10 minutes, it makes an ideal accompaniment to any broiled meat. However, cooking usually destroys the beautiful coloring.

Radicchio may be baked, broiled, or coated with batter and deep-fried. Like other members of the chicory family, radicchio goes well with ingredients with a distinctive flavor, such as fennel and citrus fruits. It is fabulous in risotto and as a pasta filling, and can be used to make soups, croquettes, gratins, and roulades. For a simple dish, stir shredded radicchio, finely chopped garlic, and olive oil into freshly cooked pasta.

Look for fresh, bright, crisp, unblemished leaves and firm stalks. Store in the salad drawer of the refrigerator for 2–3 days. To prepare, discard any damaged leaves, rinse, and pat dry. Halve, cut into wedges, or separate the leaves according to the recipe.

IN THE GARDEN Sow seeds in compost-enhanced soil 3 weeks before the last frost of spring or, in mild winter areas, in fall for a winter harvest. Thin seedlings to 8 inches apart and keep the soil evenly moist. Dry soil makes the leaves more bitter. Harvest when the heads feel firm. Cut the head from the base of the plant and remove the outer leaves.

RADICCHIO RECIPES ON PAGES 378–385

CARDOONS
CARDI

Little known outside the Mediterranean, cardoons are related to globe artichokes and have a similar subtle and slightly sweet flavor. They are grown for their leaf stalks, however, instead of their flower buds and resemble a huge bunch of celery in appearance. They are almost always precooked before being used in flans, salads, fritters, and *bagna cauda*, a warm dip served with fresh vegetables.

Look for pale green, firm stalks. Store in a cool place for up to 1 week. Remove and discard the tough outer stalks because only the inner ribs and tender hearts can be eaten. Cut off the tips, cut the stalks into 2–3 inch pieces, and remove all strings, then immediately dropping them into a pan of acidulated water. Remove the woody covering of the heart, chop, and add to the pan. Add a pinch of salt, bring to a boil, and simmer for 30–45 minutes or until tender, then drain.

IN THE GARDEN Cardoon plants grow 7 feet tall and wide and are a perennial in mild winter areas. A few weeks before the last frost, sow seedlings 2 feet apart in rows 4 feet apart in well-drained, compost-enhanced soil. Plants grow best under cool, moist summer conditions and can grow in part shade. Mulch with straw to conserve soil moisture and prevent weeds from growing. When the plants are 2 feet tall, blanch by wrapping newspaper around them for 3 weeks, then harvest by cutting the leaf stalks at the plant base. New leaves may emerge in late summer and can be blanched and harvested again in fall and winter.

CARDOON RECIPES ON PAGES 386–392

BRUSSELS SPROUTS
CAVOLETTI DI BRUXELLES

The small, sweet, nutty-flavored members of the cabbage family are not traditional in the Italian kitchen, although they are now becoming more popular. At one time, they were almost invariably blanched and then sautéed with pancetta, or gently fried in butter and served in a creamy cheese sauce, but now they are also beginning to feature in pasta sauces, gratins, and purees.

Brussels sprouts have an affinity with sweet nuts, such as chestnuts and almonds, and warm spices, such as nutmeg. They are a delicious accompaniment to pork, game, and poultry, and taste wonderful when braised in the cooking juices of a roast.

Look for fresh-looking, small, hard sprouts with tightly wrapped leaves. Avoid any with loose leaves or signs of yellowing. Store in the salad drawer of the refrigerator for a few days. To prepare, trim the base of the stalk and remove the outer leaves. Cutting a cross in the stalk is not necessary. Cook in salted boiling water for 10 minutes, until just tender.

IN THE GARDEN Brussels sprouts look like miniature cabbages growing around a tall stalk. One stalk yields more than 50 sprouts, so you only need a few plants for a good supply. Plant young plants in well-drained, compost-enhanced soil 18 inches apart in rows 2 feet apart. Mulch with straw to conserve soil moisture and prevent weed growth. Support tall plants with stakes and remove the top of the plant in early fall to encourage faster sprout formation. At the onset of cool fall weather, harvest firm sprouts with a sharp knife, starting from the bottom of the stalk and working upward. Remove the bottom leaves as you harvest.

BRUSSELS SPROUTS RECIPES ON PAGES 393–397

CABBAGE
CAVOLO

Popular varieties of cabbage include the green and red cabbage, in this country as well as the savoy, with its tender, green curly leaves. However, Italians also eat *cavolo nero*, meaning "black cabbage", with curly, very deep green leaves and a hint of bitterness. It is known as black kale or Tuscan kale. In Italy, cabbage is widely used in soups, such as *ribollita*—a type of rustic bread soup—and pork or sausage casseroles. It is also blanched to make roulades and bundles with a meat and sausage or cheese and vegetable filling. Cabbage can be shredded for salads and simply dressed with olive oil and lemon juice.

Cabbage should be firm and fresh-looking with unblemished leaves and stalks without bruises. Firm cabbages can be kept in a cool place for awhile, but savoy cabbages and Tuscan kale can be stored for only a few days. To prepare, remove the outer leaves, cut into quarters, and cut out the cores, then slice or shred. To cook, put the shredded cabbage into a pan with a little olive oil or butter and a few tablespoons of water. Cover and cook briefly, shaking the pan occasionally, until tender. Red cabbage requires a much longer cooking time and is usually braised in the oven.

IN THE GARDEN Select early, mid, and late season cropping varieties to extend the harvest. Sow seeds or plant transplants a few weeks before the last spring frost in well-drained, compost-enhanced soil. In mild winter areas, sow again in fall for a late winter/early spring crop. Place young plants or thin seedlings to 18 inches apart in rows 3 feet apart. Mulch with straw to conserve soil moisture and prevent weed growth. Harvest when the heads are firm by cutting them off at ground level.

CABBAGE RECIPES ON PAGES 398–405

BROCCOLI
BROCCOLI

Calabrese (from Calabria), with its large bluish green flowery head on large succulent stalks, is the best known type. Purple sprouting broccoli, an older Italian variety, has small flower heads on long thin stalks. The heads are often purple, turning green when cooked, but may also be white or green.

Broccoli is an excellent and nutritious accompaniment to meat and fish dishes. Lightly steamed, it can be served with butter and lemon juice, or it can be blanched and then cooked gently with garlic and chile in olive oil. It is also good in pasta sauces and soups, and florets can be eaten raw in salads. Broccoli complement cheese, anchovies, pine nuts, and golden raisins.

Look for brightly colored heads with no sign of yellowing and firm, but not woody stalks, and use as soon after purchase as possible. To prepare, trim the end and remove any discolored leaves. Break broccoli into florets and only peel the stalk if it is very thick. Cook in a little boiling water for 4–5 minutes, then drain. Cut sprouting broccoli into even lengths and steam for 4–5 minutes. Avoid overcooking any variety.

IN THE GARDEN In cold winter areas, sow seeds or transplant young plants in the spring in well-drained, compost-enhanced soil for a summer harvest. In mild winter areas, plant sprouting varieties in fall for a late winter/early spring crop. Place transplants or thin seedlings to 1 foot apart in rows 3 feet apart. Once the heads form and the buds are full but not opened, harvest the broccoli head or, in the case of sprouting broccoli, the whole plant. Once the yellow flowers appear, the flavor becomes bitter. Continue to harvest the smaller side shoots as they emerge.

BROCCOLI RECIPES ON PAGES 406–409

CAULIFLOWER
CAVOLFIORE

Its fresh flavor and attractive appearance make cauliflower a popular vegetable in the Italian kitchen. Raw or briefly blanched florets are also delectably crisp and tasty in salads. A good accompaniment to meat and fish, cauliflower is delicious served drizzled with olive oil and vinegar, or blanched, sautéed in butter, and sprinkled with Parmesan. It can also be coated in batter or bread crumbs and deep-fried. In Italy, it is often served as a dish in its own right—with cheese or ham, or made into timbales, croquettes, pies, and tarts.

Look for creamy white or brightly colored curds (the white part) without any discoloration and fresh green leaves without any yellowing. Store in a cool place for up to 2 days. To cook whole, remove the coarse leaves and cut out part of the center core, then either boil in salted water or steam for 10–20 minutes. Or separate into florets and boil or steam for 5–8 minutes.

IN THE GARDEN Cauliflower grows best if it matures during cool weather, so plant seedlings in the spring at the time of the last frost or in late summer for a late fall/winter crop. Space them 2 feet apart in rows 3 feet apart. If you have not selected self-blanching varieties, blanch white heads when they are 2 inches in diameter by tying leaves over them with twine. (Colored heads do not need blanching.) Mulch with straw to conserve soil moisture and keep the plant growing evenly. Harvest when heads are firm, but before they have a ricelike appearance, removing the whole plant.

CAULIFLOWER RECIPES ON PAGES 410–415

LEEKS

PORRI

A member of the onion family but with a milder taste, leeks
play a subsidiary role in the Italian kitchen and are mainly
used to flavor other vegetables, stocks, stews, and casseroles.
Nevertheless, they do feature in risotto, tarts, gratins, and soups.

Look for firm, white leeks with lively green leaves. They
are best eaten within a day of purchase, but can be stored for
2–3 days in the salad drawer of the refrigerator after trimming
the tops of the leaves. To prepare, cut off the green part and trim
the base. Remove and discard the outer layer and rinse. Home-
grown leeks require very thorough washing. Either slice and
rinse well in a colander under cold running water or slit along
the length and fan repeatedly under running water to remove all
traces of grit and dirt.

Leeks may be steamed, boiled, or sautéed in butter, but do
not let them brown or they will become bitter. They are ideal
partners with tomatoes, ham, cheese, and cream, and make good
accompaniments to most meat and fish dishes.

IN THE GARDEN Leeks are most easily grown from transplants.
Add compost to the soil and make a 4-inch-deep trench. Plant
seedlings 6 inches apart in rows 1 foot apart. As they grow,
gradually fill the trench with soil and mound it up around the
plants. Keep weeded and well watered. For the sweetest flavor,
wait until after a frost or cold weather to harvest. Pull plants that
are at least ½ inch in diameter and ideally have 3 inches of white
shaft. Trim excess leaves and roots.

LEEK RECIPES ON PAGES 416–418

CELERY ROOT
SEDANO RAPA

The lovely sweet, nutty flavor of celery root, also known as celeriac, belies its unprepossessing appearance—an ugly, knobby root with patchy brown and white skin. More delicately flavored than celery, it is superb in soups and gratins, combines particularly well with potato, and is delicious blanched and then fried in egg and bread crumbs. Its crunchy texture when raw or blanched makes it a valuable addition to winter salads.

Look for smaller roots, because large ones tend to be fibrous. Avoid any cracked specimens. It can be stored in a cool place for a long time. Peel carefully with a sharp knife, then slice, dice, or grate, according to the recipe, and immediately add it to acidulated water to prevent discoloration. Boil whole for 30–50 minutes and mash with other root vegetables and butter or cream. Alternatively, boil diced celery root for 10–15 minutes, until tender-crisp and serve with melted butter. It is also tasty when braised and coated with a flavorsome sauce. In spite of its humble appearance, celery root features in some elegant antipasti and salads—with piquant remoulade sauce, carpaccio with anchovies, and combined with smoked salmon.

IN THE GARDEN Celery root is easier to grow than celery. Plant seedlings 2 weeks before the last frost date in a raised bed filled with moist, fertile soil. In mild winter areas, you can also plant in late summer for a winter harvest. Space the plants 6 inches apart in rows 18 inches apart and mulch with straw to keep the soil moist. Harvest roots that are 3–5 inches in diameter in fall after a period of cool weather. Pull the plant, remove the leaves to within 1 inch of the root top, cut off the hairy roots, and clean off the soil.

CELERY ROOT RECIPES ON PAGES 419–421

RADICCHIO AND FENNEL SALAD

PHOTO PAGE 379

INSALATA DI RADICCHIO E FINOCCHIO

Preparation time: *15 min*
Serves 4

— 1 bulb fennel, cut into
   quarters
— 1½ heads radicchio
— olive oil, for drizzling
— red wine vinegar, for
   drizzling
— salt

Thinly slice the fennel, preferably with a mandoline, and put
into a salad bowl. Cut the radicchio into thin strips and add
to the fennel. Season with salt, drizzle with oil and vinegar
to taste, toss lightly, and serve.

RADICCHIO AND POLENTA SOUP

ZUPPA DI RADICCHIO E POLENTA

Preparation time: *2¼ hours,*
plus 12 hours soaking
Cooking time: *30 min*
Serves 4–6

— ½ cup dried cannellini beans,
   soaked overnight in water to
   cover and drained
— 1 carrot
— 1 small onion
— 1 stalk celery
— 1 bay leaf
— 1 tablespoon olive oil
— ½ cup finely chopped pig's
   cheek, pancetta, or bacon
— 3 heads radicchio
— 6¼ cups vegetable stock
— ¾ cup fine polenta
— salt and pepper

Put the beans, carrot, onion, celery, and bay leaf into a large
pan and pour in water to cover. Bring to a boil and cook for
about 2 hours, until tender, and season with salt toward the
end of the cooking time. Meanwhile, heat the oil in a skillet.
Add the pig's cheek, pancetta, or bacon and cook over
medium-low heat, for 5 minutes. Remove the skillet from
the heat, transfer the meat to a plate, and set aside.

Parboil the radicchio in a small pan of water for 15 minutes,
then drain and chop finely. Pour the vegetable stock into
a large pan and bring to a boil. Add the radicchio and
bring back to a boil, then sprinkle in the polenta, stirring
continuously. Cook for 10 minutes, stirring continuously,
then add the meat. Drain the beans, discard the flavorings,
and add the beans to the pan. Simmer for another
15 minutes. Remove the pan from the heat, season with salt
and pepper to taste, transfer to a warm soup tureen, and
serve immediately.

RADICCHIO AND FENNEL SALAD

RADICCHIO AND PINK GRAPEFRUIT RISOTTO

RADICCHIO AND PINK GRAPEFRUIT RISOTTO

PHOTO PAGE 380

RISOTTO AL RADICCHIO E POMPELMO

Preparation time: *15 min*
Cooking time: *25 min*
Serves 4

— 4¼ cups vegetable stock
— 3 tablespoons butter
— 1 onion, thinly sliced
— 1 head radicchio,
    cut into strips
— 1⅔ cups risotto rice
— juice of 1 pink grapefruit,
    strained
— ½ cup grated Parmesan
    cheese
— salt

Pour the stock into a pan and bring to a boil. Meanwhile, melt half the butter in another pan. Add the onion and cook over low heat, stirring occasionally, for 5 minutes, until softened. Add the radicchio and cook, stirring occasionally, for 5 minutes. Stir in the rice and cook, stirring, for 1–2 minutes, until all the grains are coated in butter. Pour in the grapefruit juice and cook until it has evaporated. Season with salt. Add a ladleful of the hot stock and cook, stirring continuously, until absorbed. Continue to add the hot stock, a ladleful at a time, stirring continuously until each addition has been absorbed, for about 20 minutes. Remove from the heat and stir in the remaining butter and the grated cheese. Let stand for 2 minutes before serving.

TREVISO RADICCHIO AND SHRIMP SALAD

INSALATA DI TREVISANA AI GAMBERETTI

Preparation time: *25 min*
Serves 4

— 3 heads Treviso radicchio,
    trimmed
— 2 avocados
— juice of 1 lemon, strained
— 11 ounces cooked shrimp,
    peeled and deveined
— 7 ounces canned palm
    hearts, drained, rinsed,
    and sliced
— 2 tablespoons olive oil
— 1 sprig thyme, chopped
— 1 sprig marjoram, chopped
— 1 sprig parsley, chopped
— salt and pepper

Make a bed of radicchio leaves on 4 plates. Peel and halve the avocado, then remove and discard the pit. Slice the avocados, sprinkle with a little of the lemon juice to prevent discoloration, and arrange in rings on top of the radicchio. Top with the shrimp and complete with the palm hearts.

Whisk together 2 tablespoons of the remaining lemon juice and the olive oil in a bowl, season with salt and pepper, and stir in the thyme, marjoram, and parsley. Pour the dressing over the salad and serve.

CHICKPEA AND RADICCHIO SALAD

PHOTO PAGE 383

INSALATA DI CECI E RADICCHIO

Preparation time: *15 min*
Serves 4

— 2 heads radicchio, preferably
Treviso
— scant 1 cup drained and
rinsed canned chickpeas
— 4–5 new potatoes, boiled and
cut into rounds
— 2½ ounces Parmesan cheese
— 6 tablespoons olive oil
— 1 tablespoon balsamic
vinegar
— salt and pepper

Cut the radicchio into large pieces and put into a salad bowl. Add the chickpeas and potatoes. Shave off some of the Parmesan and set aside for the garnish. Grate the remaining Parmesan into a bowl. Add the oil, vinegar, and a pinch of salt and whisk to a smooth dressing. Pour the dressing over the salad and stir well. Sprinkle with the Parmesan shavings, season with pepper, and serve.

TREVISO RADICCHIO SALAD WITH MUSHROOMS

INSALATA DI TREVISANA AI FUNGHI

Preparation time: *15 min*
Serves 4

— 3 heads Treviso radicchio,
trimmed
— 11 ounces porcini
mushrooms
— juice 1 lemon, strained
— 7 ounces mâche (corn salad),
trimmed
— 1 bunch dandelion leaves,
trimmed
— 4 tablespoons olive oil
— salt and pepper

Make a bed of radicchio leaves on each of 4 plates. Slice the mushrooms, sprinkle with a little of the lemon juice, and fan out on top of the radicchio. Add the mâche and dandelion leaves. Whisk together the olive oil and 2 tablespoons of the remaining lemon juice in a bowl and season with salt and pepper. Gently pour the dressing over the salad and serve.

CHICKPEA AND RADICCHIO SALAD

RADICCHIO AND CELERY ROOT SALAD

INSALATA DI RADICCHIO E SEDANO RAPA

Preparation time: *25 min*
Serves 4

— 1 head radicchio, cut into
  strips
— 1 lettuce, cut into strips
— 1 celery root, julienned
— 1 tablespoon finely chopped
  parsley

For the dressing:
— 2 tablespoons red wine vinegar
— 1 tablespoon honey
— 4 tablespoons olive oil
— salt and pepper

To make the dressing, whisk together the vinegar, a pinch each of salt and pepper, the honey, and oil in a bowl. Put the radicchio, lettuce, and celery root into a salad bowl and pour over the dressing. Sprinkle the salad with the parsley and serve.

TREVISO RADICCHIO SALAD WITH ORANGE

RADICCHIO ROSSO ALL'ARANCIA

Preparation time: *15 min*
Serves 4

— juice of 2 oranges, strained
— 3–4 tablespoons olive oil
— 1 teaspoon lemon juice
  (optional)
— 4 heads Treviso radicchio,
  cut into thin wedges
— salt and pepper

Whisk together the orange juice and oil in a bowl and season with salt and pepper to taste. Add a few drops of lemon juice to sharpen the taste if the orange juice is too sweet. Place the radicchio in a bowl and pour the orange dressing over it in a continuous stream, then toss gently and serve.

RADICCHIO CROQUETTES

CROCCHETTE DI RADICCHIO ROSSO

Preparation time: *1 hour*
Cooking time: *10–20 min*
Serves 8

— 1¾ heads radicchio
— 1 tablespoon grated
   Parmesan cheese
— 1 egg yolk
— scant ½ cup finely chopped
   lean ham
— all-purpose flour, for dusting
— 1 egg
— scant 1½ cups fresh
   bread crumbs
— ½ cup olive oil
— salt and pepper

For the béchamel sauce:
— 2 tablespoons butter
— ½ cup all-purpose flour
— scant 1 cup milk
— pinch freshly grated nutmeg
— salt

Parboil the radicchio in lightly salted boiling water for 5 minutes. Drain and gently squeeze out any excess water, then chop coarsely and set aside. To make the sauce, melt the butter in a pan. Stir in the flour and cook over low heat, stirring continuously, for 2–3 minutes, until the roux has turned pale golden brown. Gradually stir in the milk, a little at a time. Bring to a boil, stirring continuously, and cook, stirring, until the sauce is thick enough to coat the back of the spoon. Remove from the heat, stir in the nutmeg, and season with salt to taste, then let cool.

Stir the Parmesan into the cooled sauce, then add the egg yolk, ham, and radicchio. Mix well, then shape small quantities of the mixture into croquettes. Spread out the flour on a shallow dish, beat the egg with a pinch each of salt and pepper in another shallow dish, and spread out the bread crumbs in a third. Coat the croquettes first with the flour, then with beaten egg, and, finally, with bread crumbs. Heat the oil in a skillet. Add the croquettes, in batches if necessary, and cook over medium heat, turning frequently, until golden brown all over. Remove with a slotted spoon and drain on paper towels. Transfer to a warm serving dish and serve immediately.

RADICCHIO WITH BACON

RADICCHIO AL BACON

Preparation time: *10 min*
Cooking time: *10 min*
Serves 4

— 2 heads radicchio
— 1 cloves garlic, crushed
— 1½ tablespoons olive oil
— 1½ ounces bacon, cut into
   strips
— salt and pepper

Halve the heads of radicchio and blanch in a pan of salted boiling water for 2 minutes. Drain, gently squeeze out the excess moisture, and cut into 1-inch diamond shapes. Heat the oil in a pan and add the bacon until slightly cooked, then add the garlic and cook for another minute. Add the radicchio and stir-fry for five minutes. Season with salt and pepper. Cook, stirring occasionally, for 10 minutes, then transfer to a warm serving dish and serve immediately.

CARDOON SALAD

CARDI IN INSALATA

Preparation time: *25 min*
Cooking time: *50 min*
Serves 4

— juice of 1 lemon, strained
— 1 cardoon
— 4 eggs
— 1 sprig parsley, chopped
— 3 tablespoons olive oil
— 1 tablespoon bread crumbs
— salt

Pour plenty of water into a pan and add the lemon juice and a pinch of salt. Trim the cardoon, cut the inner stalk into 2-inch lengths, and remove all strings, then immediately drop the stalk pieces into the pan. Bring to a boil, then lower the heat and simmer for about 45 minutes. Meanwhile, boil the eggs until hard-cooked, refresh in cold water, shell, and chop finely. Drain the cardoon well and put in a salad bowl. Sprinkle with the chopped eggs and the parsley. Heat the olive oil in a small pan, add the bread crumbs, and cook, stirring continuously, until golden brown and crisp. Spoon the bread crumbs over the cardoon mixture, let stand for a few minutes, then serve.

CARDOON FLAN

FLAN AL CARDO

Preparation time: *1 hour*
Cooking time: *20 min*
Serves 6

— juice of 1 lemon, strained
— 1 large cardoon
— 2¼ cups milk
— 6 tablespoons butter, plus extra for greasing
— 1 vegetable bouillon cube
— ½ cup all-purpose flour, plus extra for dusting
— ⅔ cup grated Parmesan cheese
— 1 egg, lightly beaten
— salt and pepper

Bring a large pan of salted water to a boil and stir in the lemon juice. Trim the cardoon, cut the inner stalks into 2-inch lengths, and remove all strings, then immediately drop the stalk pieces into the pan. Bring to a boil, then reduce the heat and simmer for 45 minutes. Toward the end of the cooking time, add ¾ cup of the milk to the water. When the cardoon is tender, drain well. Melt 2 tablespoons of the butter in a pan. Crumble in the bouillon cube, add the cardoon, and pour in 5 tablespoons of milk. Cook gently, then season with salt and pepper. Preheat the oven to 350°F. Grease a tart pan with butter and dust with flour, tipping out any excess. Melt the remaining butter in a pan. Stir in the flour and cook, stirring continuously, for 2 minutes. Gradually stir in the remaining milk and bring to a boil, stirring continuously. Remove the pan from the heat and stir in the Parmesan, then let cool slightly. Stir the beaten egg into the béchamel sauce, then stir in the cardoon. Pour the mixture into the prepared pan and bake for about 20 minutes, until just set.

CARDOON CREPES

CRÊPES CON I CARDI

Preparation time: *25 min*
Cooking time: *25 min*
Serves 4

For the crepes:
— generous ¾ cup all-purpose
  flour
— 2 eggs
— 1 cup milk
— 2 tablespoons butter, melted
  and cooled
— vegetable oil, for brushing
— salt

— 1 large head cardoon,
  trimmed
— 3 tablespoons butter, plus
  extra for greasing
— 1 quantity béchamel sauce
  (see page 51)
— salt

To make the crepes, sift the flour into a bowl, add the eggs and 3–4 tablespoons of the milk, and mix well. Gradually stir in the remaining milk to make a fairly runny batter. Beat in the melted butter and season with salt, then cover and let rest for 1 hour. To cook, brush the base of a crepe pan with oil, then heat. Stir the batter and pour 2 tablespoons into the pan. Turn and tilt the pan so that the batter covers the bottom evenly. Cook for 3–4 minutes, until the underside is set, then flip over with and cook the other side for about 2 minutes, until golden. Slide the crepe out of the pan onto a plate. Repeat until all the batter has been used, stacking them interleaved with wax paper. Cook the cardoon in salted, boiling water for 1 hour, then drain well and finely chop. Melt 2 tablespoons of the butter in a skillet, add the cardoon, and cook over low heat, stirring occasionally, for 5 minutes. Preheat the oven to 350°F. Grease an ovenproof dish with butter. Spread a little béchamel sauce on each crepe and arrange a little chopped cardoon on top, then cover with more sauce and roll up. Put the crepes in the prepared dish, dot with the remaining butter, and bake for 15 minutes. Remove from the oven and let stand for about 10 minutes, then serve.

DELICATE CARDOON

CARDI DELICATI

Preparation time: *15 min*
Cooking time: *1½ hours*
Serves 4

— juice of 1 lemon, strained
— 1 large head cardoons
— 2 tablespoons butter
— scant ½ cup milk
— scant ½ cup light cream
— salt
— grated Parmesan cheese,
  to serve

Bring a large pan of salted water to a boil and stir in the lemon juice. Trim the cardoon, cut the inner stalks into 2 inch lengths, and remove all strings, then immediately drop the stalk pieces into the pan. Bring to a boil, then reduce the heat and simmer for 45 minutes. Drain well and transfer to a flameproof dish. Dot with the butter, pour over the milk, and cook over low heat for 30 minutes. Pour in the cream and cook, without letting the mixture boil, for 10–12 minutes, until thickened. Transfer the mixture to a warm serving dish, sprinkle with cheese, and serve.

CARDOON WITH ANCHOVY SAUCE

CARDI ALLA BAGNA CAUDA

Preparation time: *50 min*
Cooking time: *20 min*
Serves 6–8

— 4 tablespoons butter, plus
  extra for greasing
— juice of 1 lemon, strained
— 1 large head cardoon
— 1 clove garlic
— 10 canned anchovy fillets,
  drained and chopped
— ½ cup grated Parmesan
  cheese
— salt

Grease an ovenproof dish. Bring a large pan of salted water to a boil and stir in the lemon juice. Trim the cardoon, cut the inner stalks into 3-inch lengths, and remove all strings, then immediately drop the stalk pieces into the pan. Bring to a boil, then reduce the heat and simmer for 30 minutes. Meanwhile, preheat the oven to 350°F. Drain the cardoon and put into the prepared dish. Melt the butter in a small skillet. Add the garlic and cook over low heat, stirring frequently, for a few minutes, until golden. Remove with a slotted spoon and discard. Add the anchovies and cook, mashing them with a wooden spoon, until they disintegrate and the mixture is smooth. Remove from the heat. Pour the sauce over the cardoon, sprinkle with the cheese, and bake for 30 minutes.

CARDOON SFORMATO

SFORMATO DI GOBBI

Preparation time: *1 ½ hours*
Cooking time: *35–40 min*
Serves 6

— juice of 1 lemon, strained
— 1 large head cardoon
— 2 tablespoons butter, plus
  extra for greasing
— scant 1 cup milk
— 1 quantity béchamel
  sauce (see page 51)
— 4 eggs
— ⅔ cup grated Parmesan
  cheese
— salt

Bring a large pan of salted water to a boil and stir in the lemon juice. Trim the cardoon, cut the inner stalks into 2-inch lengths, and remove all strings, then immediately drop the stalk pieces into the pan. Bring to a boil, reduce the heat, and simmer for 45 minutes, then drain. Melt the butter in a skillet. Add the cardoon and cook over medium heat for a few minutes, then reduce the heat, pour in the milk, and simmer for 30 minutes. Meanwhile, preheat the oven to 350°F. Grease an ovenproof mold with butter. Remove the cardoon from the heat, transfer to a food processor or blender, and process. Combine the cardoon, béchamel sauce, eggs, and Parmesan and season with salt. Pour the mixture into the prepared mold. Put the mold into a roasting pan and pour in hot water to come about halfway up the sides. Bake for 35–40 minutes, until set. Remove from the oven and let rest for 5 minutes before turning out onto a serving plate. Serve immediately.

CARDOON WITH ANCHOVY SAUCE

CARDOON MOLDS WITH MUSHROOMS

CARDOON MOLDS
WITH MUSHROOMS

PHOTO PAGE 390

SAVARIN DI CARDI AI FUNGHI

Preparation time: *15 min*
Cooking time: *1½ hours*
Serves 4

— juice of 1 lemon, strained
— ½ head cardoon
— 4 tablespoons butter, plus
   extra for greasing
— 2–3 tablespoons bread
   crumbs
— 1 quantity béchamel sauce
   (see page 51)
— ½ cup grated Parmesan
   cheese
— 1 egg, lightly beaten
— 1 small shallot, chopped
— scant 1½ cups chopped
   mushrooms
— 4 mint leaves, chopped
— 1 sprig parsley, chopped
— salt and pepper

Pour plenty of water into a pan and add the lemon juice and a pinch of salt. Trim the cardoon, cut the inner stalks into 2-inch lengths, and remove all strings, then immediately drop the stalk pieces into the pan. Bring to a boil, then lower the heat and simmer for about 45 minutes, then drain well.

Meanwhile, preheat the oven to 350°F. Grease 4 ramekins with butter, sprinkle with the bread crumbs, turning to coat, and tip out any excess. Melt 1½ tablespoons of the butter in a skillet, add the cardoon, and cook over low heat, stirring occasionally, for 5 minutes. Turn into a food processor or blender and process to a puree. Stir the cardoon puree, béchamel sauce, and Parmesan into the beaten egg. Spoon the mixture into the prepared molds. Place on a baking sheet and bake for about 35 minutes.

Melt the remaining butter in a skillet, add the shallot, and cook over low heat, stirring occasionally, for 5 minutes. Add the mushrooms, mint, and parsley, season with salt and pepper, and cook for about 10 minutes, until all the liquid has evaporated and the mushrooms are very tender. Remove the molds from the oven and turn out onto a warm serving dish. Spoon the hot mushroom sauce over them and serve.

CARDOON WITH CHEESE

CARDI AI FORMAGGI

Preparation time: *20 min*
Cooking time: *1 ¼ hours*
Serves 4

— juice of 1 lemon, strained
— 1 tablespoon olive oil
— 1 teaspoon all-purpose flour
— 1 large head cardoon
— 2 tablespoons butter, melted,
plus extra for greasing
— ⅔ cup grated Parmesan
cheese
— 2 ½ ounces fontina cheese,
shaved
— 2 ½ ounces Emmenthal
cheese, thinly sliced
— scant ½ cup milk
— scant 1 cup heavy cream
— salt

Pour plenty of water into a pan and add the lemon juice, olive oil, flour, and a pinch of salt. Trim the cardoon, cut the inner stalks into 2-inch lengths, and remove all strings, then immediately drop the stalk pieces into the pan. Bring to a boil, then lower the heat and simmer for about 45 minutes. Meanwhile, preheat the oven to 350°F. Grease an ovenproof dish with butter. Drain the cardoon well, turn into the prepared dish, pour the melted butter on top, and sprinkle with the Parmesan and fontina. Cover with a layer of the Emmenthal. Combine the milk and cream in a pitcher and carefully pour the mixture over the top. Bake for about 30 minutes and serve.

CREAMED CARDOON WITH PROSCIUTTO

CARDI ALLA CREMA DI PROSCIUTTO

Preparation time: *1 hour, plus
10 min cooling*
Cooking time: *30 min*
Serves 4

— butter, for greasing
— juice of 1 lemon, strained
— 1 large head cardoon,
trimmed
— 3 ½ ounces lean prosciutto,
diced
— 1 quantity béchamel sauce
(see page 51)
— salt

Grease an ovenproof dish with butter. Bring a large pan of salted water to a boil and stir in the lemon juice. Trim the cardoon, cut the inner stalks into 3-inch lengths, and remove all strings, then immediately drop the stalk pieces into the pan. Bring to a boil, then reduce the heat and simmer for 30 minutes. Drain well and transfer to the prepared dish. Preheat the oven to 350°F. Add the prosciutto to the béchamel sauce and season lightly with salt. Pour the sauce over the cardoon and bake for 30 minutes. Remove from the oven and let cool for about 10 minutes, then serve.

CREAM OF BRUSSELS SPROUT SOUP

CREMA DI CAVOLINI DI BRUXELLES

Preparation time: *20 min*
Cooking time: *30 min*
Serves 4

— 3 ounces bacon, diced
— 1 pound 5 ounces Brussels
  sprouts, trimmed and halved
— 4¼ cups vegetable stock
— 3–4 tablespoons heavy cream
— salt and pepper
— grated Parmesan cheese,
  to serve

Dry-fry the bacon in a heavy skillet, stirring occasionally, for 4–6 minutes. Add the Brussels sprouts, stir in ¾ cup of water, and cook for 20 minutes. Remove the Brussels sprouts from the skillet and pass through a food mill into bowl. Scrape the puree into a pan, stir in the stock, season with salt and pepper, and heat through. Pour into a warm soup tureen, stir in a few tablespoonfuls of cream, and serve immediately, handing around the grated cheese separately.

EGGS WITH BRUSSELS SPROUTS

UOVA FRITTE CON CAVOLINI DI BRUXELLES

Preparation time: *15 min*
Cooking time: *35 min*
Serves 4

— 1 pound 2 ounces Brussels
  sprouts
— 7 tablespoons butter
— 1 thick ham slice, diced
— 1 onion, finely chopped
— 1 tablespoon all-purpose
  flour
— scant 1 cup heavy cream
— 6 eggs
— salt and pepper

Bring a large pan of salted water to a boil, add the Brussels sprouts, and simmer for 15 minutes, then drain well. Melt 2 tablespoons of the butter in a skillet, add the ham and onion, and cook over low heat, stirring occasionally, for 5 minutes. Sprinkle in the flour and cook, stirring, for 1 minute, then stir in ⅔ cup of warm water and simmer for another 10 minutes. Stir in the cream, season with salt and pepper, and heat through. Meanwhile, melt the remaining butter in another skillet, break in the eggs, one at a time, and fry for a few minutes over medium heat. Season with salt to taste. Arrange the Brussels sprouts on a warm serving dish, cover with the hot ham sauce, top with the eggs, and serve.

BRUSSELS SPROUTS AU GRATIN

CAVOLINI DI BRUXELLES GRATINATI

Preparation time: *15 min*
Cooking time: *35 min*
Serves *4*

— 4 tablespoons butter, plus
    extra for greasing
— 1½ pounds Brussels sprouts,
    trimmed
— 2 tablespoons olive oil
— 3½ ounces pancetta, diced
— scant 1 cup grated Gruyère
    cheese
— 1 quantity béchamel sauce
    (see page 51)
— salt and pepper

Preheat the oven to 350°F. Grease an ovenproof dish with butter. Cook the Brussels sprouts in salted, boiling water for about 10 minutes, then drain, set aside, and keep warm. Heat the butter and olive oil in a pan, add the pancetta, and cook, stirring occasionally, until lightly browned. Add the Brussels sprouts and 1 tablespoon of hot water and cook, stirring occasionally, for about 5 minutes. Stir half of the Gruyère into the béchamel sauce and season with salt and pepper. Put the Brussels sprouts into the prepared dish and sprinkle with half of the remaining Gruyère. Spoon the béchamel sauce on top and sprinkle with the remaining Gruyère. Bake for about 20 minutes.

PARMESAN BRUSSELS SPROUTS

PHOTO PAGE 395

CAVOLINI DI BRUXELLES ALLA PARMIGIANA

Preparation time: *15 min*
Cooking time: *20 min*
Serves *4*

— 1¾ pounds Brussels sprouts,
    trimmed
— 2 tablespoons butter
— pinch of freshly grated
    nutmeg
— scant 1 cup grated Parmesan
    cheese
— salt and pepper

Cook the Brussels sprouts in salted, boiling water for 15 minutes, then drain. Melt the butter in a pan and, when golden brown, add the sprouts and cook over low heat for a few minutes. Season with salt and pepper to taste and add the nutmeg. Transfer to a warm serving dish, sprinkle with the Parmesan, and serve.

PARMESAN BRUSSELS SPROUTS

BRUSSELS SPROUTS WITH ALMONDS

BRUSSELS SPROUT PUREE

PURÈ DI CAVOLINI DI BRUXELLES

Preparation time: *15 min*
Cooking time: *30 min*
Serves 6

— 2 ¼ pounds Brussels sprouts, trimmed
— 2 tablespoons butter
— 4 tablespoons heavy cream
— pinch grated nutmeg
— salt and freshly ground white
— pepper

Bring a pan of salted water to a boil. Add the Brussels sprouts and cook for 15 minutes or until tender. Do not overcook. Drain well and transfer to a food processor or blender and process to a puree. Scrape the puree into a pan, add the butter and cream, and cook over medium heat, stirring occasionally, for 15 minutes, until thickened. Remove from the heat, stir in the nutmeg, and season to taste with salt and pepper.

BRUSSELS SPROUTS WITH ALMONDS

CAVOLINI DI BRUXELLES CON LE MANDORLE

PHOTO PAGE 396

Preparation time: *15 min*
Cooking time: *35 min*
Serves 4

— 1 ½ pounds Brussels sprouts, trimmed
— 4 tablespoons butter
— ¼ cup blanched almonds
— 1 clove garlic
— thinly pared rind of 1 lemon, chopped
— 1 ½ teaspoons bread crumbs
— salt and pepper

Cook the Brussels sprouts in salted, boiling water for 10 minutes or until just tender, then drain thoroughly. Place on a serving dish and keep warm. Melt half of the butter in a skillet, add the almonds and garlic clove, and stir-fry for a few minutes. Add the lemon rind, season with salt and pepper, and remove from the heat. Remove and discard the garlic. Melt the remaining butter in a small pan and stir-fry the bread crumbs until golden, then stir into the almond mixture, spoon over the Brussels sprouts, and serve.

GNOCCHI WITH CABBAGE

GNOCCHI CON LA VERZA CAPPUCCINA

Preparation time: *1 hour,
plus 1 hour resting*
Cooking time: *30 min*
Serves 4

— 2¼ pounds potatoes
— 1¾ cups all-purpose flour,
 plus extra for dusting
— 1 egg, lightly beaten
— salt

For the sauce:
— scant ½ cup olive oil
— 1 onion, finely chopped
— 3½ ounces lardons or salt
 pork, chopped
— 3½ cups coarsely chopped
 savoy cabbage
— 4 tomatoes, peeled and
 chopped
— 3–4 tablespoons grated
 pecorino cheese
— 1 mild chile, seeded and
 chopped
— salt

To make the gnocchi, steam the potatoes for 25 minutes, until tender. Remove from the steamer and peel, then mash in a bowl. Stir in the flour, egg, and a pinch of salt. Shape the dough into long rolls about ¾ inch in diameter and cut into 1-inch lengths. Press them gently against a grater and spread out on a dish towel lightly dusted with flour. Let rest for 1 hour.

Meanwhile, heat 2 tablespoons of the oil in a skillet. Add the onion and cook over low heat, stirring occasionally, for 5 minutes, until softened. Add the lardons or salt pork and cook, stirring frequently, for 5–8 minutes, until lightly golden. Add the cabbage and season with salt. Cover and cook for 15 minutes, until the cabbage is just tender. Add the tomatoes, check the seasoning and add more salt if necessary, and cook briefly. Meanwhile, bring a pan of salted water to a boil. Add the gnocchi, in batches, and cook until they rise to the surface. Remove with a slotted spoon and keep warm. Put the gnocchi on a warm serving dish and spoon the hot cabbage sauce over them. Sprinkle with the pecorino and chile and serve immediately.

CAVOLO NERO SOUP

ZUPPA DI CAVOLO NERO

PHOTO PAGE 399

Preparation time: *15 min*
Cooking time: *35 min*
Serves 6

— 3 tablespoons olive oil
— 1 onion, finely chopped
— 2 cavolo nero or curly kale,
 shredded
— 6¼ cups vegetable stock
— 6 slices rye bread
— 1 clove garlic, halved
— salt and pepper

Heat the oil in a large pan or flameproof casserole. Add the onion and cook over low heat, stirring occasionally, for 5 minutes, until softened. Increase the heat to medium-high, add the cavolo nero, pour in the stock, and season with salt and pepper. Bring to a boil, then reduce the heat and simmer for 30 minutes, until the cavolo nero is tender. Meanwhile, toast the bread slices on both sides, and, while they are still warm, rub the clove of garlic over them. Place the toast in 6 individual soup bowls, ladle the soup over, and serve immediately.

CAVOLO NERO SOUP

RED CABBAGE, PANCETTA, AND ROQUEFORT SALAD

BRAISED CABBAGE

CAVOLO VERZA BRASATO

Preparation time: *15 min*
Cooking time: *20 min*
Serves 4

— 1 large savoy cabbage, cored
and shredded
— 5 ounces pancetta or bacon,
cut into small thin strips
— 1 white onion, finely
chopped
— 2–3 sprigs thyme, chopped
— salt

Bring a large pan of lightly salted water to a boil. Add the cabbage and cook for 5 minutes. Drain well and let cool. Heat a skillet. Add the pancetta or bacon and cook over medium heat, stirring occasionally, for 3–4 minutes, until the fat becomes translucent, then add the onion. Reduce the heat and cook, stirring occasionally, for 5 minutes, until softened. Add the cabbage and cook for another 5–10 minutes, then stir in the thyme and season with salt. Remove from the heat and serve immediately.

RED CABBAGE, PANCETTA,
AND ROQUEFORT SALAD

PHOTO PAGE 400

INSALATA DI CAVOLO PANCETTA E ROQUEFORT

Preparation time: *15 min*
Cooking time: *15 min*
Serves 6

—1 small red cabbage, cored
and finely shredded
— ½ cup red wine vinegar
— 4 tablespoons olive oil
— 9 ounces smoked pancetta
or bacon, diced
— 6 slices soft white bread,
crusts removed, cut into
small squares
— 3½ ounces Roquefort
cheese, diced
— salad greens, to serve

For the vinaigrette:
— ¾ cup olive oil
— 3 tablespoons white wine
vinegar
— 1 tablespoon Dijon mustard
— salt and pepper

Put the cabbage into a heatproof bowl. Pour the vinegar into a small pan and bring to a boil. Remove from the heat and pour over the cabbage. Heat 1 tablespoon of the oil in a skillet. Add the pancetta or bacon and cook over medium heat, stirring frequently, for 8–10 minutes, until crisp. Remove with a slotted spoon and set aside. Heat the remaining oil in the skillet. Add the bread squares, in batches if necessary, and cook over medium heat, stirring and turning occasionally, until golden and crisp. Remove with a spatula and drain on paper towels.

To make the vinaigrette, whisk together the oil, vinegar, and mustard in a bowl and season with salt and pepper. Drain the cabbage and put on a serving dish. Drizzle with the vinaigrette, top with the pancetta or bacon and Roquefort, and surround with salad greens. Serve immediately.

PHOTO PAGE 403

CAPUCHIN SAVOY CABBAGE

CAVOLO VERZA ALLA CAPPUCCINA

Preparation time: *15 min*
Cooking time: *1 hour*
Serves 4

— ½ savoy cabbage, cored and
   cut into strips
— 2 salted anchovies, heads
   removed, cleaned and filleted,
   soaked in cold water for
   10 minutes and drained
— 2 tablespoons olive oil
— 2 cloves garlic
— 1 tablespoon chopped parsley
— salt and pepper

Parboil the cabbage in salted, boiling water for 5 minutes,
then drain well. Chop the anchovy fillets. Heat the oil in
a pan, add the garlic, and cook for a few minutes until
browned, then remove and discard. Add the anchovies to
the pan and cook, mashing with a wooden spoon until they
disintegrate. Add the cabbage and parsley, season with salt
and pepper, cover, and cook, stirring occasionally, for about
50 minutes.

CABBAGE AND PANCETTA FRITTERS

SFERETTE DI VERZA ALLA PANCETTA

Preparation time: *30 min*
Cooking time: *45 min*
Serves 6

— 2 large savoy cabbages,
   cored and coarse leaves
   removed
— 2 tablespoons butter
— 1 egg yolk
— 1⅔ cups grated Parmesan
   cheese
— 3 ounces pancetta or bacon
— ¼ cup all-purpose flour, plus
   extra for dusting
— 2 eggs
— 1½ cups fresh bread crumbs
   vegetable oil, for deep-frying
— salt and pepper

Bring a large pan of salted water to a boil. Cut the cabbage
into quarters, add to the pan, and cook for 10–15 minutes,
until just tender. Drain well, squeeze out the excess moisture,
and chop. Melt the butter in a skillet. Add the cabbage
and stir-fry over high heat for 5 minutes. Season with salt
and lightly with pepper, remove from the heat, transfer to
a bowl, and let cool. When the cabbage is cold, stir in the
egg yolk, cheese, and pancetta, and season with salt and
pepper. Lightly flour your hands and shape the mixture into
medium-size rounds. Spread out the flour in a shallow dish.
Lightly beat the eggs in another shallow dish and spread out
the bread crumbs in a third. Coat the cabbage balls first in
flour, then in beaten egg, and finally in bread crumbs. Heat
the oil in a deep-fryer to 350–375°F or until a cube of day-
old bread browns in 30 seconds. Add the cabbage rounds,
in batches, and cook until golden brown. Remove with a
slotted spoon and drain on paper towels. Keep warm while
you cook the remaining batches. Transfer to a warm serving
dish and serve immediately.

CAPUCHIN SAVOY CABBAGE

CABBAGE AND CAULIFLOWER PIE

Preparation time: 50 *min*,
plus 1 hour resting
Cooking time: 30 *min*
Serves 6

— 1 large cauliflower, trimmed
  and cored
— 4 tablespoons butter
— 1 tablespoon olive oil, plus
  extra for brushing
— 1 shallot, chopped
— 4⅓ cups shredded cabbage
— 5 ounces fontina cheese,
  sliced
— 3 hard-cooked eggs, sliced
— salt and pepper

For the pastry dough
— 1 cup all-purpose flour, plus
  extra for dusting
— 1 cup whole wheat flour
— 7 tablespoons butter, plus
  extra for greasing
— salt

Put the cauliflower into a medium pan, pour in water to cover, and add a pinch of salt. Bring to a boil, then reduce the heat and simmer for 20 minutes, until tender but still al dente. Drain well and break up into florets. Melt the butter with the oil in a large pan. Add the cauliflower florets and shallot and cook over low heat, stirring occasionally, for 5 minutes. Add the cabbage and cook, stirring occasionally, for another 5–10 minutes, until tender. Remove the pan from the heat and season with salt and pepper.

To make the dough sift both flours with a pinch of salt into a bowl, tipping in the bran from the sifter. Add the butter, cut it into the dry ingredients, then rub in with your fingertips until the mixture resembles bread crumbs. Stir in ice water, a tablespoon at a time, until a firm, smooth dough is formed. Shape the dough into a ball, wrap in plastic wrap, and let rest in the refrigerator for 1 hour.

Preheat the oven to 350°F. Grease a 9-inch pie dish with butter. Remove the dough from the refrigerator and cut into 2 pieces, one slightly bigger than the other. Roll out the larger piece on a lightly floured counter and use to line the prepared pie dish, letting it overhang the rim. Make alternate layers of sliced hard-cooked egg, the cabbage and cauliflower mixture, and slices of fontina in the pie shell until all the ingredients have been used. Brush the pastry rim with water. Roll out the remaining dough on a lightly floured counter and lift on top of the pie, pressing down around the rim to seal. Trim the excess dough and prick holes in the surface with a fork. Brush with olive oil and bake for 30 minutes, until golden brown. Remove from the oven and serve warm.

CARAMELIZED RED CABBAGE

CAVOLO ROSSO CARAMELLATO

Preparation time: *15 min*
Cooking time: *1 hour 10 min*
Serves 8

—1 large red cabbage, cored and shredded
— ¼ cup white wine vinegar
— 2 tablespoons sugar
— salt and pepper

Put the cabbage into a large pan or flameproof casserole. Pour in scant ½ cup of water and add the vinegar and sugar. Season with salt and pepper, and bring to a boil. Reduce the heat, cover, and simmer for 1 hour, stirring frequently during the last 30 minutes, until the liquid has evaporated and the cabbage has slightly caramelized. Serve warm or cold with roasted pork.

RED CABBAGE WITH APPLES

CAVOLO NERO CON LE MELE

Preparation time: *15 min*
Cooking time: *15 min*
Serves 4

— 1 apple
— 1 tablespoon sugar
— 5 tablespoons red wine vinegar
— ½ red cabbage, cored and shredded
— 1 shallot, chopped
— 5 tablespoons olive oil
— salt and pepper

Preheat the oven to 400°F. Core and quarter the apple, place in a roasting pan, and sprinkle with the sugar. Bake, occasionally sprinkling with a little water, for 15 minutes. Meanwhile, pour the vinegar into a small pan and heat until warm. Put the cabbage into a bowl, pour in the warm vinegar, and season with salt and pepper. Spoon the cabbage onto a serving dish, sprinkle with the shallot, and drizzle with the oil. Put the hot apple quarters in the middle and serve.

DELICIOUS BROCCOLI

BROCCOLI FANTASIA

Preparation time: *30 min*
Cooking time: *10–15 min*
Serves 4

— 2¼ pounds broccoli, cut
  into florets
— 2 tablespoons olive oil
— 2 cloves garlic
— 2 leeks, trimmed and sliced
— 1 tablespoon all-purpose
  flour
— scant ½ cup heavy cream
— scant 1 cup dry white wine
— 2 tablespoons butter, plus
  extra for greasing
— ⅔ cup grated Parmesan
  cheese
— salt and pepper

Preheat the oven to 400°F. Bring a large pan of salted water to a boil. Add the broccoli florets and parboil for a few minutes, then drain and let cool slightly. Heat the oil in another large pan, add the garlic cloves and leeks, and cook over low heat, stirring occasionally, for 5 minutes, until softened. Stir in the flour and cook, stirring continuously, for 2 minutes, until lightly browned. Remove and discard the garlic. Stir in the cream, season with salt and pepper, and mix well. Add the broccoli, pour in the wine, and simmer for about 10 minutes. Grease an ovenproof dish with butter. Remove the pan from the heat and transfer the mixture to the prepared dish. Sprinkle with the Parmesan, dot with the butter, and bake for 10–15 minutes, until golden and bubbling. Serve immediately.

PASTA AND BROCCOLI IN SKATE BROTH

PASTA E BROCCOLI IN BRODO D' ARZILLA

Preparation time: *30 min*
Cooking time: *30 min*
Serves 4

For the broth:
— 2¼ pounds skate, skinned,
  washed, cut it into medium-
  size pieces
— 1 small stalk celery, chopped
— 1 carrot, chopped
— 1 onion, chopped
— salt

— 3 tablespoons olive oil
— 1 clove garlic
— 2 salted anchovy fillets
— 1¼ cups chopped tomatoes
— ½ cup dry white wine
— 1 pound 2 ounces broccoli,
  divided into florets
— 8 ounces spaghetti
— 1 tablespoon parsley, chopped
— chili oil

Place the skate into a casserole together with the chopped celery, carrot, and onion. Pour in water to cover, salt sightly, and bring to a boil. Cook at medium heat for about 20 minutes. Drain the pieces of skate and set aside. Return the leftover vegetables and skate bones to the pan and boil for about 30 minutes. Strain the liquid and set aside.

Heat the olive oil in another casserole, add the garlic clove, and fry slightly. Add the anchovies and let them melt. Add the red bell peppers, chopped tomatoes, wine, broccoli, stir and let cook for 5 minutes. Pour the strained fish broth into a pan, add a piece of the skate and after 10 minutes, add the pasta, and continue to cook for 10 minutes. Sprinkle with the chopped parsley and serve hot.

POTATO AND BROCCOLI PIE

TORTINO DI PATATE E BROCCOLI

Preparation time: *40 min*
Cooking time: *30 min*
Serves 8

— 1¾ pounds potatoes
— 1¾ pounds broccoli,
   divided into florets
— 6 tablespoons butter, plus
   extra for greasing
— 4 tablespoons warm milk
— 2 egg yolks
— pinch freshly grated nutmeg
— ⅓ cup sliced almonds
— salt and pepper

Cook the unpeeled potatoes in a large pan of salted, boiling water for 20–25 minutes, until soft. Meanwhile, blanch the broccoli in another pan of salted, boiling water for 5 minutes, then drain. Preheat the oven to 400°F. Grease an ovenproof dish with butter. Drain the potatoes, then peel and mash in a bowl. Stir in 3 tablespoons of the butter, the egg yolks, and nutmeg, and season with salt and pepper. Make alternate layers of mashed potatoes and broccoli in the prepared dish, seasoning lightly with salt and pepper after each layer, until all the ingredients have been used. Sprinkle with the almonds, dot with the remaining butter, and bake for about 10 minutes, until golden brown. Remove from the oven, turn out onto a warm serving dish, and serve immediately.

BROCCOLI WITH BOTTARGA

BROCCOLETTI ALLA BOTTARGA

Preparation time: *20 min*
Cooking time: *10 min*
Serves 4

—2¼ pounds sprouting
   broccoli, divided into florets
— 3½ ounces bottarga (dried
   striped mullet or tuna roe)
— juice of 1 lemon, strained
— 1 clove garlic, chopped
— 1 sprig parsley, chopped
— 8 basil leaves, torn
— 3 tomatoes peeled, seeded,
   and chopped
— olive oil, for drizzling
— salt and pepper
— thin lemon slices, to garnish

Cook the broccoli in salted, boiling water for 10 minutes, then drain and let cool slightly. Pound the bottarga in a mortar with the lemon juice, then gradually pound in the garlic, parsley, basil, and tomatoes. Season with salt and pepper and, when the sauce is fairly thick, drizzle with olive oil. Mix well and pour into a sauceboat. Place the broccoli on a warm serving dish, garnish with the lemon slices, and serve with the sauce.

SPICY BROCCOLI WITH YOGURT

PHOTO PAGE 409

BROCCOLETTI PICCANTI ALLO YOGURT

Preparation time: *10 min*
Cooking time: *5 min*
Serves 4

—2¼ pounds purple sprouting
  broccoli, divided into florets
— 1 sprig parsley, chopped
— 1 clove garlic, chopped
— 1 mild red chile, seeded
  and chopped
— scant ½ cup low-fat
  plain yogurt
— pinch dry mustard
— salt

Parboil the broccoli in salted, boiling water for a few minutes until just tender, then drain well and place in a large salad bowl. Combine the parsley, garlic, chile, and yogurt in a bowl, stir in the mustard, and season with salt to taste. Pour the sauce over the broccoli and serve warm.

BROCCOLI WITH ANCHOVIES

BROCCOLETTI ALLE ACCIUGHE

Preparation time: *20 min*
Cooking time: *35 min*
Serves 4

— 2¼ pounds sprouting
  broccoli, cut into florets
— 3 ounces salted anchovies,
  heads removed, cleaned,
  and filleted, soaked in cold
  water for 10 minutes, and
  drained
— 3 tablespoons olive oil
— 2 cloves garlic
— ½ fresh chile, seeded and
  chopped
— salt

Cook the broccoli in salted, boiling water for 15 minutes. Meanwhile, chop the anchovy fillets. Heat the olive oil in a pan, add the garlic and chile, and cook for 1 minute. Add the anchovies and cook, mashing with a wooden spoon until they disintegrate. Remove and discard the garlic. Drain the broccoli, add to the pan, mix well, and cook over low heat, stirring occasionally, for about 15 minutes. Serve immediately.

SPICY BROCCOLI WITH YOGURT

CAULIFLOWER POLENTA

POLENTA AL CAVOLFIORE

Preparation time: *20 min*
Cooking time: *1 hour 5 min*
Serves 4

— 2 tablespoons golden raisins
— 1 cauliflower, divided into florets
— 2 tablespoons olive oil
— 1 onion, chopped
— 1 tablespoon pine nuts
— 4 canned anchovy fillets, drained
— scant 2½ cups polenta
— salt

Put the golden raisins into a heatproof bowl, pour in warm water to cover, and let soak for 15 minutes. Meanwhile, bring a large pan of salted water to a boil. Add the cauliflower and cook for 10 minutes or until tender. Drain well, reserving the cooking water. Drain the golden raisins and squeeze out the excess liquid. Heat the oil in a small pan. Add the onion and pine nuts, and cook over low heat, stirring occasionally, for 12 minutes, until golden. Add the anchovy fillets and cook, mashing them with a wooden spoon until disintegrated. Stir in the golden raisins and cauliflower and cook for another 2 minutes, then remove from the heat, and set aside.

To make the polenta, measure out 5 cups of the reserved cooking water, adding water, if necessary. Pour into a large pan, add a pinch of salt, and bring to a boil. Sprinkle the polenta over the surface, stirring continuously. Cook, stirring frequently, for about 45 minutes, until thickened, then remove from the heat. Gently reheat the caulifower sauce, stirring occasionally. Spoon the polenta into a warm serving dish, pour the cauliflower sauce over, and serve.

SPICY CAULIFLOWER

CAVOLFIORE SPEZIATO

Preparation time: *15 min*
Serves 4

— 1 small cauliflower
— 2 carrots, cut into thin strips
— 1 clove garlic, finely chopped
— juice of 1 lemon, strained
— 1 tablespoon dry white wine
— 3 tablespoons olive oil
— ½ teaspoon cumin seeds
— pinch of paprika
— salt

Cut only the most tender florets from the cauliflower and put into a salad bowl. Add the carrots and garlic. Combine the lemon juice, wine, olive oil, cumin seeds, paprika, and a pinch of salt in a pitcher. Pour the dressing over the florets and mix well.

CAULIFLOWER FLAN

TORTINO DI CAVOLFIORE

Preparation time: *45 min*
Cooking time: *1 hour*
Serves 6

— 2½ pounds cauliflower,
divided into florets
— 2 tablespoons butter, plus
extra for greasing
— 5 tablespoons milk
— 3 eggs
— 1 quantity béchamel sauce
(see page 51)
— ¾ cup grated Gruyère cheese
— salt and pepper

Cook the cauliflower florets in a pan of salted boiling water for 15 minutes, until tender, then drain well. Melt the butter in a skillet. Add the florets and cook over low heat, stirring occasionally, for about 5 minutes, until lightly browned. Season with salt and pepper, pour in the milk, and simmer until it has been almost completely absorbed. Remove the pan from the heat and push the mixture through a strainer into a bowl.

Preheat the oven to 350°F. Grease a tart pan with butter. Stir the eggs, 1 at a time, into the béchamel, then add the grated cheese and pureed cauliflower. Pour into the prepared pan, place it in a roasting pan, and pour in hot water to come about halfway up the side. Bake for 1 hour. Remove the pan from the oven and let stand for a few minutes, then turn out onto a warm serving dish and serve.

CAULIFLOWER SALAD WITH HERBS AND MAYONNAISE

INSALATA DI CAVOLFIORE AGLI AROMI E MAIONESE

Preparation time: *30 min,
plus 1 hour standing*
Cooking time: *10 min*
Serves 4

— 1 cauliflower, divided
into florets
— 6 tablespoons olive oil
— 3 tablespoons white wine
vinegar
— 1 tablespoon chopped
parsley
— 1 tablespoon chopped
tarragon
— 1 teaspoon Dijon mustard
— 1 cup mayonnaise
— salt and pepper

Bring a pan of salted water to a boil. Add the cauliflower and cook for 10 minutes or until tender. Drain well and let cool, then transfer to a salad bowl. Whisk together the oil, vinegar, parsley, and tarragon in a bowl, and season with salt and pepper. Pour the dressing over the cauliflower and toss lightly. Let stand for 1 hour to let the flavors mingle. Stir the mustard into the mayonnaise and spoon into a sauceboat. Serve the cauliflower salad, handing around the mayonnaise separately.

CAULIFLOWER TART

TORTA AL CAVOLFIORE

Preparation time: *20 min*
Cooking time: *35 min*
Serves 4

— butter, for greasing
— 1 cauliflower, divided into florets
— 1 pound 2 ounces puff pastry dough, thawed if frozen
— all-purpose flour, for dusting
— 1 cup milk
— 4 eggs
— pinch freshly grated nutmeg
— scant 1 cup grated Emmenthal cheese
— salt and pepper

Preheat the oven to 325°F. Grease a tart or quiche pan with butter. Bring a pan of salted water to a boil. Add the cauliflower and cook for 10 minutes or until tender. Drain well and let cool. Roll out the puff pastry on a lightly floured counter and use to line the prepared pan. Put the pan on a baking sheet and bake for 5–10 minutes, until just dry. Remove from the oven and spread out the cauliflower florets in the pie shell. Combine the milk, eggs, nutmeg, and grated cheese in a bowl and season with salt and pepper. Pour the mixture over the cauliflower florets, return the pan to the oven, and bake for 25 minutes, until the filling is just set. Remove from the oven and let cool, then cut the tart into wedges to serve.

PAPPARDELLE WITH CAULIFLOWER AND GORGONZOLA

PHOTO PAGE 413

PAPPARDELLE CON CAVOLFIORI E GORGONZOLA

Preparation time: *25 min*
Cooking time: *25 min*
Serves 4

— 1½ cups cauliflower florets
— 1½ tablespoons butter
— 5 ounces Gorgonzola cheese, diced
— 3–4 tablespoons milk (optional)
— 2–3 tablespoons olive oil
— 1 clove garlic
— 1 tablespoon chopped thyme
— 10 ounces fresh pappardelle
— ⅓ cup grated Parmesan cheese
— salt and pepper

Parboil the cauliflower in salted, boiling water for 5 minutes, then drain, reserving the cooking water. Melt the butter with the Gorgonzola in a small pan over very low heat, stirring continuously and adding a few tablespoons of milk if necessary. Do not let the mixture boil. Remove the pan from the heat. Heat the oil in a shallow pan. Add the garlic clove and cook over low heat, stirring frequently, for a few minutes, until lightly browned. Remove the garlic and discard. Add the cauliflower to the pan and cook, stirring occasionally, for 5 minutes. Sprinkle with the thyme and season with salt and pepper. Cook the pappardelle in the reserved cooking water, adding more boiling water if necessary, for 2–3 minutes, until al dente. Drain, turn into the pan with the cauliflower, and stir. Stir in the Gorgonzola mixture, remove from the heat, and serve sprinkled with the grated Parmesan.

PAPPARDELLE WITH CAULIFLOWER AND GORGONZOLA

CAULIFLOWER IN BREAD CRUMBS

CAULIFLOWER IN BREAD CRUMBS

CAVOLFIORE AL PANGRATTATO

Preparation time: *30 min*
Cooking time: *10 min*
Serves 4

— 1 cauliflower, divided into
   florets
— 2 eggs
— 1¾ cups fresh bread crumbs
— 2 tablespoons butter
— 4 tablespoons olive oil
— salt

Cook the cauliflower in a large pan of salted, boiling water for 10 minutes or until tender. Beat the eggs with a pinch of salt in a shallow dish. Spread out the bread crumbs in another shallow dish. Melt the butter with the oil in a large skillet. Dip the cauliflower florets first in the beaten egg and then in the bread crumbs. Add them to the skillet, in batches if necessary, and cook for a few minutes, turning once or twice, until golden brown. Remove with a slotted spoon and drain on paper towels. Serve immediately.

TWO-COLOR CAULIFLOWER WITH BELL PEPPER

CAVOLFIORE BICOLORE AL PEPERONE

Preparation time: *20 min*
Cooking time: *20 min*
Serves 4

— 1 small white cauliflower,
   divided into florets
— 1 small green cauliflower,
   divided into florets
— juice of 1 lemon, strained
— 2 teaspoons finely grated
   lemon rind
— 6 tablespoons olive oil
— 1 red bell pepper preserved
   in brine, drained and finely
   chopped
— pinch of chili powder
— pinch of dried oregano
— 1 clove garlic, chopped
— salt and pepper

Parboil the cauliflower florets in separate pans of salted water for 8 minutes or until tender. Drain well and arrange in alternate colored layers on a serving dish. Combine the lemon juice, lemon rind, olive oil, red bell pepper, chili powder, oregano, and garlic in a bowl and season with salt and pepper to taste. Pour the dressing over the cauliflower and let stand in a cool place for 1 hour to let the flavors mingle, then mix and serve.

LEEKS AND TOMATOES

PHOTO PAGE 417

PORRI AL POMODORO

Preparation time: *20 min*
Cooking time: *40 min*
Serves 4

— 3 tablespoons olive oil
— 1 shallot, finely chopped
— 4 tomatoes, peeled, seeded, and coarsely chopped
— 1 clove garlic, finely chopped
— 1 sprig thyme, chopped
— ½ cup dry white wine
— 2¼ pounds leeks, thinly sliced
— salt and pepper

Pour the oil into a pan, add scant ½ cup of water, and heat. Add the shallot and cook over low heat, stirring occasionally, for 5 minutes, until softened. Add the tomatoes, garlic, and thyme, and season with salt and pepper. Increase the heat to medium-high, pour in the wine, and cook until the alcohol has evaporated. Reduce the heat and simmer for 15 minutes. Meanwhile, bring a pan of salted water to a boil. Add the leeks and blanch for a few minutes, then drain well. Stir the leeks into the tomato mixture, cover, and simmer for another 15 minutes. Remove the lid and let any remaining liquid evaporate. Transfer the vegetables to a warm serving dish and serve as an accompaniment to a bollito misto (mixed boiled meats).

LEEKS WITH HAM

PORRI AL PROSCIUTTO

Preparation time: *20 min*
Cooking time: *30 min*
Serves 4

— 2¼ pounds leeks, white parts only
— 3½ ounces cooked ham, sliced
— 7 tablespoons butter
— ½ cup all-purpose flour
— 2¼ cups milk
— scant 1 cup grated Gruyère cheese
— 2 tablespoons grated Parmesan cheese
— salt and pepper

Parboil the leeks in salted water for 5 minutes, then drain well. Preheat the oven to 350°F. Trim the fat from the ham and place the fat in an ovenproof dish with 2 tablespoons of the butter. Melt over medium heat, then add the leeks in 2 layers and cook, basting frequently, until lightly browned. Season with salt and pepper. Meanwhile, make a béchamel sauce (see page 51), using 2 tablespoons of the remaining butter, the flour, and milk. Stir the Gruyère into the sauce. Remove the leeks from the heat, lay the slices of ham on top, and spoon the béchamel sauce over. Dot with the remaining butter, sprinkle with the Parmesan, and bake for about 10 minutes.

LEEKS AND TOMATOES

CREAM AND LEEK RISOTTO

GNOCCHETTI DI ZUCCA AL BURRO E SUCCO D'ARANCIA

Preparation time: 20 *min*
Cooking time: 50 *min*
Serves 4

— 2 tablespoons butter
— 4 small leeks, white parts
   only, thinly sliced
— about 6¼ cups
   vegetable stock
— 1¾ cups risotto rice
— ¾ cup light cream
— salt and pepper
— grated Parmesan cheese
   to serve

Melt the butter in a pan, add the leeks, and cook, stirring occasionally, for 5 minutes. Add 1 tablespoon of water and simmer for 20 minutes, adding more water if necessary. Meanwhile, bring the stock to a boil in another pan. Stir the rice into the leeks. Add a ladleful of the hot stock and cook, stirring, until absorbed. Continue adding the stock, a ladleful at a time, and stirring until each addition has been absorbed, for about 18–20 minutes. When the rice is tender, stir in the cream and season with salt and pepper to taste. Serve with Parmesan.

LEEK TART

CROSTATA DI PORRI

Preparation time: 50 *min*
Cooking time: 25 *min*
Serves 6

— 14 ounces puff pastry dough,
   thawed if frozen
   all-purpose flour, for dusting
— 2 tablespoons olive oil
— 6 leeks, sliced
— 4 eggs
— scant ½ cup heavy cream
— scant 1 cup grated Parmesan
   cheese
— scant ½ cup diced, cooked
   ham
— 1 tablespoon chopped parsley
— salt

Roll out the dough on a lightly floured counter and use to line a 9-inch springform pan. Trim the edge and reserve the trimmings. Chill the pie shell in the refrigerator. Heat the oil in a skillet. Add the leeks and cook over low heat, stirring occasionally, for 5 minutes, until softened. Sprinkle with 3 tablespoons of water and cook for another 15 minutes. Remove from the heat and let cool. Meanwhile, preheat the oven to 425°F. Beat the eggs with the cream in a bowl, then stir in the grated cheese and a pinch of salt. Add the leeks, ham, and parsley, mix well, and pour into the pie shell. Fold the edges in toward the center of the tart. Roll out the trimmings, cut into diamond shapes, and use to decorate the tart. Put the pan on a baking sheet and bake for 25 minutes. Remove from the oven, transfer to a warm serving dish, and serve immediately.

CELERY ROOT AND PEA SOUP

MINESTRA DI SEDANO RAPA CON PISELLI

Preparation time: 20 *min*
Cooking time: 25 *min*
Serves 4

— 1 celery root, diced
— 2¾ cups shelled peas
— 1 carrot, sliced
— 4¼ cups vegetable stock
— 3½ ounces ditalini or
  other soup pasta
— 1 sprig parsley, chopped
— extra-virgin olive oil, for
  drizzling
— ⅔ cup grated pecorino or
  Parmesan cheese

Put the celery root, peas, and carrot into a large pan, pour in 4¼ cups of stock, and bring to a boil. Reduce the heat, cover, and simmer for 15 minutes. Add the pasta and cook for another 10 minutes, or according to the package directions, until the pasta is al dente. Ladle the soup into a warm tureen, stir in the parsley, drizzle with a little oil, sprinkle with the cheese, and serve immediately.

CELERY ROOT AND SMOKED SALMON SALAD

INSALATA DI SEDANO DI VERONA E SALMONE AFFUMICATO

Preparation time: 20 *min*
Cooking time: 10 *min*
Serves 4

— 2 celery roots
— juice of 1 lemon, strained
— 2 tablespoons whipped
  cream
— 5 tablespoons mayonnaise
— 5 ounces smoked salmon,
  cut into thin strips
— salt

Bring a pan of salted water to a boil. Meanwhile, cut the celery roots into slices and then into julienne strips. Stir the lemon juice into boiling water, add the celery root strips, and blanch for 10 minutes. Drain well, pat dry with a dish towel, and put into a salad bowl. Combine the whipped cream and mayonnaise in another bowl, then stir into the celery root, together with most of the smoked salmon. Sprinkle the remaining smoked salmon strips on top of the salad and serve.

CELERY ROOT REMOULADE

Preparation time: *40 min*
Serves 6

— 3 large celery roots
— 3–4 tablespoons capers,
   drained and rinsed
— 6 dill pickles, chopped
— 3 tablespoons chopped
   parsley

For the mayonnaise:
— 3 egg yolks
— 1¾ cups sunflower oil
— 2 tablespoons white wine
   vinegar
— salt

For the sauce:
— 4 tablespoons olive oil
— 1 teaspoon Dijon mustard
— 1 tablespoon white wine
   vinegar
— juice of ½ lemon, strained
— salt

First make the mayonnaise. Whisk the egg yolks with a pinch of salt in a bowl. Gradually whisk in the oil, a drop at a time to begin with, then when the mixture begins to thicken, whisk in half the vinegar. Continue whisking in the oil in a continuous stream until completely incorporated. Stir in the remaining vinegar.

To make the sauce, whisk together the oil, mustard, vinegar, lemon juice, and a pinch of salt in a bowl until thoroughly combined.

Cut the celery root into slices and then into julienne strips. Put them into a bowl, add the sauce, and toss lightly. Add the celery root mixture to the mayonnaise and stir, then add the capers, dill pickles, and parsley. Cover and chill in the refrigerator until required.

CHICKEN AND CELERY ROOT SALAD

PHOTO PAGE 421

Preparation time: *15 min*
Serves 6

— 2¼ cups cooked chicken strips
— 1 celery root, cut into thin
   batons
— ½ quantity mayonnaise (see
   recipe above)
— 3 tablespoons plain yogurt
— 1 teaspoon Dijon mustard

Put the chicken and celery root into a salad bowl. Combine the mayonnaise, yogurt, and mustard in another bowl and season with salt. Gently stir the dressing into the salad and serve.

CHICKEN AND CELERY ROOT SALAD

GLOSSARY

ACIDULATE
To add vinegar or lemon juice to water (or another liquid) for immersing some vegetables, such as globe artichokes, to prevent them from turning black before cooking.

AGRODOLCE
This dressing made with herbs, wine vinegar, sugar, onion, and garlic is served with fish, game, and vegetables, particularly onions and eggplants.

AL DENTE
The point during cooking at which pasta and rice become tender but are still firm to the bite and should, therefore, be removed from the heat and drained. Vegetables cooked al dente are tastier and retain more nutrients.

BAGNA CAUDA
Italian for "warm bath," it's a dip made from olive oil, butter, garlic, and anchovies, served warm with raw vegetables.

BLANCH
In cooking, to partially cook fruit or vegetables briefly in boiling water to make them softer or easier to peel. In gardening, blanching is the process of forcing plants to turn lighter in color and become more tender by hiding them from the sunlight at a certain point in their growth cycle. It's commonly used for cauliflower, asparagus, celery, and endive.

BOLT
When a plant goes to seed, often earlier than expected, it becomes less edible. For example, broccoli will bolt if the weather turns hot. At this point, the plant's energy goes into reproducing.

BOTTARGA
Salted, pressed gray mullet (or tuna) roe is prepared like a salami. Slices, drizzled with olive oil and lemon juice or spread on toast, make a tasty *antipasto*. Crumbled and lightly heated in oil, it makes a pleasant sauce for spaghetti. It is a Sardinian speciality.

BREAD CRUMB
To coat meat, fish, or vegetables in bread crumbs—after dipping them in beaten egg—before frying.

BUCATINI
A thick spaghetti-like pasta with a hole running through the center. The name comes from the Italian word *buco*, meaning "hole," while *bucato* means "pierced."

CARPACCIO
Raw meat or fish (such as beef, veal, venison, salmon, or tuna) generally thinly sliced or pounded thin and served as an appetizer.

CROQUETTES
A small fried food roll usually containing as main ingredients mashed potato and meat, fish, and vegetables, often encased in bread crumbs. The croquette is commonly shaped into a cylinder or disk, and then deep-fried.

DUST WITH FLOUR
Meat, vegetables, and fish are often dusted—lightly coated—with flour before frying. Baking pans, work surfaces, and pastry dough are also dusted with flour to stop the pastry from sticking to the rolling pin.

FEED
To assist plants to grow, they must be fed with fertilizers. There are two main types: organic and inorganic.

FOCACCIA
A flat, round, or square Italian olive oil bread with a cakelike texture. It is often flavored with herbs and olives or tapenade.

FONTINA
Semisoft, deep golden, Italian cow milk cheese with a reddish brown rind. The texture is firm and a little springy. It has a delicate flavor, making it a popular dessert cheese. When matured, it can be grated.

FOOD MILL
A food preparation utensil for mashing and straining soft foods. Typically, it consists of three parts: a bowl, a bottom plate with holes like those in a colander, and a crank fitted with a bent metal blade, which crushes the food and forces it through the holes in the bottom plate as the crank is turned.

FRICASSEE
A sauce consisting of eggs and lemon poured on to veal, lamb, rabbit, or chicken. When heated, it thickens and takes on a creamy consistency. The dish must be removed from the heat as soon as it is ready, otherwise the sauce thickens excessively and develops an unpleasant flavor.

FRONDS
The leaf of a fern or a large compound leaf of a palm.

GARNISH
To decorate single plates or serving dishes of savory ingredients with cut vegetables, herb sprigs, lemon slices, or other garnishes to make them look attractive and to achieve a visual balance between the various shapes and colors and to enhance the flavor of the ingredients.

GNOCCHETTI
An Italian pasta made to look like *gnocchi*, the popular potato dumplings.

GRANITA
Traditionally a semifrozen dessert made from sugar, water, and various flavorings. Granita can also be savory.

HILLING
Hilling, also known as earthing up or ridging, is the technique in agriculture and horticulture of piling soil up around the base of a plant. It can be done by hand (usually using a hoe), or with powered machinery, typically a tractor attachment.

JULIENNE
A style of cutting food—often vegetables or citrus zest—into fine long strips.

MANDOLINE
A cooking utensil used for slicing and for cutting juliennes with suitable attachments; it can also make crinkle cuts.

MORTADELLA
A large, cooked Italian salami originating from Bologna. Made with finely ground pork, garlic, salt, and pepper stuffed into a natural casing, it is sometimes studded with pistachios or green olives.

MULCH
The loose material placed over the soil to control weeds and conserve soil moisture. Usually this is a coarse organic matter, such as leaves, clippings, or bark, but black plastic sheets, and other commercial products can also be used.

ORECCHIETTE
A kind of pasta typical of Apulia, a region of southern Italy, and shaped like small ears.

PANCETTA
Cured pork taken from the belly of the pig, like fatty bacon, but cured differently. It may be smoked or unsmoked, natural or rolled, and flavored with spices. If pancetta is not available, use bacon.

PANSOTTI
Italian for "pot bellied," a term for triangular-shaped stuffed pasta with pinked edges.

PAPPARDELLE
Large, very broad fettuccine. The name derives from the verb *pappare*, or to "gobble up."

PERENNIAL
A nonwoody plant that grows and lives for more than two years. Perennials usually produce one flower crop each year, lasting anywhere from a week to a month or longer.

PESTICIDES
These products are sold as granules, sprays, dusts, pelleted grain, or bait. They are usually applied to the ground around plants to attract and kill slugs and snails.

PISTIL
The female reproductive part of a flower. The pistil, centrally located, typically consists of a swollen base, the ovary, which contains the potential seeds, or ovules; a stalk, or style, arising from the ovary; and a pollen-receptive tip, the stigma, variously shaped and often sticky.

QUADRUCCI
A Small, square, short-cut pasta, suitable for vegetable or thin soups.

RAISED (AS IN RAISED BEDS)
Planting areas that are mounded or boxed above ground level. Raised beds are usually framed by some type of barrier, such as lumber or stones.

RICOTTA SALATA
The pressed, salted, and dried variety of ricotta is known as *ricotta salata*. A milkywhite firm cheese used for grating or shaving, *ricotta salata* is sold in wheels, decorated by a delicate basket-weave pattern.

SALSICCIA
Raw Italian sausage.

SEEDED POTATOES
Seed potatoes can be planted whole, or they can be cut into pieces. Each piece needs to have 2–3 eyes on it. Let the pieces air out for a day or two so the cut areas dry slightly before planting. If cut-up pieces of seed potatoes are planted, as opposed to the whole seed potato, they need to be placed cut side down into the ground.

SETS
Onion sets are just miniature onion bulbs, which means they get off to a fast start, having more stored energy than a seed to work with. Sets are planted fat end down so that the tip is just above soil level in March and April

SFORMATO
The Italian term for a kind of molded custard. It is similar to a soufflé, but is not as airy.

SOFFRITTO
A combination of onions, carrots, and celery (either raw, roasted, or sautéed with butter), which forms the flavor base for many Italian dishes, including sauces, soups, and casseroles.

TAGLIERINI
A type of ribbon pasta.

TALEGGIO
A semisoft, washed-rind cow milk cheese from the Valtaleggio region in northern Italy, near Lombardy. It is characteristically aromatic yet mild in flavor and features tangy, meaty notes with a fruity finish. The texture of the cheese is moist-to-oozy with a very pleasant melt-in-your-mouth feel.

TAPROOT
The main, thick root growing straight down from a plant. Not all plants have taproots.

TARTARE
A preparation of finely chopped raw meat or fish sometimes with seasonings and sauces.

THIN
The removal of excess seedlings, allowing sufficient room for the remaining plants to grow. Thinning also refers to removing entire branches from a tree or shrub, to give the plant a more open structure.

TIMBALE
Both the layered dish of rice and vegetables or eggplant and vegetables and tomato sauce.

TRANSPLANTS
The process of taking the plant from one container or place and moving it to another. It usually refers to transferring the plant from the container it came from in the nursery into a more permanent spot.

TRIFOLATO
Thinly sliced and cooked with oil, garlic, and parsley, and possibly mushrooms and lemon.

ZIMINO
A Tuscan term meaning cooked with greens, often prepared with Swiss chards or spinach.

INDEX

PAGE NUMBERS IN ITALICS REFER TO ILLUSTRATIONS

DIRECTORY

The following sources specialize
in high quality Italian produce.

USA

Zingerman's
422 Detroit Street
Ann Arbor, MI 48104
+1 734 663 3354
www.zingermansdeli.com

*Di Pasquale's Italian
Deli & Marketplace*
3700 Gough Street
Baltimore, MD 21224
+1 410 276 6787
www.dipasquales.com

Buon Italia
Chelsea Market
75 9th Avenue
New York City, NY 10011
+1 212 633 9090
www.buonitalia.com

D Coluccio & Sons
1214–20 60th Street
New York City, NY 11219
+1 718 436 6700
www.dcoluccioandsons.com

Di Palo's Fine Foods
200 Grand Street
New York City, NY 10011
+1 212 226 1033
www.dipaloselects.com

Faicco's
260 Bleecker Street
New York City, NY 10014
+1 212 243 1974

Leo's Latticini
46–02 104th Street
New York City, NY 11368
+1 718 898 6069

Raffetto's
144 West Houston Street
New York City, NY 10012
+1 212 777 1261

Todaro Brothers
555 Second Avenue
New York City, NY 10016
+1 212 532 0633
www.todarobros.com

Corti Brothers
5180 Folsom Boulevard
Sacramento, CA 95819
+1 916 736 3802
www.cortibros.biz

Molinari Delicatessen
373 Columbus Avenue
San Francisco, CA 94133
+1 415 421 2337

DeLaurenti
1435 1st Avenue
Seattle, WA 98101
+1 206 622 0141
www.delaurenti.com

Vace Italian Delicatessen
3315 Connecticut Avenue
Washington, DC 2008
+1 202 363 1999
www.vaceitaliandeli.com

Convito Italiano
1515 Sheridan Road
Wilmette, IL 60091
+1 847 251 3654
www.convitocafeandmarket.com

CANADA

Moccia's Italian Meat Market
2276 East Hastings Street
Vancouver, BC V5L 1V4
+1 604 255 2032
www.moccia.ca

*Ottavio Italian Bakery
& Delicatessen*
2272 Oak Bay Avenue
Victoria, BC V8R 1G7
+1 250 592 4080
www.ottaviovictoria.com

Benito Meat and Deli
7900 Boulevard Provencher
Waterloo, 2017
Montréal, Quebec, H1R 2Y5
+1 514 723 2378
www.benitoinc.com

ONLINE GARDENING RESOURCES

— Baker Creek Heirloom Seeds
www.rareseeds.com
— Fedco Seeds
www.fedcoseeds.com
— Gardens Alive
www.gardensalive.com
— Gardeners Supply Company
www.gardeners.com
— Gourmet Seeds International
www.gourmetseed.com
— Gurney's Seed & Nursery Co.
www.gurneys.com
— Harris Seeds
www.harrisseeds.com
— Johnny's Selected Seeds
www.johnnyseeds.com
— Lee Valley Tools. Ltd.
www.leevalley.com
— Nichols Garden Nursery
www.nicholsgardennursery.com
— Park Seed Company
www.parkseed.com
— Pinetree Gardens Seeds
www.superseeds.com
— Richters Herbs
www.richters.com
— Seed Savers Heritage Farm
— Seeds from Italy
www.growitalian.com/
— Seed Savers
www.seedsavers.org
— Seeds of Change
www.seedsofchange.com
— Southern Exposure Seed Exchange
www.southernexposure.com
— Stokes Seed, Inc.
www.stokeseeds.com
— Territorial Seed Company
www.territorialseed.com
— Thompson & Morgan Seedsmen, Inc
www.tmseeds.com
— Tomato Growers Seed Company
www.tomatogrowers.com
— Vesey's Seeds Ltd.
www.veseys.com
— W. Atlee Burpee & Co.
www.burpee.com
— Willhite Seed, Inc.
www.willhiteseed.com
— Natural Gardening
www.naturalgardening.com
— Peaceful Valley Farm Supply
www.groworganic.com

RECIPE NOTES

— Butter should always be unsalted.

— Pepper is always freshly ground black pepper, unless otherwise specified.

— Unless otherwise stated, all herbs are fresh and parsley is flat-leaf parsley.

— Vegetables and fruits are assumed to be medium size, unless otherwise specified. Eggs are large, unless otherwise specified.

— Milk is always whole, unless otherwise specified.

— Garlic cloves are assumed to be large; use two if yours are small.

— Ham means cooked ham, unless otherwise specified.

— Prosciutto refers exclusively to raw, dry-cured ham, usually from Parma or San Daniele in northern Italy.

— Cooking and preparation times are for guidance only, as individual ovens vary. If using a convection oven, follow the manufacturer's instructions concerning oven temperatures.

— To test whether your deep-frying oil is hot enough, add a cube of stale bread. If it browns in 30 seconds, the temperature is 350–375°F about right for most frying. Exercise caution when deep-frying: Add the food carefully to avoid splashing, wear long sleeves, and never leave the pan unattended.

— Some recipes include raw or very lightly cooked eggs. These should be avoided particularly by the elderly, infants, pregnant women, convalescents, and anyone with an impaired immune system.

— All spoon measurements are level. 1 teaspoon = 5 ml; 1 tablespoon = 15 ml. Australian standard tablespoons are 20 ml, so Australian readers are advised to use 3 teaspoons in place of 1 tablespoon when measuring small quantities.

KEY

🐂 Contains beef
🐑 Contains chicken
🐖 Contains pork
🐟 Contains fish/seafood

Phaidon Press Limited
Varick Street
New York, NY 10014

www.phaidon.com

© 2011 Phaidon Press Limited

ISBN 9 780 7148 6117 3 (US edition)

Vegetables from an Italian Garden originates from *Il cucchiaio d'argento*, first published in 1950, eighth edition (revised, expanded, and redesigned) 1997; from *Primi piatti*, first published 2004; from *Secondi piatti*, first published 2005; and from *Antipasti e contorni*, first published in 2007.
© Editoriale Domus S.p.A.

A CIP catalogue record for this book is available from the British Library.

Designed by Astrid Stavro
Photography by Steven Joyce (recipes only) and Andy Sewell

The Publishers would also like to thank Theresa Bebbington, Hilary Bird, Linda Doeser, Carmen Figini, Lizzie Harris, Charlie Nardozzi (garden writer), Clelia d'Onofrio (curator of the Italian edition) and Jane Rollason for their contributions to the book.

Printed in China